BUILDING SAN FRANCISCO'S PARKS, 1850–1930

PUBLISHING FOR THE WORLD
125 Years
THE JOHNS HOPKINS UNIVERSITY PRESS

CREATING THE NORTH AMERICAN LANDSCAPE

*Gregory Conniff*
*Edward K. Muller*
*David Schuyler*
CONSULTING EDITORS

*George F. Thompson*
SERIES FOUNDER AND DIRECTOR

*Published in cooperation with*
*the Center for American Places*
*Santa Fe, New Mexico, and*
*Harrisonburg, Virginia*

A recently planted Portsmouth Square in 1865.

# building
# **san francisco's**
# parks,

## 1850–1930

TERENCE YOUNG

THE JOHNS HOPKINS
UNIVERSITY PRESS

baltimore and london

This book has been brought to publication with the generous
assistance of the Robert L. Warren Endowment.

The Johns Hopkins University Press
2715 North Charles Street
Baltimore, Maryland 21218-4363
www.press.jhu.edu

*Library of Congress Cataloging-in-Publication Data*

Young, Terence (Terence G.)
Building San Francisco's parks, 1850–1930 / Terence Young.
  p.    cm. — (Creating the North American landscape)
Includes bibliographical references and index (p.    ).
ISBN 0-8018-7432-7 (hardcover : alk. paper)
1. Parks—California—San Francisco—History. 2. Landscape
architecture—California—San Francisco—History. 3. Parks—Social
aspects—California—San Francisco—History. I. Title. II. Series.
SB482.C22S268 2004
712'.5'0979461—dc21          2003006247

A catalog record for this book is available from the British Library.

Frontispiece photograph from John P. Young, *San Francisco: A History
of the Pacific Coast Metropolis* (San Francisco, 1912), opposite p. 444.

FOR KC

# contents

---

> Golden Gate Park is in the most literal sense pure creation,
> a thing wrought by human hands . . . out of nothing more
> substantial than a dream and a faith, on a foundation no
> more constant than wind-blown sands.
>
> Katherine Wilson
> *Golden Gate: The Park of a Thousand Vistas*

etween 1850 and 1930, the swelling cities of industrializing America created unprecedented systems of large and small parks. Although in a handful of cities large cemeteries provided public greenspace, in 1850 no municipality included a developed public park. By 1908, however, only one of the 157 American cities with a population in excess of 30,000—Butte, Montana—lacked a park. America's best-known urban parks originated during the latter half of the nineteenth century. These included Boston's Franklin Park, Brooklyn's Prospect Park, Chicago's Washington and Jackson Parks, Los Angeles's Griffith Park, New York's Central Park, Philadelphia's Fairmount Park, San Diego's Balboa Park, and San Francisco's Golden Gate Park, as well as thousands of locally known, small greenspaces. Often treated as a dispensable urban amenity during the latter half of the twentieth century and into the twenty-first, parks played a preeminent role in the nineteenth- and early-twentieth-century debates about creating a better American society. Proponents and opponents argued vehemently during these decades over the roles of saloons, education, housing, race, immigration, class relations, and various institutions in the creation of social "harmony" and the "good life." Parks stood out as a battleground. Many excellent park, garden, landscape-architectural, and ornamental-horticultural studies about the late nineteenth and early twentieth centuries emphasize scientific and aesthetic concerns, but few address how the good society was supposed to flow from greenspace. This study examines the social and moral issues commonly associated with American parks during this era. According to the literate and powerful San Franciscans who served as the historical informants for this book, an improved urban environment, in this case a naturalized one, would secure residents a better future, by altering both the material and behavioral aspects of their lives.[1]

Many studies have analyzed human-induced environmental changes in terms of such social forces as class, ethnicity, and economic structure, but this book takes a different tack, delving into shifting ideas and their physical counterparts. In particular, it explains park landscape designs based on what an influential group of San Franciscans *believed* to be good, true, and beautiful about public greenspaces in urban life. San Francisco's park activists retained their faith in the reforming power of public greenspaces for over sixty years, but they changed their ideas about which park designs, features, and locations would best achieve reformists' goals. In pursuit of social reform, park advocates aggressively intervened in local politics, making parks one of the more significant elements of municipal government, and they transformed San Francisco's physical environment between 1850 and 1930.[2]

This book examines the meaning and geography of San Francisco's parks in two sections: a social-scientific investigation into the theoretical and historical issues surrounding American park making (Chapter 1); and then the case study (Chapters 2–6). Chapter 1 begins with the social characteristics common to those promoters who most strongly advocated parks, the reasons they claimed to justify actions, and the definitions of nature and society they employed. Continuing in this vein, the chapter considers for whom the parks were made, where they were to be located, and the links between them and ideas about nature and social order. The chapter concludes with a word about the history of the American park movement before 1870 and some of its best-known advocates, particularly Andrew Jackson Downing and Frederick Law Olmsted.

The remaining chapters interpret San Francisco's two major park periods: the romantic, which spanned the 1860s to the 1880s, and the rationalistic, which began in the 1880s and continued into the 1920s. Chapter 2 analyzes Frederick Law Olmsted's sensible, environmentally appropriate, and aesthetically thoughtful plan for a park system centered in the Western Addition. In 1866, he proposed several smallish greenspaces and one large one that would be linked by wide, greened and sunken promenades, but the plan was rejected, creating the opening for the creation of Golden Gate Park in 1870. The chapter then examines the political and personal origins of this park. Chapter 3 scrutinizes the physical refashioning of a natural, if unattractive, landscape into romantic Golden Gate Park, the city's first, and for three decades the only, substantial park. Small parks and squares existed and were planned in San Francisco before 1870, but they were of little consequence to the city's park advocates, who thought Golden Gate Park alone fostered social reform. Chapter 4 begins with the reaction of visitors, newspapers, and horticulturists to romantic Golden Gate Park, turns to the economic and political events that disturbed the park in the mid-1870s, and then presents examples of the connections that activists and supporters made between the park and the good society. Chapter 5 looks at Golden Gate Park as the setting for a contest between romantic park supporters and the new rationalistic park advocates. The latter ultimately transformed Golden Gate Park's eastern landscape along the lines they prefered, which included an international exposition in 1894, but the results were unsatisfactory for both groups. Romantic park uses limited and marginalized rationalistic designs while the latter constrained and interfered with the former. Chapter 6 examines the strategy that arose to reduce this tension: the development of the existing small greenspaces and the creation of new ones in many city neighborhoods. The quality and number of San Francisco's parks, squares, and parkways increased dramatically after 1900, creating a system of greenspaces that by 1930 included both romantic and rationalistic sites. This system remained the framework for additional large and small parks, growing into the network known today.

Parks are a window onto the complex and dynamic relationship between nature and culture in America. From our current vantage point, we see that many ideal qualities once attributed to San Francisco's parks were not timeless but historically specific. Nevertheless, Americans have generally retained the original designs of their urban parks, unlike other features of the built environment, allowing them to persist as an essential and largely unaltered element within the urban landscape. If a 1900 San Franciscan could visit Golden Gate Park today, she would likely be as impressed by the growth of the trees and shrubs as by any new structures. Living islands in a sea of buildings, San Francisco's parks have not been isolated, decontextualized, and preserved like museum artifacts or demolished and replaced, like the unwanted buildings in an urban-renewal zone. Instead, they remain valued, nurtured, and nurturing places that many San Franciscans see as natural even though they are clearly constructs. San Francisco did not become the oppressive, continuous urban grid imagined by some of its earliest residents, but an attractive, appealing, and much-beloved landscape peppered with myriad greenspaces, because of nineteenth- and early-twentieth-century park advocates. Despite their faults, prejudices, and misconceptions, they earned our recognition and gratitude, and their handiwork deserves our support and protection.[3]

# acknowledgments

T his book began as a doctoral dissertation in the Geography Department at the University of California, Los Angeles. I owe many thanks to my committee members, Professors Eric Monkkonen, Norris Hundley, Jonathan Sauer, Michael Curry, and J. Nicholas Entrikin, who alternately encouraged and cajoled, but always supported me. Nick, in particular, taught me how to begin the long journey with a single step, to first summarize the project in one sentence, then repeatedly expand it. After many iterations and well after life took me away from UCLA, the project has become this book.

The encouragement and insights of other faculty and scholars were also invaluable, and I owe special thanks to Mark Bassin, Rich Berman, Michael Black, Paul Boyer, Gray Brechin, Raymond Clary, Craig Colten, Steve Daniels, Lary Dilsaver, Marjorie Dobkin, Lance Howard, Patty Kellner, Phil Klein, Todd May, Ted Muller, Garth Myers, David Schuyler, Peggy Shaffer, Don Vermeer, Kent Watson, and Jim Wescoat. I know I am forgetting many others; I hope they will forgive me my poor memory. I also appreciate the insightful comments of the anonymous reviewers who read early drafts of the manuscript to make it a much better study. Many thanks are due to the libraries and archives that care for the variety of unique and wonderful documents and images I needed for this project, and to their hardworking, helpful, and often fun-loving staffs—the Bancroft Library, the California Historical Society, the California State Library, the Helen Crocker Russell Library, the Huntington Library, the Library of Congress, the San Francisco Maritime National Historical Park, the San Francisco Museum and Historical Society, the San Francisco Public Library, and the Society of California Pioneers. I especially want to thank Stephanie Shew for her careful and patient creation of the maps. She did a yeoman job without ever complaining about my fussiness. Anne Whitmore, of the Johns Hopkins University Press, substantially improved my prose.

George F. Thompson, president, and Randy Jones, editor and publishing liaison, of the Center for American Places were steadfast supporters of this project. Their faith kept me going through more than one low point.

A project of this scope does not flourish on intellectual curiosity, engaging materials, and a supportive publisher alone. It needs financial and other forms of support. I am grateful for funding from the Geography Department and the Academic Senate at UCLA, the History and Geography Department and the College of Architecture, Arts and the Humanities at Clemson University, The Graham Foundation, the California Association of Nurserymen, and the Starkey Fund of the Association of American Geographers. In addition, several friends supported my research, especially when I had very little to work with. Special thanks go to Tam and Sam Bryan for letting me make their home my own on the many, many trips to the San Francisco Bay area. I extend similar thanks to Vern Sanders and Carol Mallicoat. Additionally, Maxine Meltzer deserves my deep gratitude for her support.

Lastly, my warmest appreciation goes to three souls who joined me through much of this odyssey. Our cats, Loon and Otter, stood (or more accurately lay) beside me for more days than I can count. Their inter-specific friendship brought warmth and company to an often lonely task. And, of course, I offer my greatest thanks and affection to Kitty, whose unfailing encouragement kept me working. I never could have completed this project without her.

BUILDING SAN FRANCISCO'S PARKS, 1850–1930

# chapter 1

# THE AMERICAN PARK MOVEMENT

The past is everywhere. All around us lie features which, like
ourselves and our thoughts, have more or less recognizable
antecedents. Relics, histories, memories suffuse human experience. . . . Whether it is celebrated or rejected, attended to
or ignored, the past is omnipresent.

David Lowenthal
*The Past Is a Foreign Country*

A city without parks is probably unimaginable to most twenty-first century Americans. One hundred and fifty years of park advocacy and public support have left people with the impression that parks are an obvious, natural part of cities. An uninterrupted gridiron of streets and buildings stretching for miles would collide with current aesthetic, social, and ecological sensibilities. Americans have forgotten how unobvious, abnormal, and contrived parks seemed in 1850, when only a tiny handful of observers sensed their value. San Francisco overcame this inertia during the last third of the nineteenth century. The details of San Francisco's park development are unique, but they fit into the social, cultural, and historic framework of the American park movement.

From the beginning of American park making, public parks generally developed only when and where supported by a significant portion of a city's population. Moreover, park supporters had to be led by advocates who could imagine a proposal's details then actively and effectively argue for it. Without advocates articulating supportable positions and responding convincingly to trenchant criticisms, a proposal was unlikely to succeed. Before 1930 in San Francisco, a relatively small band of native-born, white, middle-class males actively promoted various types and sizes of parks. For example, Frank Soulé, who was an author and worked for the *Alta California* newspaper, pleaded for parks in the 1854 *Annals of San Francisco;* William Ashburner, a mining engineer, helped bring park designer Frederick Law Olmsted to San Francisco; and, Joseph Austin, a local merchant, served on the San Francisco Board of Park Commissioners. Their social and professional positions, when combined with their ideas about parks, justified and shaped decisions about the landscapes in San Francisco's parks—how many would be built and where, as well as who would use them and how. The advocates shared the goal of social reform, but by no means was there a collective will or fully shared range of positions among them, let alone among the larger group of park supporters. For instance, the early struggle to select the location for Golden Gate Park engaged a relatively small coterie of white, middle-class, male advocates; yet the working classes, foreign-born residents, non-whites, and women successfully contested some of the advocates' later plans. Nevertheless, this book focuses almost exclusively on the relatively small number of park advocates and their ideas, because they had the greatest control over San Francisco's parks.[1]

## PARKS AND SOCIAL REFORM

Park advocates struggled for greenspace because they believed parks could eliminate many social ills, particularly disease, poverty, crime, and social division, since these evils were thought to be caused by the negative impact of urban surroundings. Parks overcame a city's corrosive influence because, as a mid-nineteenth-century park report explained, a park was designed to produce "a certain [positive] effect upon the mind and the character of those who approach it." Forty years later, Charles Mulford Robinson, a City Beautiful leader, continued to reiterate this link between society and its surroundings when he charged, "social problems are to a large degree problems of the environment." Create parks where children can be energetic, he claimed, where adults can find "brightness, entertainment, and fellowship without throwing them into temptation . . . and many of sociology's hardest problems will be solved." Urban disorders did not arise because society was evil *by nature* but because its members were *out of touch with nature,* a source of goodness. Poverty, poor health, and other urban problems developed when cities grew too large and left residents only occasionally, if ever, in contact with nature. Creating public greenspace in a city was an act of social reform. Park advocates in San Francisco and elsewhere were not the only social reformers attempting to transform urban environments. According to historian Paul Boyer, housing reformers and playground proponents shared the park advocates' mechanistic view of the environment-society relationship, but the groups identified different environmental causes and therefore proposed different solutions.[2]

Park boosters characterized the improved society that was supposed to emerge with parks by four social ideals, or what I will call the virtues: public health, prosperity, democratic equality, and social coherence. Parks were machines to transform a flawed society and these four commendable qualities or traits were held up as the principal features of the good society being pursued. The potential realization of them was a major factor motivating park advocates throughout the United States. The four virtues divide into two pairs with the first set, public health and prosperity, relating to the material well-being of society. Parks were said to improve the general public's health in various ways, for example, by producing fresh air. Park air, especially before the turn of the century, counteracted "miasmas," the vaporous emanations that were thought to be the sources of disease before germ theory. The second virtue, prosperity, was usually connected to parks through real estate and tourism. On the one hand, wealthy residents were attracted to parks and competed for housing locations around them, prompting property values nearby to rise. This benefit, however, was not confined to the neighborhood immediately adjacent to a park, because the rising property values generated local tax revenues, which, advocates pointed out, paid for the creation and maintenance of the park and lowered taxes elsewhere in a city. At the same time, parks induced prosperity by drawing tourists, who rented local rooms, ate in local restaurants, and shopped among local merchants. Again, a wide variety of residents in San Francisco and other American cities benefited, as tourist consumption led to increased profits and wages in many economic sectors.

The second set of virtues addressed the more behavioral concerns of democratic equality and social coherence. In the case of the former, for instance, park advocates frequently expressed a concern that rising class divisions heightened class awareness, distinctiveness, and a sense of social rank, threatening the municipality and larger republic. Parks would "naturally" close social gaps when visitors left their class-sensitive employments and residences to meet in the leveling openness of a public greenspace. Finally, city living not only endangered the institution of democracy, warned advocates, it menaced daily life, as growing cities alienated an increasing number of social groups from the whole. Under these conditions, society lost its sense of unity in principles, relationships, and interests. This explained, for example, why adolescents, who saw themselves as distinct, committed crimes against adults. Parks, argued the landscape architect H. W. S. Cleveland in 1873, reinforced and augmented social coherence by strengthening "the local pride and affection of the inhabitants."[3]

The virtues, however, were never distinct ideals. Advocates in San Francisco and elsewhere never quantified them nor identified clear criteria for success in achieving them. However much the virtues were widely desired and steadily pursued with public park funds, they remained elusive, just beyond the horizon like the legendary Seven Golden Cities of Cibola or the Fountain of Youth.

## WHAT IS NATURE?

Park advocates remained committed throughout the nineteenth century and early twentieth century to the idea that parks would encourage these virtues, but park making developed in two phases—the romantic and rationalistic periods—because the advocates changed their understanding of *how* parks fostered the good society. San Francisco's transition from the romantic period to the rationalistic occurred during the 1880s. In a number of eastern cities to which parks came earlier than to San Francisco, for example, Buffalo, the transition began as early as the late 1860s; while in other locations, such as Los Angeles, the transition followed in the 1890s. No matter the timing, the rationalistic period drew extensively upon the romantic period. No sharp boundary differentiates one period from the other, but they can be distinguished by the differing sets of practices and attitudes about the shape and content of park landscapes, about who should use parks, and about how many small and large parks were appropriate and where they should be built. These contrasting practices and attitudes arose as people in the rationalistic period changed the definition of nature.[4]

*Romantic versus Rationalistic Definitions*

Depending on the period, park promoters viewed nature as either external to or inclusive of humanity. Romantic proponents, like many contemporary artists and scientists, saw nature as an interrelated world of mind, body, and being, an organic whole that included God, people, and the physical world. Social problems, they concluded, came from the physical disjunction that developed between nature and people in any city large enough to be dominated by streets and buildings. Despite the numerous positive connections between urbanization and progress recognized by park backers and others, they nonetheless viewed the city as a dangerous environmental aberration that could lead to the dissolution of society. Parks were the necessary corrective because they brought nature, which was God's handiwork, balanced and inherently good, back into cities. As the famous minister Henry Ward Beecher enunciated in 1869, for "the multitude," natural beauty was a gift of God "without price." It could "confer pleasure and profit from merely the looking at it." Lawns, flowers, shrubs, trees, and "the finest effects in landscape," provided "pleasure for all those who need the solace and ministration of the divine element of beauty." Focusing on the visual aspects of parks, romantic advocates believed that parks should mostly be composed of water features, lawns, shrubs, and trees, with the occasional random smattering of flowers. They thought it neither necessary nor desirable to have clearly organized plantings or activities within parks. Such things as athletics and large flower beds were banned or marginalized because they interfered with a visitor's ability to be improved by contemplating the beauty of the larger landscape scene.[5]

Rationalistic park advocates, by contrast, tended to see themselves as separate from nature, treating it as a system of component parts. These boosters rejected the notion that the scenic landscape in a park reformed society, because they did not believe nature to have been designed or its parts necessarily in harmony. As this Darwinian, mechanistic view of nature replaced a romantic, teleologic one, the physical world came to be seen as unbalanced, morally ambiguous, and, like any mechanism, subject to human design and assembly. Consequently, the importance of contemplating nature faded and parks were reborn as favored settings for organized leisures. Rhododendron dells and tulip beds, art museums, baseball, and children's play became common park features as rationalistic park champions pursued their formula for encouraging the good society. "There is no use trying to treat a place in the middle of a crowded city on the wilderness motif," urged one advocate. "The thing to do is to frankly recognize that its beauty, if it is to have any, must be civic beauty." No longer would social improvement be left to the beguiling charms of a passive park visit. For the rationalistic park advocate it was time to take charge of society's directional change.[6]

### Nature and Space in Parks

San Francisco's rationalistic park advocates saw their romantic Golden Gate Park as underdeveloped, not mis-designed, so they did not seek to replace the existing park features. Their new vision of the nature-society connection was both figuratively and literally built out of, upon, and beside the existing, romantic one. For instance, in the course of changes made during the 1880s, most of the grass, shrubs, trees, water, and rocks in Golden Gate Park remained but their meanings and roles were redefined, even as new elements, such as ball fields and museums, were added. This tendency toward minor reconstruction and renovation of urban parks continues to the present. San Francisco's nineteenth- and twentieth-century parks, like most American parks, persist largely intact, despite the expense of maintenance, the enormous monetary value of the open land, and a nearly continuous series of proposals to build new features upon them.[7]

Despite much other continuity during the transition between park-making eras, the space in parks increasingly became socially and spatially segmented during the rationalistic period. Areas within large and small parks were dedicated to specialized uses—archery, children's play, or picnicking, for example. In the romantic period, by contrast, most American parks had subordinated their few specialized areas to the whole. This earlier focus on holistic parks had guided the best-known, most influential design team of the nineteenth century, Frederick Law Olmsted and Calvert Vaux. "The Park throughout is a single work of art," they asserted in the 1858 "Greensward" plan for New York City's Central Park, "and as such, subject to the primary law of every work of art, namely, that it shall be framed upon a single, noble motive, to which the design of all its parts, in some more or less subtle way, shall be confluent and helpful." In practice, this holism led park designers to create nondistinctive spaces linked repeatedly to similarly nondistinctive spaces. A visitor to any portion of a park was supposed to feel that he or she was in some unspecified and unbounded rural landscape. In the rationalistic period, however, a visitor would not have expected every park space to look the same and be used in a similar fashion. Rationalistic users and advocates wanted their parks to include athletic fields, gardens, museums, playgrounds, and other specialized features. For rationalistic park advocates and supporters, a great deal was gained and nothing lost by the addition of these specialized "improving" spaces to existing romantic parks.[8]

As the spatial segmentation of Golden Gate Park proceeded, San Francisco's authorities created numerous new greenspaces throughout the city utilizing both romantic and rationalistic characteristics. For example, many small, neighborhood parks with ball fields appeared, as did municipal street trees, boulevards, and parkways. This spatial diffusion of parks and other greenspaces allowed for the uneasy coexistence of the romantic and rationalistic elements within the city's park system. Without San Francisco's many new or invigorated small to medium parks and squares, such as Alta, Duboce, and Lincoln, the pressure to transform a romantic Golden Gate Park into a fully rationalistic facility would have prompted many more conflicts than occurred. However, the parks created after 1890, particularly the smaller ones, tended to be entirely rationalistic in orientation, which allowed for the continuation of many romantic characteristics in Golden Gate Park.[9]

## THE CONTOURS AND CONTENT OF AMERICAN PARKS

By the time the construction of Golden Gate Park began in 1870, park advocates and supporters expected the natural and built elements in any new park to conform to an elaborate set of landscape principles, which created the opening for the landscape architects' profession. Their predecessors, landscape gardeners, such as Andrew Jackson Downing, had arranged greenspaces, but the emergence of public parks and park making transformed the "modest elegance" of the landscape gardeners into the "exacting professional discipline" of the landscape architects. As progressivism swept the country during the late nineteenth and early twentieth centuries, landscape architects became *the* park and greenspace experts in American cities.[10]

During the romantic period, a park was supposed to be an ecumenical, bucolic, green landscape consisting mostly of trees, shrubs, grass, rocks, and water, arranged by landscape architects into "naturalistic" landscape scenes. According to Frederick Law Olmsted,

> The landscape character of a park . . . is that of an idealized, broad stretch of pasture,
> offering in its fair, sloping surfaces, dressed with fine, close herbage, its ready alter-
> natives of shade with sunny spaces, and its still waters of easy approach, attractive
> promises in every direction, and, consequently, invitations to movement on all sides,
> go through it where one may.

In opposition to the geometric regularity of the urban grid, the park landscape would be curvilinear and have few structures. Numerous expansive, meadowlike areas surrounded by masses of trees lay interspersed with an assortment of natural surprises or "wonders," like a waterfall or a rocky outcrop. Water in the form of streams and small lakes would in one place divide and at another unite meadows and woods. Romantic parks were designed so that visitors would feel they had left the urban landscape and entered some sort of rural, natural place.[11]

In addition, park advocates argued that the greenspace had to be sufficiently expansive and vertical to block out a visitor's view of the city, because a park's reforming ability came from its natural scenery. In the words of Olmsted, a park had to include "depth of wood enough about it not only for comfort in hot weather, but to completely shut out the city from our landscapes." If a visitor glimpsed urban landscape, then personal improvement diminished. Parks were *rus in urbe* (country in city) rather than *rus et urbe* (country and city)—a visitor was renewed and society reformed as he or she became immersed in its nature. In addition, no "riotous" or "boisterous" urban activities like running and yelling children, baseball, or football were permitted of park visitors. Park authorities encouraged quiet, rural recreations such as picnicking, painting, reading, and, of course, landscape contemplation.[12]

Rationalistic advocates, by contrast, were less antiurban and embraced lively activities as appropriate, even necessary. They claimed that games such as baseball uplifted, but most especially when played within the natural beauty of a park. According to George Burnap, a Washington, D.C., landscape architect, parks needed both "beauty and utility. [They] must serve many purposes of use as well as pictorial pleasure." Rationalistic proponents minimized the romantic era's concerns for curvilinearity, irregularity, organic wholeness, and the greenness of plants to instead feature straight roads and paths, regularity of design, specialized activity areas, and colorful plants. They treasured such structures as museums, whose purpose was education and whose architecture was derived from orderly, classical models such as Roman and Greek temples. Plantings were no longer understated but unabashed, demanding attention. For example, flower gardens of all sizes and shapes were planted in a style known as "bedding out." Flower beds displayed plants massed primarily for their attractive colors, usually in abstract, geometric patterns, but sometimes in representative and whimsical shapes, such as the rowboat and boater that plied the lawn in Chicago's Washington Park or the sundial in Golden Gate Park. The romantic period's concern for the visual banishment of the city also declined during the rationalistic era and, as a result, parks could be smaller. A city no longer needed to focus nearly all its attention on one large park but could create a complex, extensive, hierarchical system that supported many smaller, neighborhood greenspaces, each suited to a given set of circumstances. In San Francisco, for example, new small parks appeared in the emerging Sunset, Parkside, Bernal Heights, and Mission districts, while many of the squares in the older Pacific Heights and Western Addition districts, which had mostly been vacant lots, were finally developed.[13]

## PARK USERS

According to Frederick Law Olmsted, a romantic park had no specific class, age, or behavioral audience but instead was "intended to furnish healthful recreation for the poor and the rich, the young and the old, the vicious and the virtuous" so that the virtues would flourish throughout society. However, it is also clear that park advocates, especially during the romantic period, thought adult men benefited most from parks, because it was they who were most threatened by their daily involvement in public, commercial activities.[14]

Although park champions typically embraced the wealth generated by urban business, they also condemned commerce and industry as causing poor health, saying it was "exhausting," leading to a loss of "vitality." The portion of the population engaged in business activities, warned Olmsted in 1866, was "wearing itself out with constant labor, study and . . . anxieties." This exhaustion undermined prosperity. "Cases of death," he continued, "or of unwilling withdrawal from active business, compelled by premature failure of the vigor of the brain . . . [can] cause losses of capital . . . as much as fires or shipwrecks." The solution, of course, was regular visits to a park, where the man would be "refreshed" and "braced" for another round of commercial activity.[15]

Romantic park advocates rarely connected women or children to parks. Women increasingly entered the public arena after the Civil War, but through much of the romantic period they carried out their social duties mostly in the private, domestic world, so park advocates believed that women were not wearied by urban life because they were less immersed in it. According to social historian Gary Cross, a middle- to upper-class home during the romantic period was "bereft of economic purpose," having become—like a park—a haven or leisure center, as industry and commerce, which had once flourished in the home, migrated to their own urban spaces. At the center of this domestic urban retreat stood the married woman, who, according to sociologist Galen Cranz, organized family recreation and acted to "cushion the individual [adult male] from many urban stresses." In this view, women and parks served similar social functions. Like nature, which is what parks represented, women were "divinely designed," wrote Mary Dodge in 1872's *Woman's Worth and Worthlessness,* for a "state of repose, ease, leisure." Consequently, when women park users were mentioned by park boosters, issues of female domesticity generally arose and they were encouraged to use parks as a tool in their recreative chores. For example, women park users were referred to as "ladies with their families" and "ladies who may wish to enjoy themselves in a homelike manner" in the 1874 report of the San Francisco Board of Park Commissioners. Park advocates also infrequently mentioned children, because the latter were supposed to spend most of their leisure time in the superior recreational space of home. When children were mentioned, a park advocate usually expressed a concern for little more than their personal safety or orderliness, especially since "boisterous" children disturbed landscape contemplation.[16]

In the rationalistic era, the vision of park promoters expanded to include many of the types of users discounted by romantics. Playgrounds appeared as childhood came to be seen as a critical developmental stage. Juvenile crime, warned this new generation of park champions, increased when youths matured in a poor environment without parks. Play areas, especially those in parks, fostered social coherence and deterred crime among the poor and ethnic populations in densely built neighborhoods. J. Horace McFarland, the president of the American Civic Association, proclaimed that Chicago had learned "the truth as to this relation between crime and . . . the small park . . . ; for in 1909 it was discovered that within a half-mile radius of her twelve [parks] . . . juvenile delinquency had decreased 44 per cent, while in the same year it had increased 11 per cent in the city as a whole." With enough parks, a city could eliminate much of its crime, because it was in children's groups, park advocates argued, that self-government and the value of law were learned, making play areas beneficial, even necessary. However, they cautioned, play should not occur just anywhere; it was best in a natural setting. Since it was impossible to send thousands of city children into the countryside, nearby parks were the optimal alternative.[17]

Economic links to children and adolescents also energized rationalistic park proponents. They claimed taxpayers would be able to keep more of their income if tax dollars were spent on parks, because properly developed, law-abiding youths would demand fewer public expenditures in the form of policemen, the courts, and incarceration. Besides, capable and decorous adults would contribute to the overall wealth of the city and be responsible, involved citizens.[18]

Rationalistic park exponents also finally expressed a concern for the impact of parks on women. While advocates assumed that women would continue their traditional family roles, they encouraged women to think about their health and to "pursue exercise" in parks and elsewhere "as a vigorous remedy for their complaints." However, this shift by park proponents was not from one certainty—women do not need parks—to its opposite. Instead, the rationalistic position was ambivalent. For example, Luther Gulick, a founding member of the Playground Association of America, supported female athletics as a means to prepare women for the competitive workplace, yet he also ignored them in his discussion of adult play. As a result, the opportunities for females to exercise were largely confined to athletics, and even there women remained relatively disadvantaged, since only bicycling, golf, and tennis were available to both sexes.[19]

Further expanding the list of who should be using parks, the rationalistic promoters shifted the emphasis from individuals to groups of users. With the arrival of large numbers of immigrants, rationalistic park advocates replaced the romantics' interest in the enervated, native-born entrepreneur with a plan to develop among recent immigrants, who had been coming in large numbers since 1870, both an American identity and a sense of group cooperation and competition within the overall population. Rationalists argued that active pastimes, such as sports, led to improved health and trained the mind and the body for greater individual and group efficiency as well as success in America's increasingly managerial business environment.[20]

In concert with the changes in gender, age, and group emphases came a new focus on museums and other educational facilities. According to many park boosters, education should persist beyond adolescence because development continued throughout life. Museums, maintained the rationalists, offered the public "an opportunity for education, recreation, and the appreciation of the arts." Moreover, museums were best located in parks, because, on the one hand, "every great museum in the world is in a park," claimed M. H. de Young, the founder of Golden Gate Park's museum. As examples he named the Metropolitan Museum of Art in New York's Central Park, the British Museum in Bloomsbury Park in London, and the Berlin Museum in the Tiergarten. On the other hand, people go to museums when they have spare time, "they do not go downtown, where the streets are dead and where there is no life. They go to their parks. And that is the logical place for a museum."[21]

## WHERE TO LOCATE PARKS

Both romantic and rationalistic advocates believed parks fostered the virtues, but they disagreed about the optimal location for parks. The edge of the built environment was ideal for a large, romantic landscape, like the solitary Prospect Park in Brooklyn and San Francisco's Golden Gate Park, or for the large to medium rings of parks, like those around Albany, Buffalo, and Chicago. A romantic-era city, like the period's parks, was a relatively homogeneous entity in which poverty, disease, crime, and class conflicts were diffused. Park champions made little of areal distinctions, because they felt that every urban district equally needed the virtues; a new park improved users no matter where they resided, as long as it was nearby. Although sectional coteries within individual cities frequently offered political, economic, and other justifications for locating a new amenity in their part of the city, none questioned the justification of positioning a new park or parks along the urban edge.

Rationalistic park advocates, however, came to see cities as increasingly composed of socially and spatially discrete populations, and poverty, disease, crime, and class conflicts as concentrated in certain districts, especially the crowded, ethnic ones. From the rationalistic advocate's perspective, it no longer made sense to rely on one, spatially peripheral park to transform distant clusters of malignant population. Instead small parks, squares, parkways, and other greenspaces needed to be located either within or proximate to a disorderly district to best foster the virtues. Furthermore, the two definitions of nature in parks made it logical to design specialized parks sensitive to their surrounding context. For instance, small neighborhood parks with ball fields and play areas but only a touch of greenery were common in densely populated areas, as were parks with rich beds of flowers and benches but no playground or other activity spaces.[22]

The mantle of social reform through positive environments eventually passed from urban parks to the nonurban regional, state, and national parks. In the eyes of park advocates, after the 1920s urban parks were no longer *the* promoters of moral order. Consequently, the urban park changed little, and the rationalistic vision continues to dominate it today. This examination of San Francisco's parks therefore concludes around 1925–1930, the point when urban parks also came to be controlled more by bureaucrats than by park advocates.[23]

## SAN FRANCISCO IN AMERICAN PARK HISTORY

The history of San Francisco's parks diverges at several points from the American park development schema outlined above. First, Golden Gate Park represented an unusually large proportionate area of 1870 San Francisco. Its 1,019 acres made it the second largest park in the United States although San Francisco was only the tenth largest city; San Francisco provided nearly twice as much park acreage per person as did the next most generous city, Philadelphia. The creation of such an inordinately large park did not go unnoticed at the time. The February 1871 issue of *California Horticulturist and Floral Magazine* denounced the park as "far more extensive than San Francisco requires." Approximately twenty years later, the situation remained largely the same. Minneapolis, Detroit, and St. Louis each had more park space per person than San Francisco, yet San Francisco had added almost no new greenspace since 1870.[24]

The vast size of Golden Gate Park undoubtedly delayed San Francisco's full embrace of the rationalistic approach, especially its emphasis on small parks. Boston, Buffalo, and Minneapolis had created systems of numerous specialized and localized parks as early as the late 1860s, but San Francisco only began to develop a system of many small- to medium-sized parks during the first decade of the 1900s because Golden Gate Park's extent made possible a variety of concurrent activities in one location, reducing the demand for additional parks. For instance, a baseball game could be played in one part of Golden Gate Park without disturbing users in other areas who wanted to admire the landscape, smell the flowers, or visit the museum. In addition, Golden Gate Park's construction and maintenance expenses, which were $250,000 for 1897, absorbed money that might have been directed toward creating other parks, until a new city charter in 1898 reorganized budgets. Only when San Francisco's population reached nearly 350,000 in 1900 did its park acreage per resident finally drop below that of Buffalo in the 1870s and Boston in the 1880s.[25]

San Francisco's distinctive park history may also stem from its ethnic diversity. The average U.S. city in 1870 was 34 percent foreign born, but San Francisco stood well above that, at 49 percent, making it the least native-populated large city in the country. According to geographer David Ward, the arrival of immigrants, with their non-American traditions, was a reason the native-born began to consider cities disorderly. San Francisco's higher-than-average number of foreigners may have prompted the relatively early effort by the city's native-born to create a park.[26]

San Franciscoalso was not as socially or spatially divided as most American cities around 1870. Social and spatial segmentation is associated with both the rapid population increase and the industrialization of the late nineteenth century. While San Francisco grew swiftly, from 56,802 in 1860 to 233,959 in 1880, it held little manufacturing or the residential districts that typically accompanied it. Instead of being a manufacturing center, 1870 San Francisco functioned primarily as an entrepôt for the supplies destined for the gold and silver fields to the east. Consequently, the port was its clearest spatial segment before 1880. According to historians William Issel and Robert Cherny, "manufacturing in San Francisco [was] both directly and indirectly the handmaiden of commerce" during the 1860s and 1870s. However, the demise of the Nevada silver fields and the economic depression that struck San Francisco and elsewhere in the early 1870s led to a rapid diversification into manufacturing. These economic changes in turn contributed to the increasing spatial differentiation of San Francisco and its parks during the rationalistic period.[27]

After 1880, San Francisco increasingly mirrored other American cities. The percentage of foreign-born residents peaked in 1880 then declined to 32 percent by

1910, nearer the U.S. average of 29 percent. By the mid-1880s the spatial segmentation typical of U.S. cities had become discernible in San Francisco. A central business district with financial, administrative, wholesale, and retail sectors had developed around the eastern terminus of Market Street. According to one historian, "a traveler alighting from one of the ferries at the foot of Market Street . . . would have found surroundings familiar to residents of other port cities, whether Boston, New York, Philadelphia or Baltimore." To the northwest and west were middle- to upper-class residences while most working-class people lived and labored to the south.[28]

Yet San Francisco stands out from all other cities during the rationalistic period for one reason. On April 18, 1906, one of the most devastating earthquakes in American history struck San Francisco, leaving approximately 3,000 of the city's 450,000 residents dead and 200,000 homeless. In the period immediately following the quake, more than 20,000 refugees took up residence in Golden Gate Park and other public greenspaces. The parks and squares were back to normal by 1908, however: San Franciscans were generous, but they also had an abiding belief in the link between parks and the good society, one they would not compromise even for refugees.[29]

## LANDSCAPE DESIGN BEFORE GOLDEN GATE PARK

The large American parks created during the nineteenth century, including Golden Gate Park, were designed using three landscape art genres initially developed in Great Britain during the eighteenth century—the Beautiful, the Picturesque, and the Sublime—and each was yoked to a set of unique attributes. Smallness, roundness, smoothness, delicacy, and color best captured the Beautiful, making it the favored genre for parks with extensive lawns or water features bordered by shrubs and trees. The Sublime countered the Beautiful, being linked to terror, obscurity, difficulty, power, vastness, majesty, and infinity, but it remained the realm of painters and writers rather than landscape architects because the restricted space in parks, even the largest ones, was insufficient to create it. The Picturesque mediated the two extremes, expressing the pleasure gained by abrupt, unexpected, or rude forms and textures, as well as the "roughness" that could exist at any scale. Many parks incorporated picturesque elements as a stimulating contrast to beautiful ones, but the former rarely dominated.[30]

After the 1906 earthquake, public parks served as temporary homes, shops, government offices, and graveyards. Here San Franciscans camp in Jefferson Park. Reproduced by permission of The Huntington Library, San Marino, California.

A romantic landscape school using the three genres emerged in the United States during the 1830s and 1840s. These new romantics contended that the premier prerequisite for landscape artists was an ability to perceive nature "as is" and to represent its inherent truths. Since nature reflected a benevolent God, the creation and perception of "natural" landscape became a moral venture for many romantics.[31]

### Andrew Jackson Downing

A. J. Downing (1815–1852) was the first writer on American landscape gardening to systematically introduce romantic notions into the subject. A horticulturist as well as designer, he lived along the Hudson River, in Newburgh, New York, publishing his first book, *A Treatise on the Theory and Practice of Landscape Gardening Adapted to North America; With a View to the Improvement of Country Residences*, in 1841. It included ideas and designs drawn from the best-known English landscape designers, especially Humphry Repton and John Claudius Loudon. An overwhelming success, *A Treatise* brought Downing widespread fame and permanently influenced American landscape design. Over the next eleven years, he published several more titles and revised the previous editions of his books repeatedly even while editing the influential *Horticulturist and Journal of Rural Art and Rural Taste*.

During his lifetime and for many years afterward, Downing was, in the words of historian George Tatum, "the undisputed arbiter of American tastes in matters relating . . . to garden design," and his ideas framed the park debates that began around 1850.[32]

Downing also contributed to the American park movement when his discriminating public commentaries ultimately led to the creation of the country's first large park, New York City's Central Park. Beginning in 1848, but especially after an 1850 visit to England, Downing regularly condemned American cities', especially New York's, lack of park space, in his *Horticulturist* editorials. Cities, he declared, were necessary but did not have to be barren, leaving the public alienated from nature. "It is needful in civilized life for men to live in cities . . . [but] it is not . . . needful for them to be so miserly as to be utterly divorced from all pleasant and healthful intercourse with gardens, and green fields." A park would be a "green oasis" in "this arid desert of business and dissipation." As evidence of the demand for large parks of a rural character, Downing pointed to the recreational use of Greenwood Cemetery, a privately owned but publicly accessible space for Brooklynites which had been designed in what was then called the "English" or romantic landscape style. The cemetery was not accessible to many New Yorkers, so a similarly large—that is, over 500-acre—landscape was needed in the city's gridded setting. "In that area there would be space enough to have broad reaches . . . with a real feeling of the breadth and beauty of green fields, the perfume and freshness of nature." In this type of setting urban dwellers could escape to find the "greatest happiness . . . [in] parks and pleasure-grounds."[33]

Downing, like the romantic and rationalistic park advocates who followed him, saw society as a product of its environment and thought beautifully designed parks would create the good society. The public needed to understand "the value and influence of beauty of this material kind, on our daily lives." Downing implored, "we *must* believe it, because the BEAUTIFUL is no less eternal," that is, a divine product and therefore no less important to pursue, "than the TRUE and the GOOD." Tightening his environmentalist focus, he also felt the public needed to recognize

how much these outward influences have to do with bettering the condition of a people. . . . Nay, more; what an important influence these public resorts . . . must exert in elevating the national character, and softening the many little jealousies of social life by a community of enjoyments. . . . Let our people once see for themselves the influence for good which [a public park] would effect . . . and I feel confident that the taste for public pleasure-grounds . . . will spread as rapidly as that for cemeteries has done.[34]

Like many later park champions, Downing expected parks to foster the virtues, but unlike them, he articulated only three virtues; prosperity would not be enunciated by him. Parks promoted democratic equality, he observed, by eliminating social differences.

Shame upon our republican compatriots who so little understand the elevating influences of the beautiful in nature and in art, when enjoyed in common by thousands and hundreds of thousands of all classes without distinction! They can never have seen, how all over France and Germany, the whole population of the cities pass their afternoons and evenings together, in the beautiful public parks and gardens. How they enjoy together the same music, breathe the same atmosphere of art, enjoy the same scenery, and grow into social freedom by the very influences of easy intercourse, space and beauty that surround them.

In Downing's view, parks equalized because they could meet needs of each class: "soften and humanize the rude, educate and enlighten the ignorant, and give continual enjoyment to the educated. Nothing tends to break down those artificial barriers [of social class] . . . so much as a community of rational enjoyments." Downing's park advocacy assumed that the recent rise in social class differences had developed from unequal access to good environments. The poor and foreign born were "rude" because they lacked opportunities to immerse themselves in art and landscape. They could not escape the city, but a publicly supported, idealized country landscape could be created to equalize class opportunities and then make the poor and foreign born more like the middle classes, who supported parks.[35]

Downing also saw parks as the promoters of social coherence and public health, an opinion based on his knowledge of German parks. For example, in a *Horticulturist* editorial he praised the positive power of Frankfurt's public park, which, being open to all visitors, was a true "republican" setting. There, in the fresh air, people mingled and learned to get along with each other without tension or strife. "In short, these great public grounds are the pleasant drawing-rooms of the whole population; where they gain health, good spirits, social enjoyment, and a frank and cordial bearing toward their neighbors." The reference to health was especially notable in Downing's day because there had been repeated, severe epidemics of cholera in crowded New York during the 1830s and 1840s. Open spaces within the urban fabric were seen as a public health measure, providing air purified of disease-bearing "miasmas." By 1852, Downing's efforts had made him the best known, most significant landscape designer in the United States. Americans had been building public parks since at least the eighteenth century, but until Downing their essential social functions and designs had never been so clearly and forcefully articulated. According to one biographer, Downing's "theories of beauty in the landscape . . . dominated . . . every public park in America" from the 1840s until the 1940s.[36]

Finally, Downing influenced the direction of the American park movement through his impact on the lives of Calvert Vaux (1824–1895) and Frederick Law Olmsted (1822–1903), who met in Downing's office during the summer of 1851. Olmsted, who had once been a farmer, had read the *Horticulturist* long before he met Downing and, according to historian David Schuyler, attributed, "his own recognition of the role of art and taste in civilizing American society" to Downing's articles and commentary. Although Olmsted would later reject some of Downing's design principles, it was Downing who taught Olmsted the difference between a garden and a park. The former could obviously be decorative and artificial but the latter had to be the antithesis of the city, a natural-appearing landscape. At the same time, Downing personally encouraged Olmsted's interest in landscapes and gardening by publishing the latter's first writings. Vaux, however, had a more intimate relationship with Downing—he worked for him. In 1850, Downing had traveled to England and France to obtain first hand experience in European ways of gardening and while on this trip had met Vaux and hired him as his architectural assistant. Over the next two years, Vaux shared Downing's office in Newburgh, assisting Downing in the design of numerous houses, estates, and commercial buildings, but most importantly of Washington Park in the District of Columbia. As had been the case with Olmsted, Vaux absorbed from Downing a strong sense of the role that art could play in transforming American society. Together Olmsted and Vaux would design America's first large public park, New York's Central Park.[37]

## NEW YORK'S CENTRAL PARK

After Downing's death, in 1852, Calvert Vaux took over the design business in Newburgh; but in 1856 he moved to New York City, where he joined those agitating for

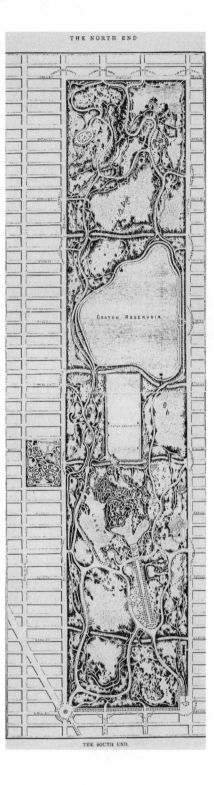

Frederick Law Olmsted and Calvert
Vaux's 1858 Greensward plan for New
York City's Central Park. From Clarence
C. Cook, *A Description of the New York
Central Park* (1869; reprinted, New York,
1979).

Central Park and for a competition to determine its design. Unknown to him or anyone else involved with this park, it would become one of America's most significant park landscapes, influencing the design of Golden Gate Park as well as many others. When the Board of Central Park Commissioners conceded in August 1857 to a design competition, Vaux convinced Frederick Law Olmsted, who became the superintendent of the new park in September of that year, to work with him on a design, the "Greensward" plan. Their plan won the competition, in 1858. Together they made a knowledgeable and effective team. Vaux brought architectural training and a knowledge of English-style landscapes; Olmsted intimately knew the site's topography; and they both agreed that natural landscapes could improve society. According to Francis R. Kowsky, Vaux's biographer, he "fervently advocated the power of art to refine and elevate the human spirit. . . . he believed that well-planned, picturesque buildings and naturalistically laid-out parks and grounds enhanced the lives of all who used them." Olmsted, in addition to reading the *Horticulturist* and absorbing many of Downing's views about society and landscape, had been exposed to Uvedale Price, Repton, and other English landscape artists during his youth. In addition, historian Charles Beveridge notes, Olmsted had "avidly read John Ruskin's *Modern Painters,* absorbing its aesthetic doctrine." Clearly Olmsted and Vaux felt Central Park would promote public health, democratic equality, and social coherence.[38]

The "virtue" of prosperity was not commonly associated with parks until after Central Park had been built, but Olmsted had been aware of the link before entering the design competition. When touring England in 1850, he had visited Birkenhead, a 185-acre park in a suburb of Liverpool. Designed by Joseph Paxton (1801–1865) and Edward Kemp (1817–1891), Birkenhead was the first park Olmsted ever saw, and he much admired it, later making it the subject of his first article on parks. According to Laura Wood Roper, an Olmsted biographer, the site had previously been a farm of level fields; but as its future lake was excavated, the removed earth was arranged to create an uneven surface in the central area of the park then landscaped to include "shady glens, open meadows dotted with trees, rock gardens, cricket and archery grounds, ornamental buildings, avenues of trees . . . the whole accessible by good hard roads and footpaths." It was immensely popular with the public. In contrast to the central area, however, the site's margins had been set aside for residences, where lots had been "graded and landscaped, streets had been laid, several fine houses with private entrances onto the park had been built." By the time

Olmsted arrived, "local land values had . . . soared." The creation of Birkenhead led to a direct increase in the wealth of nearby residents, who consequently paid higher taxes as property values increased, lowering the tax burden on the larger community. Thus, both distant and local property owners benefited financially from Birkenhead Park. Olmsted brought this knowledge of the connection between prosperity and parks with him as he worked on Central Park.[39]

In the late 1850s, some wealthy New Yorkers who shared Downing's vision of Central Park as an explicitly didactic landscape wanted the park to inculcate their traditional values and behaviors among those they deemed less fortunate. This contingent pressed for statues, monuments, and other works of art to be included in the park. In opposition were the popular press, who supported a setting for athletic competitions and mass spectacles of cricket, baseball, and footraces. The park commissioners responded by calling for specific items from both camps in the competition's design proposals. Olmsted and Vaux's plan for Central Park, however, was a novel design rather than a blend of the local, conflicting views over how a park should be arranged. Based on Downing's ideas without slavishly reproducing them, the Vaux and Olmsted plan included many of the required features even as it rejected as inappropriate the broader implications of both the elite and popular views. Olmsted and Vaux laid out a "naturalistic" setting into which the city and its elements would not intrude.[40]

Like Downing, Vaux and Olmsted believed that natural park scenery positively altered an individual's mental and physical state, "relaxing" and "unbending" minds made "tense by the strain, noise and artificial surroundings of urban life." According to Charles Beveridge, Olmsted consciously manipulated park environments to eliminate nearly every urban view from inside the park so as to

> heighten the psychological effect of the landscape on the visitor. In fact, Olmsted designed [his landscapes] to facilitate the visitor's complete immersion in the scenery—an immersion so deep that the scenery would act on those in its midst in a profound, subconscious manner. . . . That immersion in scenery was what Olmsted wished to provide American city dwellers in his parks. The most important aspect of those parks was the opportunity they offered, by careful design, for what he later called "*unconscious, or indirect recreation.*"

Two of Greensward's elements were aimed at "distancing" the visitor from urban scenes. First, the city was "planted out" by a barrier of trees and shrubs placed along the park's perimeter; this reduced street noises, screened the built environment, and obscured the long straight sides of the two-and-a-half-mile by half-mile park. Encased in thick vegetation, the park would seem larger from within, because the eye would be tricked into thinking the greenery extended indefinitely in every direction. Second, the design competition's rules had called for four transverse roads to cross the park, because the commissioners did not want the city's crosstown traffic to be blocked for over two miles. The roads, however valuable, would nevertheless bring the city inappropriately into the park, ruining its ability to transform visitors. Olmsted and Vaux's ingenious response was to sink the roads into cuts and tunnels, removing them from sight.[41]

The Greensward design incorporates natural scenery both "pastoral"—a variant on Downing's Beautiful—and picturesque. Olmsted and Vaux expected the former to have "a quiet, soothing effect" on visitors, writes Charles Beveridge, while the latter would generate "a heightened sense of the bounteousness and mystery of nature." Wherever possible they planned pastoral scenes, broad expanses of gently rolling lawn interspersed with groves of trees and tranquil bodies of water. The terrain north of the park's two reservoirs, for example, was naturally well suited for pastoral effects, so they planted it only slightly and left it relatively free of structures. The area south of the reservoirs, in contrast, was peppered with stony outcroppings and marshy valleys, so it was more difficult to promote pastoral scenery there. Nonetheless, by blasting and excavating extensively, they created open spaces and a smoothly rolling terrain. Two of the deepest valleys became water bodies; a meadow emerged as one of three required playgrounds for children and sites for family picnics; and another large, open area was designated the Parade Ground for local militia. In contrast to these many opportunities for pastoral effects, few situations were suitable for picturesque scenery. On the handful of sites, Olmsted and Vaux "employed rich and varied plantings that created 'complexity of light and shadow near the eye'" to set off the pastoral's delicate forms and indefinite boundaries. The principal location, an area called The Ramble, was immediately south of the reservoirs and was chosen so that it would contrast clearly against nearby pastoral spaces to produce picturesqueness.[42]

In order that park scenery might "act powerfully" upon people, the park's walks and drives were laid out to enhance visibility. As a visitor strolled or rode, he or she would be brought to a particular scene's best vantage points. Like the walks and drives in other English-style landscapes, those in Central Park were curvilinear and deployed so as to make easy, "unconscious" movement possible. As if on a theme-park ride, the circulation system gave coherence to the whole by organizing a visitor's experience; he encountered the pastoral or picturesque scenery in a preordained, orderly fashion. At the same time, incongruous and distracting elements, particularly uses, styles, or structures that interfered with the quiet contemplation of landscape, were kept at a distance or isolated from the scenes. To protect the playground, Parade Ground, water bodies, and Ramble from visual inconsistencies, Olmsted and Vaux designated the park's southeast side a "dress ground," and placed there the incompatible activities, plantings, and structures they did not want but were required to include by the competition rules. In their design, nearly all the eastern flank of the park was isolated from the rest of the park and made the domain of features and activities that intruded on the park's scenic qualities, despite being otherwise desirable. Cut off from the more important, scenic interior, this marginal area became, for example, the location for a flower garden with a fountain and an arboretum.

A park, of course, incorporates many major and minor structures, such as bridges, seats, and shelters, for the convenience of visitors. To preserve the primacy of the naturalistic scenery, Olmsted and Vaux designed many of their edifices to play subordinate roles in the larger, unified composition. A bridge or seat, for instance, sometimes might take on a rocky look so that it appeared to be a part of the earth, while shelters were constructed in a rustic style in which unsawn, unfinished tree limbs were pegged together. The Promenade, or Mall, one of the park's largest artificial features, was also arranged so that its synthetic character would be less obvious. A place to see and be seen, the Mall was designed as a quarter-mile-long, straight walkway flanked by seats and a series of parallel trees. Clearly artificial in plan, the Promenade nevertheless appeared relatively natural on the ground, because an observer could only tell that the trees were parallel by looking along the axis. From other angles, its trees blended visually with others in the area. At the north end of the Promenade sat a carriage concourse and the clearly architectural Terrace, whose steps took one down to a lake. Again avoiding an architectural intrusion, the scene was disposed so that the Terrace could not be seen from the Promenade. From atop the Terrace, one looked across the 20-acre lake in the foreground to see the Ramble's picturesque hillsides beyond.[43]

Once opened, Central Park drew enormous numbers of visitors; nearly 8,000,000 came in 1865. Whether or not the park improved the health, equality, or coherence

A rocky, rustic seat in Central Park, constructed of stones, an unfinished tree trunk, and thick plantings. Reproduced by permission of the Stuart Collection, Rare Books Division, The New York Public Library, Astor, Lenox and Tilden Foundations.

of New York remains open to debate; but as Olmsted had known they would, property values soared around the park, with both owners and the city reaping a financial bonanza. For Olmsted and Vaux, Central Park was a romantic vision of the best way to live in cities, designed to relieve visitors of the cares and concerns generated by life in a gridded, crowded, industrializing city. This *rus in urbe* was among the earliest efforts to consciously shape and form an urban environment to achieve social reform, and it became the model for numerous subsequent parks. These other parks, including Golden Gate Park, consisted of "naturalistic" landscapes of pastoral and picturesque scenery which were supposed to foster prosperity, public health, democratic equality, and social coherence. Plans usually included dense plantings of vegetation along perimeters, sunken thoroughfares or ones directed around the park, curvilinear circulation systems, marginal locations for inappropriate uses, styles, and structures, and malls. However, many cities today, including San Francisco, possess park systems—large and small parks, some connected by greenbelts, serving various functions and neighborhoods—rather than just a single large park. Unsurprisingly, Olmsted and Vaux initially developed the idea of the park system through their work in the cities of Brooklyn and Buffalo. These projects complete the context into which fit the many parks of San Francisco.[44]

## BEYOND CENTRAL PARK

Brooklyn's Prospect Park, authorized in April 1860, became the first opportunity for Olmsted and Vaux to refine their Central Park experience. Brooklyn, like its sister across the harbor, had chosen a site beyond the urban landscape; but unlike Central Park, the new park's perimeter was irregular. Instead of a long rectangle, Prospect Park was bounded by nine streets and bisected by Flatbush Avenue. An initial plan for the site was developed in 1861 by Egbert L. Viele, a civil engineer who had worked on Central Park; but when the Civil War began later that year, the park's development halted. During the war, the head of the park commission, James S. T. Stranahan, dissatisfied with Viele's plan, consulted Calvert Vaux. Following a number of sessions with Stranahan, Vaux submitted an alternative, if preliminary, plan to the park board. Olmsted, who was working in California, received a copy and judged the plan "excellent." He subsequently agreed to return east to collaborate with Vaux on a complete plan for Prospect Park, and in May 1865 the Brooklyn Park Commission appointed Olmsted, Vaux & Company its landscape architects.[45]

Olmsted and Vaux's Prospect Park comprised 526 acres, roughly one-third less area than Central Park, yet it included many of its predecessor's features. It was naturalistic, incorporated a curvilinear circulation system, rustic bridges and shelters, lacked museums and statuary, and was ringed by a verdant, imperceptible

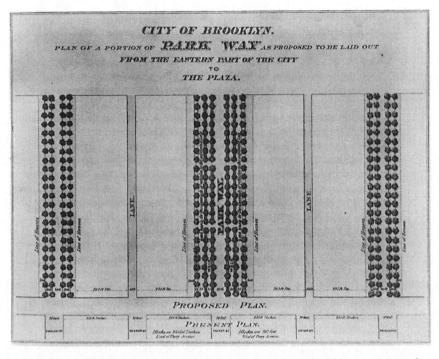

Olmsted, Vaux, & Company's parkway plan for Brooklyn. Reproduced by permission of the Brooklyn Historical Society.

perimeter created by planting thickly atop mounds along much of the park's margin. Its interior was graced by the pastoral scenery of the Green (later renamed the Long Meadow) while nearby loomed the Ravine, whose picturesqueness recalled Central Park's Ramble. Opposite the Green lay the irregularly shaped Lake with its two large architectural features, the Concert Grove and the Refectory, for group activities. Although Olmsted and Vaux were unable to shape Prospect Park completely to their vision, they created what Olmsted called "a formidable rival to the Central Park" despite its smaller domain. Nevertheless, the landscape architects felt they had to extend Prospect Park into the urban landscape if it were to achieve its maximum ability to transform society.[46]

Following the creation of Central Park, Vaux and Olmsted recognized a problem—it was virtually inaccessible to the majority of Manhattan's population, especially those seen as most in need of its "civilizing" effects, the working classes and poor in the tenements. By the mid-1860s, many working-class families did live near the park; but the majority, especially the Irish, continued to live near the island's southern tip, and the cost of traveling up to Central Park was prohibitive. For example, a family of five would have had to pay fifty to sixty cents for a round trip by street railway. Such an expense represented approximately one-third of a day's wages for unskilled laborers. In addition, most laborers worked long hours and six days per week, limiting their use to Sundays alone. Parks were less likely to benefit society if those most in need could visit only once or twice a year. In response, Olmsted and Vaux soon conceived of "parkways" and park systems and suggested that Brooklyn construct a comprehensive system of parks, rather than Prospect Park alone.[47]

In their 1868 report, Vaux and Olmsted persuaded the Brooklyn park commissioners that parkways would solve the distance problem by acting as "routes of approach to and extensions from the Park." Like tree roots into surrounding soil, they integrated the park into the city through a series of broad thoroughfares "designed with express reference to the pleasure with which they may be used for walking, riding, and driving of carriages; for rest, recreation, refreshment and social intercourse." Each would stretch 260 feet across with a central roadway, service roads, and pedestrian paths separated from each other by plots of grass and six rows of trees. Commercial traffic would be segregated from residential traffic, walks would be shaded, the desirability of adjacent lots (and their value) would increase even as the entire development acted as a fire barrier. Prospect Park would no longer sit alone, distant from much of Brooklyn. The parkways would bring its benefits into closer contact with the populace. Moving ahead, Olmsted and Vaux identified two routes, the Ocean and the Eastern Parkways, but a shortage of funds soon curtailed their program. In 1873 they terminated their relationship with the city because of its financial condition. However, they were seizing an opportunity to create an integrated park plan elsewhere even as their relationship with Brooklyn deteriorated.[48]

During summer 1868, Olmsted visited Buffalo at the request of several local residents who wanted city parks but had no plan. In their company, he selected three sites for development, then with Vaux prepared a preliminary report, which they submitted in the fall. Like their previous plans, this one declared parks "healthful recreative" areas, but unlike the plans for New York and Brooklyn, this one immediately proposed a comprehensive system of parks and parkways.[49]

The primary component in the Buffalo plan was "The Park" (later renamed Delaware Park), located just north of the city. Encompassing 350 acres, the site

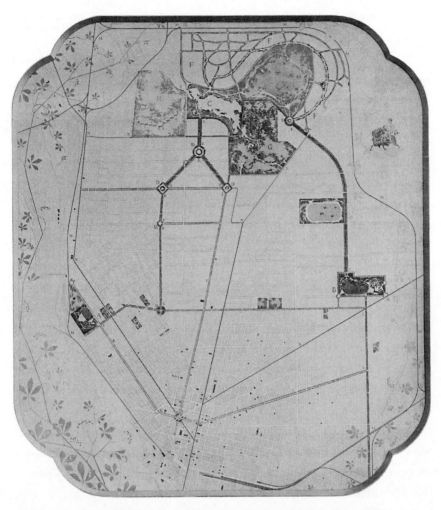

Olmsted, Vaux & Company's park system plan for Buffalo, New York. "The Park" is at the top, "The Front" along the left, and "The Parade" along the right. Reproduced by permission of the Olmsted National Historic Site, Brookline, Massachusetts.

already included a meadowlike area, a creek, and a major, bisecting thoroughfare. Working with these features, Olmsted and Vaux repeated elements from their earlier efforts, creating the Meadow, a 150-acre expanse of pastoral scenery bordered by the Lake, which was created by damming a portion of the creek. While these areas would be largely pastoral in effect, the plan also designated part of the lake's shoreline as "a profusion of plants, 'picturesque and varied in form.'" A curvilinear circulation system ran through the entire park and, reminiscent of Central

Park, the roadway's grade was lowered and its border planted thickly to block it from view.[50]

This naturalistic landscape provided some residents an opportunity for passive recreation, but Olmsted and Vaux knew it could not meet everyone's needs, so they urged park leaders to see the Park as only the most important feature in a comprehensive and proper park system. Buffalo, their report declared, also needed small, accessible parks "to which many can resort for a short stroll, airing, and diversion." They recommended acquisition of additional sites for the Front and the Parade. The Front was a 32-acre tract on the Niagara River near the densest part of Buffalo. Elevated on a bluff, it provided spectacular views of Lake Erie and the river and a playground for team sports, a carriage concourse, amphitheater, and an architectural terrace for music. On the eastern edge of town, the Parade's 56 acres encompassed a level ground for military exercises, play facilities for children, and a refectory for "gregarious" recreation. Finally, to connect the three sites and several areas of the city, the report suggested a series of 200-foot, linking parkways. Comprehensive and articulated, the plan differentiated and strategically located Buffalo's recreational spaces. Based on Olmsted and Vaux's report, Buffalo acquired the three sites, hired the partners to design the parks, and began construction in 1870, under the superintendence of a civil engineer. Progress was steady, and by 1876 Olmsted was able to call Buffalo "the best planned city, as to its streets, public places and grounds, in the United States." At nearly the same time, but on the opposite coast, San Francisco began a similar undertaking that would also trace its first vision to the pen of Frederick Law Olmsted and would, after many twists and turns, provide that city with its own park system.[51]

# SAN FRANCISCO'S PARK
# MOVEMENT BEGINS

The Board of Supervisors . . . have utterly refused to do any
definite thing. Olmstead [*sic*] prepared a plan for a Park, but
the Board of Supervisors would not adopt it. And now,
instead of making a reservation for a Park, they desire to
obtain authority to do just what they please.

*Daily Evening Bulletin*, March 21, 1868

In the years immediately following the 1848 discovery of gold in the Sierra
Nevada, San Francisco ballooned. For example, from January 1848 to December
1849, the population soared from 1,000 to 25,000, prompting the historian Gunther Barth to term San Francisco an "instant city." With this hasty growth came
intensive social instability—such as the routine racist persecution of Chinese residents or the attacks by the nativist Committee of Vigilance on Irish Catholics in
the mid-1850s. Rapid and largely unregulated development also sprawled the city
north, west, and south from its core around Portsmouth Square.

At least as early as 1854, San Franciscans began to grumble about the shortage
of available greenspace in their swiftly expanding city. Writer and social observer
Frank Soulé commented, "Over all these square miles of contemplated thoroughfares there seems to be no provision made . . . for a public park." William Eddy's
1849 planning map called for only four small spaces—the existing Portsmouth
Square, what would become Washington and Union Squares, and an unrealized
square near Folsom and Seventh Streets—no large park, and platted most of the

city for sale as private property. The situation was outrageous in Soulé's view, because parks promoted at least one of the virtues, public health. According to him, and many others then and later, parks were "the true 'lungs' of a large city," producing and diffusing fresh air. Louis Pasteur was developing the germ theory of disease during Soulé's day, but for many decades, authorities continued to believe that "filth" spontaneously generated diseases, which were then transmitted by noxious, invisible gasses called a "miasma." This belief gave rise to the maxim, "Cleanliness is next to godliness." Parks were open, green, and clean spaces where spontaneous generation of disease did not occur because purifying vegetation and the site's openness broke up miasmas. Like lungs, a park brought in fresh, healthful air and expelled tainted, dangerous gases. Soulé was therefore as much a public health advocate as a journalist when he critically noted, "Portsmouth Square, and two or three other diminutive squares, delineated on the plan, seem the only breathing holes intended for the future population of hundreds of thousands. This is a strange mistake and can only be attributed to the jealous avarice of the city projectors." Not only were there few public spaces, he fumed, but everyone knew that the squares were "by no means verdant, except in patches where stagnant water collects and ditch weeds grow." The squares lacked purifying greenery and were a breeding ground of dirty water where disease developed. Worse than a wasted opportunity, they were a public threat, which could not be ignored with impunity. Soulé's biting criticism struck home, and the city refurbished Portsmouth Square in November 1854 with "handsome gravel walks" and a variety of trees. More importantly, by 1856 it had designated six new small parks, plazas, or squares. Nevertheless, San Francisco remained park poor during the 1860s. Advocates were able to establish and develop only a handful of greenspaces, which ranged in size from 1.38 to 17.09 acres.[1]

These early park advocates' successes were limited for several reasons. First, despite its rapid growth, San Francisco was a relatively small, low-density city in the mid-1800s. When Andrew Jackson Downing had argued in 1851 for an expansive park in New York, that city was large and dense, with a population of just over 500,000. Many New Yorkers could not obtain Downing's "real feeling of the breadth and beauty of green fields, [nor] the perfume and freshness of nature." San Francisco, by contrast, included less than 40,000 souls when Frank Soulé condemned the park situation in 1854; and although the city grew to nearly 60,000 by 1860, the number and density of population remained very different from New

Portsmouth Square, originally called the Plaza, in June 1854. Compare this drawing with the frontispiece photograph showing the square in 1865 after redevelopment. From Frank Soulé, *Annals of San Francisco* (New York, 1854), p. 545.

York's crush. San Francisco was uncrowded, its built environment consisting of small, low-rise buildings covering little ground. If someone found his neighborhood's appearance too urban, it was easy to walk out of even the most developed district in less than an hour. According to one contemporary historian, John Young, "there was no lack of [fresh air] in the denser parts of the City at any time in the Sixties."[2]

San Francisco's dearth of green and open places also may have been a consequence of the frequent abuse and misuse of the public spaces it did have. Newspapers in particular often attributed the shortage of parklike spaces to the recurrent occupation of any open space by impoverished squatters. The practice of squatting, an outgrowth of the highly unstable character of the early, mining-oriented population, was not limited to the poor and politically impotent. According to the *Daily Evening Bulletin,* people from all sorts of backgrounds and walks of life would move onto undeveloped ground. For example, a former street commissioner,

Washington Square (*foreground*) was among San Francisco's first public greenspaces. Landscaping for it had recently been designed and planted when this photograph was taken in 1867. Reproduced by permission of the California Historical Society (FN-19354).

John Addis, was accused of illegally setting up his home in Union Square in November 1854. Such influential squatters, as we will see later in this chapter, could easily cloud titles and tie up the ownership of property, public or private, for indefinite periods. Furthermore, even if a public space failed to attract uninvited occupants, it often became a trash dump, which was perceived as more than merely unsightly to people who believed in the spontaneous generation of disease in refuse and miasmas.[3]

Additionally, the need for a public park was nullified in southern San Francisco by the appearance of a private development, South Park. The owners of these homes, who were of the same influential social background as the later park advocates, could easily satisfy a desire for verdant space by simply stepping out the front door. South Park was a residential neighborhood created by an English immigrant, George Gordon, who in 1852 had begun buying lots between Bryant and Brannan Streets and Second and Third Streets, an area about one and one-quarter miles from the city center. Described by historian Albert Shumate as "the only level spot of land free from sand in the city's limits," this spot was also, unfortunately, without any appealing vegetation; so the developer placed an oval garden of approximately three-quarters of an acre in the center of the development, surrounding it with the residences. In the 1854 *Prospectus of South Park,* Gordon indicated that he intended to lay out "ornamental grounds and building lots on the plan of the London Squares, Ovals or Crescents or of St. John's Park or Union Square in New York." As in similar developments with a private garden, an iron fence enclosed the park and only the residents had keys to the gates. Today South Park is unfenced public property offering a mixture of short trees, on a swath of lawn. Surrounded by low-rise professional and commercial businesses, the space is used daily as a playground as well as a picnic and relaxation area by tourists, office workers, and neighborhood residents of all ages. In the 1850s, however, it looked quite different. Initially the garden was bare, but Gordon planted assiduously to create greenery. By December 1854, approximately 1,000 trees and shrubs had been transplanted,

South Park provided a private greenspace for San Francisco's earliest elites. Here the development with its oval garden is shown at its peak of popularity, in approximately 1860. This view is from Third Street looking east. Reproduced by permission of the California History Room, California State Library, Sacramento.

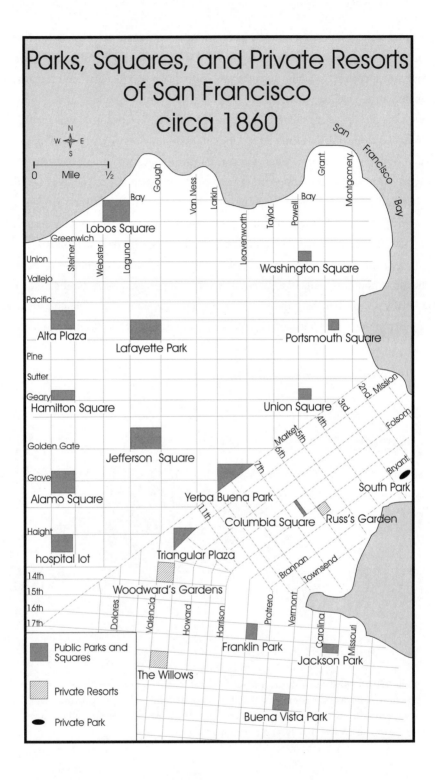

Parks, Squares, and Private Resorts of San Francisco circa 1860

and soon the vegetation was a dense display of evergreens, particularly conifers, and deciduous species arranged in a gardenesque style about the two circular walks accessed through the gates at either end. By the 1860s, South Park was dominated by its rising trees.[4]

Gordon sold lots slowly during the 1850s and into the early 1860s, attracting the local elite, including Robert B. Woodward, creator of Woodward's Gardens, discussed below. South Park's advertisements, like the statements made by later public park advocates, appealed to the virtue of public health and stressed the local scenery. They described the development as not only "healthful for private residences" but as having "unobstructed views of the Bay, Alameda, and the City and its surroundings." Nevertheless, nearby commercial development undermined the neighborhood's appeal to elites, and by 1881 it was being described as "a relic of bygone days." The garden became a public park in 1897.[5]

The presence in San Francisco of small, privately owned resorts and pleasure gardens, which sold what parks would later provide free, also helps to explain the lack of interest in public parks during the 1850s and 1860s. For example, the Willows and Russ's Garden were considered out-of-town sylvan retreats where one could purchase refreshments, enjoy such entertainments as singing and dancing, and watching tight-rope walkers. The Willows, located approximately two and a half miles from downtown, bounded by Valencia, Mission, Eighteenth, and Nineteenth Streets, was accessible at first by foot, horse, buggy, and omnibus. These modes of transportation were relatively slow and tiring, so the resort remained quiet during the 1850s. However, in 1860 the Market Street Railroad introduced a steam-driven street railway that ran from Battery and Market Streets, southwest along the latter, and then south on Valencia Street. This innovation rapidly swelled the crowds at the Willows, since it now took only ten minutes and cost ten cents each way from downtown.[6]

In June 1861, when the *Mining and Scientific Press* ran a feature on the Willows, it had a new owner, François Pioche, who was most interested that the Willows

FACING PAGE:
Many of these small public parks and squares were poorly developed, if at all, and often difficult to visit because of the steep terrain. At this time, public transportation clung to the low ground, generally from the eastern core area around Portsmouth Square toward the south, and then southwest to where the private resorts dominated.

project a French air and attract large crowds. Under his management, this "second Arcadia" included a quiet garden where a visitor could,

> ramble along the shady avenues and walks, beneath the thick luxuriance of beautiful willow trees, to find arbors and nooks, whose cool recesses—furnished with chairs and tables, where the poet may unloose his Lyre, the lover proclaim the ardor of his honorable passion, or the *bon vivant* indulge in champagne lunches—provide all the delightful seclusion that could be wished.

In addition to relaxation or romance in the garden, visitors could play games, such as rifle shooting, or inspect the small menagerie, which included the usual monkeys and native California wildlife but was most renowned for its exotic emu. This bird was so novel and popular that it became a local celebrity and inspired Bret Harte to write,

> O say, have you seen at the Willows so green,
> > So charming and rurally true,
> A singular bird, with the manner absurd,
> > Which they call the Australian emu?

According to John Young, the true "drawing card" at the Willows was not the animals but the singing and dancing. Still this resort was not to remain attractive for long. Over the course of the decade it declined so precipitously that in 1871 Mark Twain derided the place as a "dingy horror" in *Roughing It*.[7]

Russ's Garden, located in the same area as the Willows, was as German as its counterpart was French. Its founder, Christian Russ, opened his beer garden resort along the Mission Road in the early 1850s to take advantage of traffic funneled onto the highway by the hilly terrain. Consisting of a variety of buildings, including a stable and exhibition and dance hall, Russ's Garden was the site for frequent ethnic festivals, especially the German observation of May Day. In 1854, for example, between two and three thousand revelers gathered to eat, drink, and enjoy the day's entertainment of gymnastics, singing, and instrumental music. Like the Willows, Russ's Garden had a popular garden with trees and shrubs, but apparently the plants received little attention, because John Young describes them as "not always refreshingly green." In 1863 Russ's Garden moved to the southwest corner of Sixth and Harrison Streets, because its owner felt that the new location, which was along the recently opened Central Railroad Company's horsecar line, would draw even larger crowds; he was correct. Russ's Garden was so successful at this location that it kindled Robert B. Woodward's nascent urge to create yet another pleasure ground.[8]

Without question, the most famous of this period's resorts was Woodward's Gardens. From its creation in the 1860s until Golden Gate Park overshadowed it in the 1880s, it was San Franciscans' first choice for outdoor recreation. Woodward had come to San Francisco from Rhode Island during the Gold Rush, but unlike most of his fellow travelers was more eager to provide services than to seek gold. His first venture was a coffee house on what is today called Waverly Place, in Chinatown. Its success inspired him to build an inn, the What Cheer House, on Sacramento at Leidesdorff Street. A strict moralist, Woodward allowed no liquor or women into his establishment; but he did provide guests with three unique features—a free library of two to three thousand books on a variety of subjects; a clipping file of California, eastern U.S., and European newspapers; and a museum. With these attractions, the hotel drew many well-known visitors, including Mark Twain and Bret Harte.

Woodward amassed such a fortune with the What Cheer House that he decided to build himself a new, well-appointed house and garden. Woodward and his family were living in elite South Park at the time but thought the increasing number of row houses made it feel too crowded. As an alternative, he selected a large western tract of nearly two square blocks at Fourteenth and Mission Streets, adjacent to the horsecar tracks of the City Railroad Company, a firm he owned with Isaac Powell and E. T. Pease. In 1866, while the new house was under construction, Woodward began to lay out a beautiful, extensive garden with fountains, a lake, a conservatory, grottoes and caverns, plus lawns, colorful flowers, shrubs, and trees. As the house neared completion, he hired Virgil Williams, a California landscape painter, to purchase statues, paintings, and other indoor and outdoor ornaments for him in Europe.[9]

If Woodward's life had continued as it was going, the new estate might well have remained exactly what it had been designed to be—a beautiful house and garden. Soon after all was complete, however, Woodward was asked if a large contingent of local Civil War veterans could hold a reunion on his estate. He generously agreed and, as historian Louise Taber surmises, "perhaps it was this that put a new idea into his mind." The affair was most successful. Word of it quickly got around, and

In 1864, a North Beach and Mission Railroad horsecar prominently displays its "To the Willows" sign as it picks up riders on California Street at Montgomery Street. The Willows, a private garden, was a popular refreshment and entertainment greenspace during the 1850s and 1860s. Reproduced by permission of the San Francisco Maritime National Historical Park, Lawrence Houseworth Collection (A22.40.056 NL).

soon other organizations were asking Woodward to use his beautiful gardens. Rather than refuse, and having recognized the draw of Russ's Garden, Woodward the hotelier decided to transform his attractive estate into a profitable resort.[10]

Striking for both its size and the variety of its attractions, Woodward's Gardens, which opened in 1868, were styled by one contemporary as "the Central Park of the

Pacific. The grounds comprise only five acres, but [are] so arranged by the disposition of galleries and buildings, and the planting of trees and shrubs as to appear fully twice the size." The centerpiece of the resort was its museum. Installed in the original home, it housed a natural history collection whose size, inclusivity, and dense display recalled a European kabinet. Woodward was a catholic collector who steadily expanded his collection to include seashells, coins, stamps, and stuffed mammals, birds, and reptiles. Among the more outstanding exhibits were the mineral and geological specimens. According to Louise Taber, this last collection "created the keenest interest throughout the years." Since San Francisco was a major entrepôt for valuable metals, Woodward was able to amass many fine samples from the mining districts of the Sierra Nevada. A few steps away lay the aquarium, San Francisco's first. One of Woodward's favorite features, many patrons considered it the most attractive element in the gardens, since it displayed both local and exotic fish.[11]

Russ's Garden, seen here in 1854, was another privately owned garden that served refreshments and offered entertainments. Like other privately owned but public amusement "gardens," it satisfied the desire of San Franciscans for greenspace in the era before Golden Gate Park. From Frank Soulé, *Annals of San Francisco* (New York, 1854), p. 653.

Woodward's Gardens was by far San Francisco's most popular private amusement center during the 1860s and 1870s and was inspired by the success of Russ's Garden. It is seen here from the southeast, at Fourteenth Street and Mission Street (*on the right*) in approximately 1880. Reproduced by permission of the San Francisco Maritime National Historical Park, C. E. Miller Collection (P88-090.14 PL).

On elevated ground near the aquarium sat a great pavilion. Connected to the resort's central area by an ornate flight of stone steps, it acted as a theater, dance hall, and skating rink as needed. In the pavilion one could obtain a meal and then retire to listen to the massive wind organ pealing in the theater. This capacious room had 5,000 seats arrayed in a rising circle around the central arena. Most week days roller skaters careened around the floor, but on weekends gymnastic and acrobatic acts appeared, including, writes Ethel Malone Brown, Woodward's granddaughter, "the Famous French tight rope walker, Blondin, [who] cooked and ate his omelet while balanced over the heads of the awestruck." Dancing was also common, and the latest extravaganzas, such as Gilbert and Sullivan's *Pirates of Penzance,* were frequently performed on the stage. Near the foot of the pavilion steps was a unique amusement, the circular boat, linked into a continuous loop of small boats. Patrons sat on a bar and could row or not as they pleased because three or four sails usually were set and, this being windy San Francisco, motion was assured. Although nothing delighted or thrilled visitors more than this unusual, early amusement park ride, the overall effect of the resort would have been diminished except for the thoughtful use of plants. The museum, aquarium, pavilion, and other features did not seem crowded on the five-acre site, because ornamental plants filled much of the garden. In many spots, low-growing shrubs and statues mingled with flowers to distract from the density of architecture. Elsewhere the vegetation was the draw, because it was so thick one had a sense of being in an eastern American glade rather than arid, dune-encrusted San Francisco.[12]

An underground tunnel, passing below Fourteenth Street, connected the garden proper with the less verdant amphitheater or "amusement section." In the center of the raised seating for a thousand rested the racecourse where Roman chariot races, hurdle races, and foot races were run. When a competition was not in progress, one might find troupes of jugglers, acrobats, and, once, the famous midgets, "Commodore Nutt" (George Washington Morrison), Minnie Warren, and "General Tom Thumb" (Charles S. Stratton). The zoo was situated nearby with its roaring and crying lions, tigers, leopards, grizzly bears, sacred cows, and numerous other creatures. Adjacent lay a field for balloon ascensions, goat carts, donkey rides, and, of course, popcorn stands. All the stimulations and pleasures of Woodward's Gardens were available for a 25-cent entrance fee, and to guarantee plenty of guests, Woodward even built and operated a horsecar line down Mission Street to Fourteenth. Nevertheless, as the founder's granddaughter noted, Golden Gate Park would draw away many of the garden's patrons during the 1870s and 1880s, paving the way for its demise.[13]

The final deterrents to construction of parks in San Francisco were a couple of constraints on the city government. The San Francisco government would have been unlikely to respond to any pre-1865 calls for parks, because, as in the case of Brooklyn's Prospect Park, the Civil War delayed public construction as capital and other resources were directed to the war effort. Additionally, the People's Party controlled the municipal government for most of the period between 1856 and 1875, and they pursued extreme fiscal conservatism. A local institution, the party drew its membership from the Republican and Democratic businessmen who had united in response to preceding, irresponsible administrations. Politicians who had put the augmentation of their own wealth before public service had dominated the first years of the city. The People's Party had moved into control after a campaign vilifying their opponents. The party was composed of conservatives, many from the Committees of Vigilance, who were suspicious of Irish Catholic voters, wished to impart greater "respectability"—that is less openness—to the political system, and longed for the lowest tax burden possible. They questioned all public expenditures, stood vocally against corruption, and viewed the best government as "businesslike" in its organization and administration. Upon assuming control, they passed the Consolidation Act of 1856, which reduced tax rates and public spending, dropping the city's expenditures by a dramatic 86.6 percent, from $2,646,000 in 1855 (mostly salaries) to $353,000 in 1857. The Department of Streets, Sewers, and Squares, which held responsibility for the city's existing public spaces, had the budget for its triad of responsibilities slashed a devastating 99.8 percent, from $479,000 in 1854 to $605 in 1857. Next, the new administration ordered that municipal expenditures always balance with revenues. In the words of one party executive, they wanted the city's finances to be "on a 'pay as you go' basis," with any new expenditures coming only at the expense of existing ones. Under these fiscal constraints, it was nearly impossible for San Francisco to create a public park, because the large initial and continuing costs would overwhelm the city's budget for any year. The only solution would have been to float long-term bonds, but this mechanism was also forbidden.[14]

The power of the People's Party arose from fiscal concerns but its appearance also signaled a cultural change among San Franciscans. As the war wound down, the recklessness and day-to-day living that had characterized the city's early years gave way to a greater respect for civil order. "There was a visible diminution of what may be termed the brazenness of evil," related John Young. "Instead of attempting to force all to a common [that is, low] level, there was a growing disposition to respect the man who avoided drinking places and refused to gamble." It was into this soil, where there was a growing concern about the good society, that the idea of a large city park was planted.[15]

## FREDERICK LAW OLMSTED
## AND THE FIRST SAN FRANCISCO PARK PLAN

Although private conversations undoubtedly preceded the public discussions that ultimately led to a major park for San Francisco, public debate clearly began on July 25, 1865, when the editor of the *Daily Evening Bulletin*, George K. Fitch, asked his readers if it was not time for the city of San Francisco to create a true park. Referring to another article in that day's *Bulletin*, "The Parks and Pleasure Grounds of Capital Cities," Fitch insisted San Francisco needed a park, not just a scattering of squares, private gardens, and amusement centers, if it was ever to join the ranks of the world's great cities. Thoughtful, provocative, and articulate, Fitch's editorial quickly generated a detailed reply, in a letter printed on August 4 that was signed "*Rusticus in urbe*" (a country man in the city) but was none other than Frederick Law Olmsted.[16]

Olmsted had lived most of his life in the northeastern United States but was in California at the time after resigning his post as the head of the U.S. Sanitary Commission in August 1863 to become the manager of a Mariposa gold mine. According to historian Victoria Post Ranney, Olmsted accepted this lucrative job managing a 44,000-acre estate to free himself from financial concerns and, "by proving his abilities as a practical businessman, to command the respect of influential men for his ideas." His two years in California, however, had failed to come even close to meeting his expectations. It turned out that the mine had played out before he and his family arrived, and shortly after he was hired, the company cut off his capital supply. Soon they even refused to pay his salary.[17]

As the mining company spiraled into collapse, Olmsted hunted about in California for new opportunities, including landscape architecture projects. He worked briefly on two private-estate designs on the San Francisco peninsula but little came of them. He directed his major efforts eastward, across San Francisco Bay, where he began two projects in 1864. At the first, the directors of the Mountain View Cemetery in Oakland asked him for a plan that would "make their 200 acres . . . into the finest cemetery in the state." Accepting the commission, Olmsted sent initial designs in early 1865. They recalled Central Park's plan: an east-west axial mall commanded the center, while curvilinear roads and walks, here more closely spaced than in the New York park, snaked about to the north and south. The plan was eagerly embraced and implemented; the cemetery was dedicated in May and its initial improvements completed in August 1865. Olmsted's second commission came for the College of California, the forerunner to the University of California, in nearby Berkeley. The college's trustees aspired to a plan that would improve the campus proper even as it attracted prosperous, influential, and tasteful residents to the adjacent neighborhood. On September 4, 1865, Olmsted proposed a suburban campus, later producing a plan that sought to balance the isolation of a rural campus with the "overheated" nature of an urban one. Unfortunately, it was never implemented.[18]

About the time Olmsted was working on the College of California's plan, he sent the letter that the *Daily Evening Bulletin* published on August 4. Unsurprisingly, Olmsted supported Fitch's proposition and took the opportunity to link a large, public park to the four virtues. "[The] citizens of San Francisco," he declared, "need a recreation ground and would be more benefited by it than those of any other city of equal importance." Drawing on the example of New York's Central Park, he explained that a San Francisco park would increase local prosperity, because real estate values would rise; residents who might have moved away, "particularly . . . citizens of wealth and large tax payers," would remain; and new population, "particularly of wealthy citizens," would be attracted. Experts, he stressed, had also demonstrated that parks encouraged public health. Cornelius Agnew, a physician and colleague of Olmsted on the U.S. Sanitary Commission, had stated that "the poorer classes" as well as the wealthy, and "especially the women and children," showed a "marked improvement in health and vigor" from regular visits to a park. "There is no doubt that the park has added years to the lives of many." Olmsted was more progressive than his peers when arguing that women and children were the special beneficiaries of a park. As we shall see, for several more decades, few other activists would express serious concerns about the value of parks for women. Turning to the virtue of democratic equality, Olmsted suggested that a park was *the* place for all of society to gather amicably. "Not only its popularity with all classes, but the degree of propriety, civility, good order and decorum with which all classes meet and enjoy themselves in it, has far exceeded the most sanguine expectations of its original projectors and advocates." Finally, taking sight on the virtue of social coherence, he declared a park to be an incubator of safety and social order. Despite the well-known "bad reputation" of New Yorkers, he wrote, they were nonetheless exceedingly law abiding in the park. "The truth is . . . there is no park in Europe that is made as good use of by the people, none where the proportion of offenses against good order and good taste is so small, or the respect for the regulations necessary for the best use of a park, so great as in the park of New York." In Olmsted's utopian vision, parks sat squarely at the center of the good society.[19]

As Olmsted was pitching the virtues of a San Francisco park, he knew that the authorities and public were "favorably disposed to the project" but were being delayed by two concerns. On the one hand, the city's fiscal structure resisted change, necessitating "extraordinary caution in undertaking improvements which may involve large expenditure." A park in San Francisco, Olmsted counseled, was certain to be expensive, since Central Park's site had cost New York over $7 million for just the land and purchasing expenses. Nevertheless, the cost was "no reason for neglect." As he had noted when linking a park to prosperity, wealth would flow from a park, not into it, making delay the worst possible policy for those concerned about costs.

> If a park is to be made for San Francisco at any time and to be within a convenient distance of the present populous part of the city, it is as certain as anything in the future can be that every year's delay in acquiring land for it, and in determining the general plan, so that the grading of streets, the construction of railroads, or sewers, of buildings, the laying of gas and water pipes, etc., may be adapted to it, will greatly add to the expenditure which will be involved.

On the other hand, Olmsted acknowledged that the public and municipal authorities were justified in being cautious because they felt that San Francisco's "treeless, wind shorn and sandy suburbs" offered "no fair opportunity of forming a park." These were reasonable concerns. Olmsted himself entertained no doubts that the site was difficult and challenging, but in contrast to the San Franciscans, and the majority of landscape designers in his day and since, Olmsted did not consider the humid-environment models that jumped into people's minds to be appropriate. "It must be admitted that the attempt to form a park in the style of the Central Park or the parks of London and Paris, would be absurd. . . . That it would need to be of an original and quite peculiar style is probable." But the discussion need not end there, he observed, because alternative designs were possible. "Though, it would perhaps require much careful study to secure it, it is not unreasonable to believe it practicable."[20]

In order to keep the public discussion heated, William Ashburner and Frederick Billings, two of Olmsted's influential acquaintances from the Mariposa mine, soon circulated a pro-park petition that adopted the landscape architect's ideas and concerns. On the sixth of November, "a large number of citizens and taxpayers" presented this petition to the San Francisco Board of Supervisors. "The great cities of our own country," it declared, "as well as of Europe, have found it necessary at some period of their growth, to provide large parks, or pleasure-grounds, for the amusement and recreation of the people. . . . No city in the world needs such . . . grounds more than San Francisco." A "great park," like Central or Prospect Parks, would be wonderful, but it would fly in the face of Olmsted's editorial suggestion that such an approach was unsuitable to the site. Instead, the petitioners suggested,

"the great want of the city" is "a series of small parks, connected by varied and orna-
mented avenues." Everyone knows that "until some provision is made to meet this
want . . . San Francisco . . . will not be an attractive place." So, they inquired, why
were the authorities not pressing forward? The project was sensible, delay expensive, and with the need for a park "patent to everybody . . . it would seem to be wisdom . . . to have some general plan adopted as early as possible." Again repeating
Olmsted's view, they argued for a comprehensive plan now, to keep costs down later.
"However slowly or rapidly the work on the grounds may be prosecuted, all the
other developments of the city . . . will then be adapted to the plan of the Park, and
thus the great expense of subsequent charges will be avoided." Wrapping up their
appeal, the petitioners requested a consultation between the supervisors and Frederick Law Olmsted about the matter.[21]

Less than two weeks later, another major newspaper, the *Daily Alta California,*
added its voice to the rising chorus in support of parks, but in contrast to Olmsted
and the petitioners, it did not support the idea of a system. Instead, the paper
wanted a large park where one could lose sight of the surrounding landscape.
Under the banner of "A Great Public Park Wanted in San Francisco," the *Daily Alta
California* maintained that the city and its site were barren, devoid of the real and
necessary nature that occurred in places like Central Park.

> Looking at our city from the bay, or the Golden Gate, in the summer and fall, we see
> a mass of yellow houses on yellow hills of yellow sand or yellow rock. . . . We want a
> place where, under the protection of our hills, we can have fifty, a hundred, or two
> hundred acres, sown with grass, planted with trees and laid off with roads pleasant
> for walking and driving. We need the reviving influences of beautiful nature.

The future affairs of the city, warned the paper, must not be postponed. If they
were, "the unwise policy of to-day will bear an abundant crop of *evil* to-morrow"
(emphasis added). A few weeks later, still another major newspaper, the *Daily
Morning Call,* also came out in support of "a magnificent public park" but it was
even more expansive about the size of the park needed—"an aggregate of one
thousand acres, in one or more bodies."[22]

The *Alta California*'s characterization of San Francisco's physical site as "yellow
. . . yellow . . . yellow" was warranted in the 1860s. The city is located in a Mediterranean climate where over 85 percent of its scant 21 inches of annual rainfall arrives
during the winter months, making the native plants, which are adapted to long,

San Francisco in the 1860s was a visually stark environment. This view looking west from Telegraph Hill in 1864 illustrates why the grid of the streets, the lack of ornamental vegetation, and the shrubbiness of the sparse natural vegetation failed to satisfy San Franciscans' desire for a "nature" that looked like New York's Central Park. Point San Jose (now Black Point in Fort Mason) is in the middle distance with North Beach to the east of it. Reproduced by permission of the San Francisco Maritime National Historical Park (A11.14.143 N).

dry spells, often unattractive to an uneducated and unprepared eye. Only a small portion of the site bore the lush green requisite to the majority of residents who had migrated from humid environments. In addition, the western half of San Francisco consisted mostly of sand dunes, which moved with the winds, especially near the coast, and were yellow-white in color. The remaining land was composed of yellow, orange, and reddish soils cloaked largely in coastal scrub and coastal prairie, although other vegetational communities occasionally interrupted these.

Coastal scrub consists of a mixture of seasonal grasses and herbaceous species mingled with low shrubs. During the winter and spring months, when the rain falls, the grasses and herbs put forth luxuriant, rich green growth, but once the rains dwindle and summer arrives, their leaves dry, veiling the hills in yellow-brown. Interspersed among the grassy species are the shrubs. Some, like toyon (*Heteromeles arbutifolia*), are evergreen and dark in color; but many others, such as California sagebrush (*Artemisia californica*) and coyotebrush (*Baccharis pilularis*), are grey or grey-green all year. Co-dominating with the coastal scrub, especially near the northern portions of the city, was coastal prairie. Above the shoreline cliffs and landward from the edges of various sandy beaches stretched perennial grasses such as California oat grass (*Danthonia californica*), bracken (*Pteridium aquilinum* var. *pubescens*) and other herbaceous species, like summer lupine (*Lupinus formosus*), which masked the earth in green and the many colors of winter and spring flowers. However, this vegetation complex rarely contained trees or large shrubs, so when summer arrived, yellow-browns predominated.

On the eastern side of the peninsula, close to the shores of the bay, coastal forest provided some aesthetic relief during summer. Broadleaf trees such as hazelnut (*Corylus cornuta* var. *californica*), coast live oak (*Quercus agrifolia*), and blue elderberry (*Sambucus mexicana*), as well as shrubs like California coffeeberry (*Rhamnus californica*), California blackberry (*Rubus ursinus*), and, no one's favorite, western poison oak (*Toxicodendron diversilobum*) remained green when the coastal scrub and prairie turned brown. These pleasant woodlands, however, were tightly limited in their extent, occurring mostly in the damper lowlands where streams flowed and spread out near the bay. On a few of the moister ridges also, evergreen bishop pine (*Pinus muricata*) and coast live oak trees mixed with various manzanitas (*Arctostaphylos* spp.), coyotebrush, California coffeeberry, western poison oak, and evergreen huckleberry (*Vaccinium ovatum*) to provide some summer greenery.[23]

Nevertheless, most of the dry, hilly land without the dominant coastal scrub and prairie was blanketed in chaparral, a type of vegetation characterized by tough-leaved, evergreen shrubs adapted to a dry habitat. The principal species are chamise (*Adenostema fasciculatum*), various manzanitas, several *Ceanothus* species, toyon, scrub oak (*Quercus berberidifolia*), and western poison oak. Chaparral is rarely above nine feet in height and usually dense, making it difficult to penetrate, as well as highly resinous, harsh against the skin, and extremely vulnerable to fire. During winter months, chaparral will be richly green and laced with equally green and sometimes colorful grasses and herbs, but when the summer drought arrives, the shrubs go dormant, get stiffer, and lose their rich green even as the grassy species turn brown. And, everywhere, the dust rises.

To someone raised in the northeastern portion of the United States (the majority of native-born Americans in San Francisco were from this region), San Francisco's site appeared stunted, desolate, and even dead. The natural environment had evoked a similarly grim reaction in Richard Henry Dana, the author of *Two Years Before the Mast* and a Massachusetts native, Frank Soulé, a Mainer, and Frederick Law Olmsted. Arriving in December 1835, Dana described the site as "dreary sand hills, with little grass to be seen, and few trees, and beyond them higher hills, steep and barren, their sides gullied by the rains." Soulé, who was even more scathing in his condemnation, felt the city's particular location was "about the most barren part of the district; and the immediate vicinity consists chiefly of low sand-hills, covered with coarse shrubs and scattered patches of grass." Olmsted, a landscape architect who had traveled to Europe, East Asia, and Central America, and was familiar with diverse vegetation, nonetheless was put off at first sight. Writing to his wife, Mary Perkins Olmsted, in October 1863, he described the hills he saw as he initially sailed into San Francisco Bay as "perfectly bare of trees or shrubs—and almost awfully bleak." In addition to possessing a naturally severe site, San Francisco had grown through the 1860s without the softening effect of ornamental vegetation, since almost no one planted street trees, shrubs, gardens, or yards. Some public spaces, notably older ones like Portsmouth Square, had been improved somewhat; but they did little to relieve the barrenness presented to eyes trained in a lush, humid environment. It is no wonder park advocates called for new, extensive greenspaces—they sought relief from an environment that struck them as profoundly alien and ugly.[24]

In response to the park activists, especially their petition, People's Party mayor Henry P. Coon, City and County Attorney John H. Saunders, and Supervisors Gerrit W. Bell and Frank McCoppin contacted Olmsted on November 11, 1865, to "obtain his views and recommendations as to extent of grounds required, and suitable location for a Park . . . the expense of said Report, not to exceed $500." This interaction was the first *official* exchange between Olmsted and city officials but not the earliest contact between them. At some time earlier in 1865, Mayor Coon reported to the city supervisors, he had invited the landscape architect "to make a careful inspection of this peninsula, with the intention of getting from him plans for a public park. I conducted Mr. Olmsted over every part of surrounding country and promised to send him maps and other memoranda to guide him in making the plans." If what the mayor said is true, it seems clear that he, William Ashburner, and Frederick Billings, along with the organizers of the November 6 petition, Olmsted, and perhaps others, had privately orchestrated the demand for a public project. On March 31, 1866, Olmsted submitted a preliminary plan that attempted to accommodate the semiarid environment of San Francisco and demonstrated his concept of a park *system* for the first time. As he and Vaux would do for Brooklyn later in 1866 and Buffalo in 1868, Olmsted proposed a series of separate but connected spaces designed to meet a range of recreational needs.[25]

The centerpiece of the Olmsted plan was an irregularly shaped, sheltered expanse called the "Rural Ground" consisting of approximately 200 acres located along the western edge of the built portion of San Francisco (centered around the current Duboce Park). Readily accessible from town and central to the surrounding suburbs, the Rural Ground connected eastward to a hub (situated near the current intersection of Eddy Street and Van Ness Avenue) by the continuous, linear Promenade. From the hub, the Promenade turned north to the proposed Marine-Parade and Saluting Ground on the shoreline at Point San Jose (now Black Point where Fort Mason and the Aquatic Park meet) as well as southeast toward an open end (at Market and Larkin Streets). The plan also suggested how the designs could extend to the south and southwest but did not recommend immediate construction, just land purchases for later development. Olmsted carefully avoided the term *park* for any portion of the project, calling the entire plan a "Pleasure Ground," because from his technical perspective a park incorporated a large expanse of grass, shrubs, trees, rocks, and water. Such a landscape was inappropriate in semiarid San Francisco, and Olmsted recognized that it would be costly to maintain. Instead, he drew on his "dim memories of Italian villas" retained from an 1856 visit to Italy and personal observations in San Francisco to create a regional style of landscape design appropriate for the Mediterranean climate.[26]

As Olmsted's Central Park did, his San Francisco Pleasure Ground had planted perimeters, but they served two purposes instead of one in San Francisco. The "thick plantations" of trees and shrubs created the desired visual barrier between the refreshing, verdant interior and the exhausting urban environment so that San Franciscans, just like New Yorkers, could "escape" from city into rural life; living in this western outpost was no less frantic and harried than living in any other rapidly growing American city. Also, in San Francisco's unique physical site, the boundary of greenery served as a windbreak. Located abreast of the Pacific Ocean's cold California Current and on the tip of a peninsula, San Francisco is buffeted by bitter, often driving northwesterly winds, particularly during the summer when the hot interior draws sharp drafts through the Golden Gate. At these times, the leafy

Point San Jose (now Black Point in Fort Mason) in the 1860s was the site for the Marine-Parade and Saluting Ground in Frederick Law Olmsted's 1866 proposal for a San Francisco park system. Reproduced by permission of the Bancroft Library, University of California, Berkeley.

margin acted as a buffer between the prevailing bluster and the interior plants and visitors.[27]

The stretches of Promenade were thoughtfully designed for gathering, strolling, and riding in a cold but dry climate. The primary segment was the one that ran northeast and then north out of the Rural Ground to the tip of the peninsula. Olmsted noted that a number of potential routes were possible for this corridor but as an example described a 390-foot-wide course along Van Ness Avenue with 55 feet on each side reserved for streets and a terminus at San Francisco Bay. The center of the Promenade and its surrounding ornamental horticultural grounds would run in a cut at least 20 feet deep with planted, sloping sides. The median would consist of a 24-foot-wide pedestrian mall with planted borders that had a carriage and horse roadway on either side—the reverse of Brooklyn's parkways, where Olmsted and Vaux would situate the roadway in the center. Turf and flowers would blanket the adjacent, lower slopes, and there would be shrubs and trees above and "a thicket

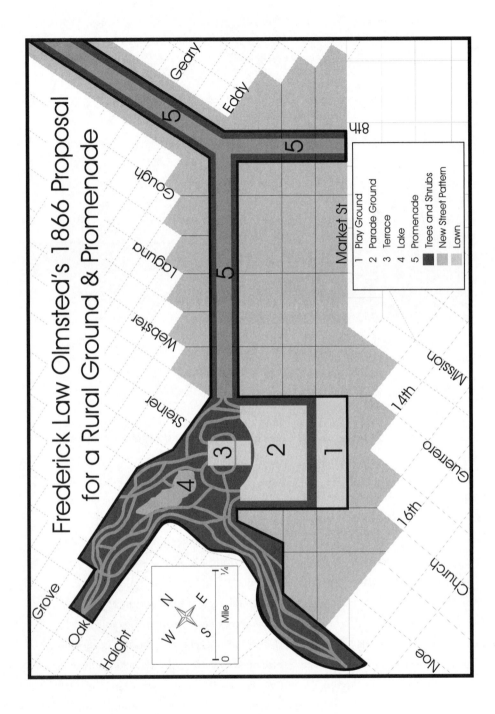

# Frederick Law Olmsted's 1866 Proposal
## for a Rural Ground & Promenade

Legend:
1 Play Ground
2 Parade Ground
3 Terrace
4 Lake
5 Promenade

Trees and Shrubs
New Street Pattern
Lawn

Streets: Geary, Eddy, 8th, Gough, Laguna, Webster, Steiner, Grove, Oak, Haight, Market St, Mission, 14th, Guerrero, 16th, Church, Noe

N W E S

0  Mile  ¼

of hardy evergreens all along the top." Hydrants sat at regular intervals along the edge of adjacent streets "so that, (with hose and punctured pipes, such as are used for watering the lawns and roads of the Bois de Boulogne [in Paris]), the dust could be kept down, and the turf and plantations readily sprinkled as often as necessary."[28]

The beauty of the Promenade was horticultural rather than scenic. Olmsted felt that the plantings along the Promenade had to be compact in design, protected from the deforming, drying winds, and "rich in detail, close to the eye." Strangers to San Francisco, he had noticed, were "usually much attracted by the beauty of certain small gardens, house courts and porches." This beauty relied on boldness, proximity, and novelty rather than subtlety, expanse, and regularity. An eclectic plantsman, Olmsted's plan mingled native and exotic species, including cacti, roses (*Rosa hybrida*), ceanothus (*Ceanothus*), rhododendrons (*Rhododendron*), ivies (*Hedera*), geraniums (*Pelargonium*), tulips (*Tulipa*), callas (*Zantedeschia*), and more. In some places he arranged the elements formally but in others the design was naturalistic. Most species would be set in the ground, but some of the more formally treated ones would sit in containers, which might be on pedestals, walls, or the ground. Large sections contained native California species, but alternate areas might illustrate the plants of "Australia, China, Japan, or Siberia, in so far as they would suit the situation." This sort of beauty had to be examined closely, since it would, in Olmsted's opinion, be lost in "such expanded landscapes as form the chief attraction of parks."[29]

The northern end of the planned Promenade terminated in the Marine-Parade and Saluting Ground. San Francisco, unlike Brooklyn and Buffalo, was a major harbor, and this segment of the Pleasure Ground could provide a waterside place to receive arriving dignitaries formally. A quay extended into the bay from the Ground's plaza, with a swath of lawn both large enough for people to stand and sit when guests arrived and bordered by evergreens on the west to block the wind. Alongside the plaza was a pavilion for receiving guests. In effect, this segment of Olmsted's plan was "the sea-gate of the city."[30]

The Rural Ground was a protected valley with moist soil and abundant growth; it contained the segment of the Pleasure Ground that was most like a park. The Rural Ground included "those parts of the general system of pleasure grounds which require considerable lateral [rather than linear] extension." Along its southern edge was an extent of low, level ground for a moderately sized playground and parade ground. Olmsted supported the need for a full-sized parade ground but argued that it should be separate from the rest of the Pleasure Ground and located some miles from the city. An area large enough for military maneuvers would, were it a part of the Pleasure Ground, cost too much and "be otherwise objectionable." In the protected hills to the north and west of the play- and parade ground he proposed a "secluded garden" containing a curvilinear system of roads and paths. On the upper portion rested a grove of trees and a picturesque setting of rocks and terraces planted in shrubs and vines—Olmsted likened it to the Ramble in Central Park—while the lower part was a pastoral scene including a small lawn and a placid lake. "From within this garden, no carriage road or buildings, except those of a rural character, inviting rest, should be seen." This was the only area that would be scenic, so Olmsted warned that "no pains should be spared to make it a spot of pure and tranquil sylvan loveliness."[31]

Between the secluded garden and the play- and parade ground was the Grand Terrace. A place for people to mingle and contemplate the scenery, it incorporated dense parterres, or formal flower gardens, with fountains, and it had two levels— one for pedestrians and one for equestrians. Connecting the Terrace with the play-and-parade ground was a bandstand and public-speaking platform, a place of entertainment and civic events. The stand faced away from the secluded garden and toward the ground where "a crowd of many thousand persons might be assembled."[32]

Laura Wood Roper, an Olmsted biographer, describes his San Francisco plan as "brilliantly imaginative," a demonstration of "thoroughness and foresight" that entitles Olmsted "to be regarded as a pioneer city planner." An insightful, creative, and bold response to a novel and challenging environment, it is also the first demonstration of the park-system approach he would employ frequently at other sites. Nevertheless, Olmsted's plan was never implemented, falling victim to an aggregation of forces. First, by March 1866 when Olmsted sent his plan to the San Francisco supervisors, he had again taken up residence in New York. He had left San Francisco in October 1865 to form a partnership with Calvert Vaux to design Brooklyn's Prospect Park. Therefore, he could not personally engage in discussions of his San Francisco plan's merits and weaknesses. Second, a communication delay upset the possibility of immediate state support for the plan. The supervisors' contract, including maps and notes, was sent via Wells, Fargo, & Company on November 11, 1865, but did not leave San Francisco for months. Olmsted received it in New York on February 26 and, working as hastily as possible, expressed his plan back to San Francisco on March 31. Nevertheless, on May 9, 1866, shortly after he had received Olmsted's report, Mayor Coon wrote to tell Olmsted that the supervisors had been unable to "procure the necessary legislation for carrying your report into practical operation." The express office foul-up had delayed the events so much that when Olmsted's plan arrived, it was, according to the mayor, too late "to be submitted to the last [session of the California] legislature." Given the city's charter, no project as large as Olmsted's could be pursued without state support. Since the legislature was out of session, the project was thrown into limbo. By June 29, 1866, the situation had further deteriorated. Writing again to Olmsted, the mayor admitted, "It is quite uncertain what action will be taken in future in reference to a public park—an impression seems to exist that your plan will cost more than the city will be able to afford for some time to come." Although the mayor approved of the plan, he found that there was "great opposition" to it.[33]

The source of this opposition may have been people who, like the writers in the *Daily Alta California* and the *Daily Morning Call* mentioned above, preferred a single, large park to a series of smaller, linked facilities. Driven by multiple motivations, some were in sympathy with George Fitch, the editor of the *Daily Evening Bulletin,* who wanted San Francisco to be like New York, a world-class city. The latter, they noted, did not create a system of parks but a single, large park. Why should San Francisco be any different? They thought it would be best to stick to a proven formula rather than to experiment.

Many of the opponents to the Olmsted plan also favored other sites as much as they disapproved of his design. For several months prior to contacting Olmsted, the "Mission Crowd," the "North Beach Clique," and a "western group" had been lobbying for a park located not southwest of the city but either immediately south, northwest, or due west of the urban core around Portsmouth Square. After the supervisors' request for a proposal had been mailed to Olmsted, an expectant lull developed in anticipation of his response; but when his proposal arrived, was reviewed, and found unsatisfactory by these groups, it simply stirred them to greater efforts in support of their favorite locations. Each group wanted the immediate rise in property values that they believed would accompany a new park. Owners in and beyond the Mission District allied themselves with the Rincon Hill and South Park inhabitants, whose addresses were among the most prestigious in San Francisco at the time, to strongly contend for a southerly location. Arrayed against them were residents and property owners towards North Beach who collaborated with others on Russian Hill and Nob Hill to secure nearly 1,400 acres on the Presidio Military

Reservation for a park to the north of the city. It was, in the words of one observer, "a great fight: public meetings; halls overflowing; store-box overflow meetings in the streets; processions with banners and transparencies, lamp flambeau, and tar torches; newspaper columns carrying long articles and rampant editorials." This particular conflict, however, would soon fade, as a third faction, the western site advocates, began to prevail. In the end, this group would win, not because their location was the most accessible nor the most promising in terms of design, but because a park in their area became the means for settling the nettlesome problem of the Outside Lands.[34]

## THE OUTSIDE LANDS

The Outside Lands were a sizeable area west of what is now downtown and beyond the charter line of 1851. Including today's Richmond and Sunset Districts, the vast majority of these roughly 8,400 acres was covered in loose, blowing sand dunes that extended from the municipal boundary on the south, to the Seacliff District on the north, and east from the Pacific Ocean through the low points between the hills almost to San Francisco Bay. The sand blocked streams in the west to create a series of tidal and freshwater ponds and lakes, the most significant being Lake Merced, Laguna Puerca (Pine Lake), Laguna Honda, and Mountain Lake; smaller bodies lay scattered about elsewhere. As sand was blown about, the stability of the dunes was constantly challenged. Even if a dune became "fixed" in place by a rich mat of intertwined plants, a strong wind could uproot enough of these sand binders to cause a "blowout" and the dune's complete breakdown. The mobility of the sand depended on the plants rooted in it and on the quantity of organic matter and clay it contained. Plant survival was always threatened, as strong winds carried salt spray well inland, retarding growth. Also, the sands held water poorly and were generally deficient in the nutrients plants need. Furthermore, the surface of the sands, being light in color, mercilessly reflected heat back at the plants, especially on clear, sunny days, leading many species to evolve light-colored surfaces and other moisture retaining strategies. These were demanding conditions for vegetation.[35]

Despite the adverse environment, vegetation here was rich in diversity, with a variety of grasses, herbaceous species, and a few shrubs; but trees did not develop, because their roots could not anchor them sufficiently in the loose sand, which allowed the frequently high winds to blow them over. The most effective binder was dune grass (*Leymus mollis*) but salt rush (*Juncus Lesueurii*), Pacific wild rye (*Leymus pacificus*), and sand-dune blue grass (*Poa douglasii*) were common. Low-growing, often matting species, like sand verbena (*Abronia latifolia*), California salt bush (*Atriplex californica*), beach strawberry (*Fragraria chiloensis*), and sea plantain (*Plantago maritima*), also helped to stabilize dunes. Yellow bush lupine (*Lupinus arboreus*) and chamisso beach lupine (*Lupinus chamissonis*) were the most conspicuous shrubby plants, the latter being most common where sand gave way to dirt. Elsewhere, one could also expect to come across coastal sagewort (*Artemisia pycnocephala*) and coyotebrush.

Since the signing of San Francisco's charter of incorporation in 1851, the ownership of this austere and shifting land had been in dispute. In court after court, San Francisco had held that this was city land subject to its disposal, since the area had been part of the original pueblo. In opposition, the federal government claimed that the land was outside the pueblo and therefore the property of the United States. Slowed by distance, complexity, and the Civil War, the case dragged along until the U.S. Circuit Court ruled in San Francisco's favor in May 1865. However, the issue was not laid to rest by the decision.[36]

During the thirteen years of court battles, self-proclaimed "settlers" had moved onto the land, trusting for a decision in favor of the United States. If the federal government won, these squatters hoped to establish homesteads of up to 160 acres and profit handsomely when the railroad arrived and the city expanded westward. A handful of the squatters were sufficiently wealthy and influential to prevent the city from profiting from the decision of the federal court. When San Francisco won, this cadre apparently persuaded U.S. senator John Conness, a Republican from Sacramento, and Congressman John Bidwell, a Republican from Chico, to support a congressional bill that effectively reversed the court's decision. The bill was passed and signed into law in March 1866. The new law relinquished the federal government's claim to all the disputed lands, which is what the city had wanted and expected; but then it directed that the property "be disposed of and conveyed by the city to parties in its *bona fide* actual possession," that is, the squatters. The law came as a terrible blow to many in the city because it not only deprived the municipality of revenue from land sales but prevented other San Franciscans from purchasing small lots at the reasonable prices the city authorities would have set. The only exceptions in the law were for any parcels that might have been sold legally and for any which were needed for federal or municipal purposes, including, most suggestively, for a public park. In a stroke of ingenious, if backroom, politics, the Outside Land squatters had the federal government transform them into the property's owners and deal them a high card in the local park site game. On the heels of this act, neither the northern, the southern, nor the Olmsted proposals made any further headway; and on March 27, 1868, the episode closed, when California's governor signed the final bills conveying the Outside Lands to San Francisco for disposal.[37]

Despite the public consternation the federal act of March 1866 caused, it could not have been a surprise to San Francisco's authorities. The U.S. Congress would not have passed a bill affecting the most significant city in California without any local discussion. These dialogues were never public, but the San Francisco authorities' inaction strongly suggests they occurred. If the supervisors or the mayor had been opposed to the legislation, they could have blocked it before passage or overturned it later. Similarly, the squatters could have protested federal interference but they were quiet. The major private voices were mute and the city's authorities did nothing because they must have been involved in the legislation's creation. Historians Lewis Francis Byington and Oscar Lewis suspected the hand of the Outside Land cadre when they wrote that with the bill's passage "only a small group managed to enrich itself." Even John Young, who was generally a sanguine, Whiggish historian and not accusatory on this specific issue, admitted that the squatters were politically powerful and determined to benefit from any settlement between San Francisco and the United States. William Hammond Hall, a keen chronicler of the events surrounding the park site selection, also sensed the influence of the Outside Land squatters, suggesting that the authorities were a part of the deal. According to him, people said at the time that the members of Congress had been misled and defrauded by private interests about the wishes of San Franciscans and their local authorities. Congress had only been doing what it thought was wanted, and now the city was stuck with the results. The municipal authorities, in Hall's view, felt they had two options open to them after the act had passed, either fight it in court, losing municipal revenue for years and hampering development, or accept the title settlements, the park site, the city's other share of the lands, and an immediate growth in municipal revenue. They chose the latter, explained Hall, because they "seemed to think that a coterie of men who were resourceful and powerful enough to delay the city before the State Legislature, as had been done for years past, and then to go to Congress and have an Act passed, which, purporting to confirm yet really set aside a United States Circuit Court decision and decree, surely was a power which a mere Board of Supervisors should settle with on the best terms possible." The real fraud, Hall insisted, lay not in the congressional act but the quiet acceptance of it by city authorities.[38]

The March 1866 act, however, neither dictated a method for determining which land to include in a public park nor indicated if the city had to pay those currently residing on it, and if so, how. These issues remained unaddressed and subject to further court battles. Even so, city supervisor Frank McCoppin recognized an opportunity to settle these nettlesome issues and seized it to advance his political career. McCoppin represented the Outside Lands area, so he likely knew what the now legalized landholders were planning, was on the committee that had negotiated an Outside Lands settlement, and was also a member of the supervisorial committee communicating with Frederick Law Olmsted about a park plan. Uniquely privy to these three sources of information, McCoppin decided an Outside Lands park could be the resolution to both questions and a plank on which he could be elected mayor. He was correct on all counts, becoming mayor in 1867 and then organizing the complex land and money exchange that would create a park. McCoppin also saw an Outside Lands park as a solution potentially profitable for himself. He was the principal stockholder in the San Francisco Grading Company, and he "reasoned that if the park were located in the hilly section of the Outside Lands, he could get the contract to level it." This ingenious deal, however, would also generate yet another wave of public disputes.[39]

The first Democratic mayor elected since the rise of the People's Party in the 1850s, Frank McCoppin ran as a reformer who favored government support for projects that benefited the public, in particular a new city hall and the park, and in opposition to the restrictions of the Consolidation Act of 1856, which had been proposed, passed, and defended with single-minded devotion by the People's Party. The act "bristled with obstacles to extravagance," declared John Young. "The strictest economy . . . was attained . . . by the introduction of a rigid system of checks, which made expenditures for any except the most ordinary purposes practically impossible." However, in addition to reining in expenditures, the Consolidation Act impeded the creation of a large park. Its strict provisions against the creation of any debt or liability hamstrung the municipality, preventing it from pursuing the path taken by New York City when creating Central Park—the selling of long-term municipal bonds. Consequently, observed Young, the act "made it impossible to initiate an enterprise, no matter how desirable, without the intervention of the legislature." A successful park proposal would have to remain within the limits of the Consolidation Act and be acceptable to Sacramento. In effect, the state indirectly ruled the city. In 1869, after lengthy negotiations, Frank McCoppin, the members of a municipal committee, and the Outside Land holders finally struck an innovative bargain that allowed San Francisco to obtain over a thousand acres for a large park without using up the city's entire annual budget or going beyond a current year's revenues.[40]

On May 18, 1868, the San Francisco Board of Supervisors received the majority and minority reports of the Committee on Outside Lands Upon the Reservations of Land for Public Uses. The committee was charged with recommending locations for a park or parks; it had returned a split decision even though the members agreed on a number of points. Both reports cited Olmsted's 1866 plan as support for their recommendation, referring to the landscape architect's thoughts about the need to protect the park and its visitors from the wind and to create a "system of walks, rides, drives, and resting places." At the same time, neither the majority nor the minority view favored Olmsted's system of small parks connected by parkways, never even mentioning this alternative or Olmsted and Vaux's proposal for parkways in Brooklyn. It may be that the committee members were unaware of the eastern development, since the plan had only been presented to the Brooklyn Park Commissioners in January 1868 and the news may not have reached the West Coast in four months. But it may also be that they were unimpressed with the proposed Brooklyn park system, since the parkways existed only in blueprints and remained in that state as late as 1873. The committee did discuss New York's Central Park but did so only in a very favorable light, saying they were determined to create "a rural retreat and places of sylvan seclusion." Such a park, they argued, could never achieve ruralness if it was anything less than a half-mile wide: "Central Park of New York is a few feet over half a mile; and a map of it shows that the width is none too great for proper arrangement and decoration."[41]

Both reports recommended a San Francisco park shaped like Central Park's elongate rectangle, and the entire committee unanimously supported the following propositions:

1. That the park should not be more than 1,000 acres in extent.
2. That it should extend to the ocean beach.

3. That it should be situated so as to include at least a part of the tract finally selected by a majority of the Committee.

The first point, in particular, is noteworthy, because it represents a concern for the future. The committee recognized that San Francisco's population would increase, and that although the acreage was more than was immediately needed, it might not be enough someday. At the same time, the committee identified an upper limit, knowing that they could not request much more without setting off resistance within the Outside Land holders. In addition, they recognized that this was their only chance to obtain the land at a reasonable price, since any of the property in the future would cost much more once the park had started raising nearby values. Furthermore, they knew that 1,000 acres would be very expensive to develop, even noting the costs to improve Central Park's 843 acres and concluding that their park would be at least as expensive. Notwithstanding their agreements, the committee was still divided about the best site for a park. The minority favored two unlinked sites totaling 1,043 acres. The first parcel was 66 acres just south of Haight Street between Masonic Avenue and Divisadero Street. The supervisors accepted this recommendation and it would shortly be named Buena Vista Park, but they rejected the minority's second site in favor of the majority's proposition. The minority's large parcel encompassed 977 acres and would have been about the same size and in the same location as the majority's single park, but it was slightly narrower from north to south in order to extend farther east to encompass the area beyond Stanyan Street between Grove Street, Masonic Avenue, and Haight Street. Instead, the supervisors embraced the majority's slightly larger location, soon to be called, "the Golden Gate Park."[42]

Once the supervisors agreed where to locate the new large park and what shape it would take, they had to negotiate an agreement with the Outside Land holders that would quiet all property titles, create the park, and not violate the Consolidation Act's proscriptions against debt. As we have seen, the landholders held a solid legal position going into these negotiations and, according to Frank McCoppin, the core group "had influence enough to block the city through the Legislature, in whatever it might attempt. . . . therefore, it was necessary to have, in so far as it could be obtained, the assent of their leaders to the principles of a plan of settlement before its details were unfolded." With an eye to gaining this support, the municipal authorities, with Mayor McCoppin at the head, called a conference to

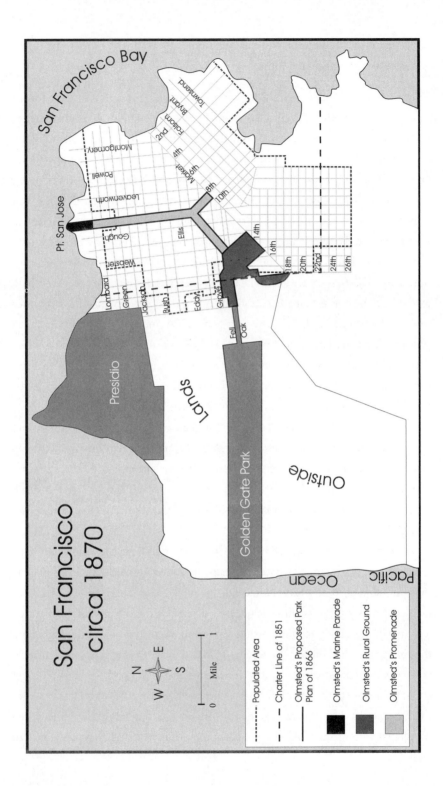

San Francisco
circa 1870

San Francisco Bay

Pt. San Jose

Presidio

Lands

Golden Gate Park

Outside

Pacific    Ocean

Montgomery
Powell
Leavenworth
Gough
Webster
Lombard
Green
Jackson
Bush
Eddy
Grove
Fell
Oak
Ellis
2nd
4th
Folsom
Bryant
Townsend
Market
8th
10th
14th
16th
18th
20th
22nd
24th
26th

N
W E
S

0    Mile    1

Populated Area
Charter Line of 1851
Olmsted's Proposed Park
Plan of 1866
Olmsted's Marine Parade
Olmsted's Rural Ground
Olmsted's Promenade

ask if the settlers would be willing to relinquish 10 percent of their holdings for a park if the city would unite with them to procure state legislation confirming their titles. Such legislation appealed to the Outside Land holders because it removed the uncertainty clouding ownership and allowed them to sell their settlements free, clear, and without dispute. Several months' negotiations led to a settlement with the landholders that provided public property for Golden Gate Park, Buena Vista Park, Mountain Lake Park, the land that would eventually become McCoppin Square and Parkside Square, and Lincoln Park (originally designated as a cemetery). The settlement also included land for another square (bounded by Bush and Sutter Streets and Masonic and Presidio Avenues), which never developed, and more than 100 institutions, such as schools and hospitals. In addition, the agreement called for a 10 percent tax on the assessed value of the remaining property—the first taxes the settlers had ever paid—to raise the money needed to purchase the parcels conceded to public use by the landholders. A number of small Outside Land holders opposed the settlement at several public meetings, but the agreement held. In the end, the city incurred no debts, since the agreement raised nearly all the funds necessary to pay for the property at the time of the park's creation. The supervisors ratified the agreement in 1869 and the state confirmed it in 1870. The legislature created for the park its own, self-governing body—the San Francisco Board of Park Commissioners—who were appointed by Democratic governor Henry Haight on April 19, 1870, and authorized to sell up to $225,000 of municipal bonds to begin the initial park improvements. A secretary and a superintendent served the board, while all other employees, whose posts would be created as necessary, answered to the superintendent.[43]

Newly created Golden Gate Park sat about one mile west of the city and had a size and shape quite similar to that of New York's Central Park. The former covered approximately 1,019 acres and possessed an axial ratio of 1:6.1, excluding the Avenue (today known as the Panhandle), while the latter encompassed 843 acres with a ratio of 1:5.5. No records indicate exactly why Golden Gate Park is rectilinear, but it may be explained by reference to several complementary possibilities. First, the 1868 site selection committee had been unanimous in their support for a park that extended to the ocean. If the Pacific had to be the western edge, any shape other than an east-west trending, elongated rectangle would have left the eastern (proximal) edge of the park inaccessibly far west of the built portion of San Francisco. Second, the unaltered natural landscape did not suggest a park with a

This 1865 photograph taken near today's Cliff House reveals the extent to which the western portion of the Outside Lands was mostly shifting sand dunes. Golden Gate Park would be created in this dune field. From John P. Young, *San Francisco: A History of the Pacific Coast Metropolis* (San Francisco, 1912), opposite p. 432.

rectilinear shape, but the city had surveyed the Outside Lands and projected its future streets as a rigid grid. If the park boundaries followed lot lines, rather than cutting across them to work with the natural features, fewer legal disputes were likely to develop. Consequently, the main body of Golden Gate Park was designed to fit neatly within an area delimited by the Pacific Ocean, Stanyan Street, Fulton Street (which at the time was called D Street from approximately 8th Avenue to the ocean), and H Street, while the Avenue extended east out of the park proper to fill the rectangle bounded by Stanyan, Fell, Oak, and Baker Streets. Third, Golden Gate Park like Central Park is one-half mile in width. The national reputation of the latter and the references to it in the site-selection committee's reports suggest it was the model. Fourth, many of the disputants on both sides of the settlement knew that property values rose following the creation of Central Park and other parks. They supported the agreement because they recognized that their remaining properties would become more valuable, that the rise would be sharpest along the immediate margins of the park, and that a long rectangle maximized a perimeter's extent. Golden Gate Park's elongate shape promised an abundance of increased property values for both the landholders and the city.[44]

The settlement, however, generated disputes and criticisms from various quarters. Common were complaints that the city had paid too much for the park, that the citizens would be burdened with maintaining the facility, and that the settlers were being assessed at too high a rate. However, the most frequent critique was that the site would make for a poor park because it was mostly sand dunes.[45]

## THE ORIGINAL PARK SITE

John Young's resigned assessment of the park site is probably the fairest one: "The land for the new park was not selected with reference to its fitness for the purpose, but it was the best that could be obtained." This certainly seems to be the case when

This 1868 bird's-eye view looking eastward over San Francisco and surrounding country captures the extent of the sand dunes on the western side of the peninsula. Golden Gate Park would extend east from just south (*right*) of Sutro Heights (*foreground left of center, at ocean's edge*) to the southwestern edge of Lone Mountain (*small peak at center of drawing and at western edge of street grid*). Point Lobos Road, today mostly Geary Boulevard, can be seen running from the city to Sutro Heights. Toned lithograph, *Birds-Eye View of the City of San Francisco and Surrounding Country,* after George H. Goddard. Reproduced by permission of the Amon Carter Museum, Fort Worth, Texas.

one considers that shifting sand dunes covered all but about 270 acres at its east end. Of those acres, approximately 200 were also originally dunes but, according to William Hammond Hall, Golden Gate Park's first superintendent, "had by natural process become clothed with native growths" of grasses and other binding, herbaceous species, making them relatively fixed. Wrote Hall:

> The pronounced hills and ridges of this eastern 270 acres . . . carried a scrubby live-oak [*Quercus agrifolia* or *Q. berberidifolia*] growth, which seldom attained a height of more than 10 feet. . . . The intervening valleys in this portion of the park were unsightly, hummocky surfaces of sand, held by the rough native sand-plant growths, in which the blue lupin [likely *Lupinus chamissonis*] and prostrate escalonia [*Escallonia* spp.?] predominated. The hummocks were densely overgrown, the intervening depressions generally bare, loose sand. Through the winter and spring, water to the depth of a foot or two accumulated in the three larger depressions, making ponds each an acre or less in area, where frogs croaked and snakes wriggled through the little marshes of sedge grass around the margins. This portion of the park site presented a bright appearance in the springtime when the lupin and other flowering plants were in bloom, but the bright effect was of very short duration.

Overall, the grounds were not a lovely sight. As one critic who preferred a competing site described it, the park had "been located in the midst of sand hills that are devoid of any natural beauty or attraction—a mass of barren, desolate sands, utterly unsuceptable [*sic*] of any improvement whatever." Others were even less charitable; Thomas Magee, the influential editor of the *San Francisco Real Estate Circular,* repeatedly referred to it simply as "The Great Sand Park." Clearly, the windswept, shifting, and yellow sand dunes with their scattering of vegetation failed to approach the parks envisioned by Andrew Jackson Downing or designed by Calvert Vaux and Frederick Law Olmsted.[46]

In addition to its vegetational barrenness, the site was but sparsely populated by either people or animals. Hall's description continues:

> On the eastern point of the central hill there was a ramshackle, tumble-down little house, where an old, heavily-whiskered hermit-like man lived, with several dogs for companions. Chickens and ducks which he raised there, and large frogs which he caught in the ponds out towards the beach and sold to the French restaurants, yielded him a livelihood. . . . A few jackrabbits, cottontails and quail found refuge on the scrub-covered hills, and sustenance amid the sparse herbage of the hillocks; and coy-

otes, from the San Miguel hills, visited the neighborhood of the chicken ranch nightly and with sufficient persistence to keep the old hermit and his dogs busy scaring them away.[47]

Despite this unpromising foundation, the park commissioners and their super-intendent would make a determined effort to convert the "sand waste site" into a park along eastern lines. It would take many years and a great deal of effort, but, as John Young wryly observed, the faith that Golden Gate Park's creators had in them-selves was "unbounded."[48]

# ROMANTIC GOLDEN GATE PARK

What never has been tried no man can know. It is impossible. This park was an experimental undertaking from the
start, and due allowance must be had for possible mistakes
. . . because nothing had been planted there before, and no
man could know what would grow. Where could he get the
experience?

Frederick William Poppey,
testifying before the California legislature in 1876

F aced with the daunting prospect of creating a park upon the "sand waste site,"
the new park commissioners in April 1870 called for bids for a land survey.
Numerous offers were received, but the lowest bid, $4,860, came from William
Hammond Hall (1846–1934), a pivotal character in the creation and definition of
Golden Gate Park whom historian Robert Kelley described as "irascible and idealistic" and geographer Gray Brechin characterized as "brilliant and often troubled."
Born in Hagerstown, Maryland, in 1846, he moved with his family to California at
the age of seven. There an Episcopal minister taught him in a private academy from
1858 to 1865. His parents hoped William would attend the U.S. Military Academy at
West Point, but with the outbreak of the Civil War, they abandoned the idea. When
the war ended, he became a computer and draftsman in the offices of the U.S. Engineer Corps, participating as a field engineer in the 1865–1870 survey of the Pacific
Coast from San Diego to Washington State. This experience well prepared Hall to
perform an inexpensive examination of the Outside Lands site for the park com-

missioners, because he had already surveyed much of the San Francisco peninsula. As he subsequently noted in an interview, he "had worked over the very area of the . . . park site" only a short time before the request for bids.[1]

In August 1870 the Park Commission awarded Hall the surveying and mapping contract, and he immediately set to work with a corps of assistants to identify the boundaries, soil, and surface features of the park in relation to the existing city surveys. In February 1871, Hall presented his completed topographic survey to the commission, reporting that, of the park's 1,019 acres, only the easternmost 270 or so "were clothed with native growths" while the remainder consisted of blowing, shifting sand dunes west to the Pacific Ocean. The commissioners accepted the engineer's report, thanking him for his thorough efforts, and contemplated their next step. Obviously, if a Central Park–type landscape were ever to emerge from this unpromising site, the dunes would first have to be fixed in place or they would bury low-growing and immature plantings. But what methods would be used? And by whom? Additionally, once they settled the dune issue, who would design the park? The commissioners did not immediately conclude that Hall, a survey engineer, was their person; but unknown to them, he had begun to think about a plan for the site's transformation while he had been working on the survey.[2]

## WILLIAM HAMMOND HALL'S PLAN

Although Hall's training and experience were as a surveyor, not a landscape architect, he was determined to become an authority on park design. Since it was impossible to obtain a formal education in landscape architecture—the field was nascent in 1870—Hall became an autodidact, studying other cities' plans for the improvement of their parks even as he surveyed and mapped the Outside Lands site. A common publication in the nineteenth century, municipal park reports contained such information as income, expenses, personal statements, and landscape plans. Prominent among Hall's readings were the designs and statements of landscape architects Frederick Law Olmsted and Calvert Vaux, since he had collected park reports from New York, Brooklyn, and elsewhere. As he read the reports and surveyed the Outside Lands, Hall became convinced that a proper San Francisco park would need the guiding hand of an expert landscape designer.[3]

During the winter of 1870–71, Hall suggested that the commissioners secure the services of Olmsted, Vaux & Company to either develop or advise them on a park

William Hammond Hall, a 24-year-old civil engineer, performed the initial site survey of Golden Gate Park during the winter of 1870–1871. An admirer of Frederick Law Olmsted, Hall also produced Golden Gate Park's first design plan and was its inaugural superintendent, serving from 1871 to 1876. Reproduced by permission of the Bancroft Library, University of California, Berkeley.

plan. By this time, Olmsted and Vaux's reputation had grown because of their involvement in the Chicago parks as well as Central Park, Prospect Park, and the Buffalo parks. The commissioners considered the suggestion, but funding uncertainties and anticipated high expenses delayed any move to hire park designers. "It was supposed that the Eastern experts would charge a large fee," explained Hall, "and that some term contract would have to be made in engaging them, and that one of them would have to come to San Francisco for some time—then a formidable undertaking as compared to the present. And so, the first two years of the work wore on, with the Olmsted engagement put off."[4]

Some work proceeded on the park, because soon after Hall presented his survey map to the Park Commission in February 1871 he also gave them his provisional landscape plan for the 270 sand-free acres at its eastern end. According to Hall, he sought "to plan and plant this Avenue reservation as a park, to impart a wooded effect, and by the overlapping of suitable tree masses, to arrest the sweep of the winds through it, and, hence, his plan, made gratuitously and as a suggestion to the Commission, provided curved roads and walks only." Appended to this plan was a "memorandum" addressing the fixing of the sand dunes in place. Hall never intended his plan to be the park's definitive guide, merely a suggestion and indicator of his skill and knowledge. Although he was trying to continue his involvement with the park, this tentative effort would lead to much more.[5]

Hall's plan was based primarily upon his reading of the current literature and adjusted to San Francisco. While examining the Central Park and Prospect Park Reports, he had, as he recounted, "caught the idea of closely adapting the plan and details of [those parks'] improvement to local conditions." Hall decided that a San Francisco park would have to be different from all others because of the Mediterranean climate and the vast expanses of sand. Notwithstanding his design inexperience, Hall thought he understood Olmsted and Vaux's landscape ideas and could modify them to fit Golden Gate Park. In the appended memorandum, Hall outlined a French technique he wished to employ for fixing the sand dune problem, but again the procedure was something he had only read about rather than practiced. Other dune-fixing techniques were better known in San Francisco, so it would have been surprising if the commissioners had decided to hire Hall simply on the strength of his proposed solution. They did so because he and his plans had two important supporters.[6]

Shortly after its submission to the park commissioners, Hall's memorandum came to the attention of Paul Rousset and General Barton S. Alexander. Rousset was a politically well-connected local who owned property in the Outside Lands near the site of Golden Gate Park and who, according to Hall, "knew of his own knowledge what had been accomplished by way of . . . reclaiming sandy-dunes in France and other European countries." Alexander, an engineer, had been Hall's superior officer in the engineer corps and the director of the U.S. Pacific Coast survey in 1867. At the time, Alexander had suggested to Hall that he study the sand dune–reclamation techniques used in Holland, France, and Denmark, because they were the most efficient and cost-effective, and, in the general's view, soon to be in demand in San Francisco. Hall took the General's advice, and four years later, when he submitted his memorandum on sand dune reclamation to the park commissioners, the technique he outlined was the one Alexander had suggested. In addition, but unknown to Hall, Rousset knew of the technique.[7]

This convergence of knowledge proved critical for Hall's employment, because the park commissioners immediately turned to a recognized engineering authority, B. S. Alexander, for an assessment of Hall's memorandum. Unsurprisingly, Alexander supported the dune reclamation approach; but he then went further, encouraging the board to place Hall in charge of the park. Rousset, who had also been consulted by the commissioners, concurred, so they appointed Hall engineer and superintendent of Golden Gate Park in August 1871. "Almost before I knew that action in the matter was contemplated," Hall claimed, he was the park's chief executive, at the young age of 25. Thus, Hall came to be in charge of Golden Gate Park because he was well connected, knew the site better than anyone else, and had offered to attend to the park's immediate needs for reclamation and design.[8]

As superintendent, Hall recognized that the amateurish design he had given the commissioners and the knowledge he had gained from a smattering of park reports would not translate into either the skill or the insight needed to create a proper park. At the same time, he decided that no local was qualified to assist him, so first he wrote to reputable booksellers in Philadelphia and New York City for a wide range of park plans and "the most desireable works on Landscape gardening & Park improvement." Then on August 22, 1871, he contacted an admired and acknowledged expert, Frederick Law Olmsted. Requesting the older man's assistance and beginning a decades-long correspondence, Hall begged Olmsted,

> Please excuse the liberty I take in addressing you without being even an acquaintance. Our similarity of tastes and profession must be my excuse. . . . You must know that landscape gardening is a thing almost wholly unknown on the Pacific Coast. There is not a single specimen of a public park treated as other than a rectangular city square. . . . Will you aid me by sending me a list of such works or publications bearing upon the subject in all its branches as you may consider useful? I know that mere study of books does not make the landscape engineer. Study of nature—of effect—in planting and constructing; and, above all, *experience* are required.

To convince Olmsted that he should reply, Hall explained that he was not a complete novice but had formally trained in an allied field, landscape engineering; and he argued that even if he did not have park-making experience, he was aware of the field's best European and American examples. He pointedly acknowledged the importance of Andrew Jackson Downing in American landscape design and implied that he had personally visited Downing-inspired estates along the Hudson River in New York. He had "visited and carefully studied and noted the principal parks and grounds about London, Paris and in the United States; particularly have I roamed through your Central Park and the Fairmount [Philadelphia] and the Brooklyn and the Druid Hill [Baltimore] to say nothing of those beautiful spots on the Hudson with which that gentleman of great taste, Mr. Downing, and yourself too I am told, had so much to do."[9]

The mails being anything but rapid and because of Olmsted's busy schedule, the landscape architect's amiable but skeptical reply of October 5 did not arrive in San Francisco until later that month. "On returning to my office after a month's absence I have the pleasure to find your esteemed favor of 22d Aug.," he gently wrote to calm Hall's concern that his letter had been presumptuous. Olmsted related that he had pondered the idea of an Outside Lands park in San Francisco but was not optimistic about applying a Central Park–style design on coastal dunes in a Mediterranean environment, thus reinforcing Hall's idea that a successful development must be sensitive to local conditions. Olmsted declared:

> I do not believe it practicable to meet the natural but senseless demand of unreflecting people bred in the Atlantic states and the North of Europe for what is technically termed a park under the climatic conditions of San Francisco. Experience in Persia, Turkey, Smyrna, Spain & Portugal would afford more suggestions for what is practicable and desirable than any that could be derived from English authorities. But the conditions are so peculiar and the difficulties so great that I regard the problem as unique and that it must be solved if at all by wholly new means & methods. It requires instruction, not adaptation.[10]

Olmsted did not leave Hall with only his doubts, but provided a list of landscape designers to investigate, most of whom were English and can be characterized as part of the landscape tradition outlined in Chapter 1.[11]

Hall and the commissioners, however, could not heed Olmsted's warning about the problems of simple adaptation, because loud and persistent critics were continuing to oppose the selected location as well as its capacity to be a park, bringing intense pressure for a clearly recognizable and affordable tranformation of the site. In particular, the proponents of creating a park in the Presidio steadily militated for their choice and condemned Golden Gate Park well after the Outside Lands site had been officially accepted. These opponents, who included such notables as Mayor Thomas H. Selby, Mayor McCoppin's successor, and the San Francisco *Bulletin* newspaper, refused to abandon the fight because, in Hall's words, they "could not bring themselves to believe that a park could be made on the sands, without incurring appalling expense. The leading clubs and banks and mercantile houses were peopled with such unbelievers, and they were heavy taxpayers." In Hall's view, a Presidio park might have replaced the Outside Lands site at any time from 1870 to 1872 because of the widespread "lack of faith in the success of development of the sand-waste site." Critics also condemned the commission's and superintendent's management of the park and their policies, with one source in particular, *The California Horticulturist,* declaring the development "unsatisfactory" as late as February 1872. The park's layout and design, the journal argued, demonstrated the management's bad taste and poor judgment; and in a direct attack on Hall, it demanded that the work "be stopped until more competent men can be appointed to take charge of our Park grounds."[12]

The Board of Park Commissioners' first public report, released in January 1872, responded clearly to these pressures by declaring upfront their desire to "make the park acceptable to the people in as short a space of time as possible" and by embracing an unambiguously eastern-style design. Hall and the commissioners may have ignored Olmsted's advice when they adopted a Central Park–style plan, but it is more likely that they recognized how little time they had to educate the public about its problems in semiarid San Francisco. On the one hand, if the Outside Lands site failed to quickly become something that looked like Central Park, funding probably would have been reduced or withdrawn. On the other hand, the commission and superintendent could not develop a Mediterranean-style design, even if they had been capable, or mount an education campaign, because they were required by law to produce their first official report only four months after Hall's appointment in August 1871. Hemmed in, with no reasonable alternatives, they issued the *First Biennial Report of the San Francisco Park Commissioners,* which included a detailed lithograph of the eastern end of the park based on Hall's preliminary sketches and which was designated as *the* park plan. The foundation for nearly all later work, this plan divided the park into two elements—"The Avenue" and "The Park" proper—and included many elements typical of an Olmsted and Vaux park but with an altered arrangement.[13]

The Avenue (now known as the Panhandle) is a 275-foot by 4,000-foot extension eastward from the main body of the park. Almost reaching the edge of San Francisco's built environment in 1870, its eastern tip stretched to within one mile of City Hall. As the most accessible portion of the park, it would greet visitors with a suggestion of the landscape beyond by bringing, in the words of the *First Biennial Report,* "a portion of the Park as near the City as possible." A proposal offered prior to Hall's appointment as superintendent had suggested that the Avenue be arranged like a parkway consisting of a "straight driveway of considerable breadth, with walks flanking" and be bordered by rows of trees. Hall rejected this proposal in a July 1871 memorandum to the commissioners and in the *First Biennial Report* as being too "formal," "naked," and "bald." The Avenue, he noted, ran east to west, the direction of the prevailing winds. A long, parallel line of trees would concentrate and accelerate breezes uncomfortably. "Ought it not, " he asked in the memorandum, "be our object by every means, to render this avenue as sheltered as possible—to make it a route for getting to the park pleasantly?" Hall's plan for the Avenue instead "partook of the nature of a pleasure ground," including curvilinear walks and drives with clumps of bordering, sheltering trees and expanses of lawn. A curvilinear design, Hall declared, "avoid[ed] the sweep of the wind" and piqued the aesthetic sense as "every turn . . . develop[ed] some new feature." This approach, he felt, would bring a greater sense of visual and physical "warmth of feeling" to "our damp climate."[14]

Hall's concern for the Avenue's natural characteristics fit into contemporary landscape theories, the same ones that informed the designs of Olmsted and Vaux and their English predecessors. In language harking back to Alexander Pope's concern for "genius of the place" in the eighteenth century, Hall noted that landscape designers applied standardized rules to myriad locations but only while recognizing that every setting has its "peculiarities," which "should be an object of [the designer's] renewed study." For Hall, the two major peculiarities of the Golden Gate Park site were its sand and its wind, and he gave the latter "primary importance" as he laid out the grounds for the eastern end of the park.[15]

The most obvious impact of wind on the design was in the thick plantings in the northeast corner of the plan, where clumps and masses of vegetation would be set, with paths and drives into the interior. Hall intended these and several other "heavy woods" to perform three functions. They would direct the prevailing northwest winds off the sands, over nearby vegetation, and above the heads of visitors. Consequently, the dunes would shift less, shrubs and shorter trees would grow in less contorted forms, and people would be warmer and less often stung by sand. In addition, the woods were to be "tracts for rambling walks and something of picturesque effect," providing a landscape similar to the Ramble in Central Park or the Ravine in Prospect Park. Finally, the trees were supposed to provide a viewer outside of these woods with "a pleasing succession of distances in the foliage." They would be particularly noticeable when a visitor entered from the Avenue, for from there the woods would provide a receding middle distance.[16]

To the west of these northeastern woods lay a 15-acre, sheltered valley, which included many park features that would have blended poorly with scenic stretches elsewhere. In the center was to be a plant conservatory; one modeled after those in Kew Gardens, London, soon appeared. Given to the park in December 1877 and soon assembled at this site, it was to be surrounded eventually by formal flower gardens with fountains, while to the immediate southeast but still within the protected area was to be a Croquet Ground or Childrens' Play Grounds. That area would be surrounded by vegetation, except for a short reach on the south, so that visitors viewing scenery outside the playing grounds would not be disturbed. Only through the break in its perimeter would this isolated and protected area be visible to outsiders.[17]

Further south and west lay Golden Gate Park's 75 acres of landscape expanse, where lawns, a Parade Ground, and a Meadow rested among several lakes. These open areas filled the majority of the eastern part of the plan and were the pastoral portions of Hall's design. Park visitors seeking restful scenery would be drawn here because boundaries of clumped and intermediate-height vegetation blocked other park functions from view.[18]

Hall planned for a 12-acre botanical garden in Golden Gate Park's southeast corner but it would never be built. Instead, this area would shortly become the site of the park's nursery, where thousands of new trees, shrubs, and other plants would be nurtured before installation. Adjacent to the nursery, on the west, was to rest another Children's Play Grounds in a protected area. It would also never be built but a children's area would be installed nearby about two decades later during the rationalistic era. Along the western margin of the park area planned by Hall ran the transverse Traffic Road. Unlike the similar roads in Central Park, this was not a sunken thoroughfare but instead was placed in low ground "so that it could be built at small expense." Bridges for park drives and walks separated traffic by crossing over this road, but nowhere in the description of his plan does Hall mention how these bridges should appear.[19]

In the style of Olmsted and Vaux's Prospect Park, Hall proposed only a handful of structures in the Golden Gate Park. The Manor House and Large Pavilion appeared on the plan but their functions were not recounted. Conversely, the plan description in the *First Biennial Report* lists a structure called "Rustic Pavilion," but it did not figure on the plan. Nevertheless, rustic structures began to appear after Hall hired the carpenter Anton Gerster in early 1874. "At that time," related Hall later in life, "Mr. Gerster was recognized as the foremost worker and designer in rustic wood-work in our country. He had planned and erected the works of the kind in both Central Park, New York and Prospect Park, Brooklyn, and our having him out here was the realization of another helpful favor from Mr. Olmsted." Hall also noted in the same *Biennial Report* that the details of the plan were incomplete and that the actual park could include "a greater number of small garden pavilions, seats and arbors, and further improvements about the lakes, such as boat houses, landings, etc."[20]

In contrast to Olmsted and Vaux at Central and Prospect Parks, Hall did not intend to plant the entire perimeter of Golden Gate Park. He saturated most of the border with trees and shrubs, but stretches of 150 feet and more opened occasionally to the surrounding area without explanation. Hall may not have noticed the unbroken character of perimeter plantings elsewhere, but he also may have intentionally left the gaps for scenic views. One line in the *First Biennial Report* hints at this purpose. While discussing a wooded hill in the eastern park, Hall suggested it could "afford a favorable site for an elevated carriage concourse . . . presenting . . . fine views without," that is, beyond the park boundary. Contemporary maps indicated streets and improvements surrounding the park, but the reality was an almost complete absence of nearby infrastructure and development in 1871. Since little or no city existed outside the park to disturb a visitor's contemplation, Hall may have left open stretches where a visitor could gaze upon some distant and pleasant bit of natural scenery, like the San Miguel Hills. As we shall see in the next chapter, visitors enjoyed these long views.[21]

With an initial, gross plan in hand, Hall turned to the improvement of his park-

In romantic Golden Gate Park, many architectural features, like this bridge, were finished in a rustic style featuring unsawn lumber, which retained its bark. Reproduced by permission of the Society of California Pioneers.

making knowledge. To refine his understanding of how inventories of plants were assembled and arranged and how the other features of a romantic, pastoral park were constructed, Hall again wrote to the bookseller D. Van Nostrand, in November 1871. Included in his book order was a selection of Olmsted's suggestions, and it is clear that haste was on Hall's mind. "Send me, immediately; fast freight; overland; C.O.D. if you choose, the following list" of books. In a postscript he added, "If you have any inexpensive work on ornamental architecture, bridge construction or rustic-work, send it also. Let me know also of any maps, plans or views of Parks or Pleasure Grounds which are in the market." He was a man desperate for knowledge.[22]

It seems fairly certain that Hall quickly amassed a sizable reference library, with Van Nostrand and perhaps other booksellers providing a broad selection of materials. For example, Hall requested Humphry Repton's *Landscape Gardening and Landscape Architecture* (1840) in his letter, and the copy from his library has a Van Nostrand label glued into the inside cover. In addition, Hall's unpublished July 1871 memorandum to the Board of Park Commissioners quoted Charles H. J. Smith's

A rustic shelter located near the northeastern corner of Golden Gate Park in the 1870s.
Reproduced by permission of the Society of California Pioneers.

*Landscape Gardening; or, Parks and Pleasure Grounds* (1856), William Gilpin's *Practical Hints upon Landscape Gardening: With Some Remarks on Domestic Architecture, as Connected with Scenery* (1835), John Henry Rauch's *Public Parks: Their Effects on the Moral, Physical and Sanitary Condition of the Inhabitants of Large Cities* (1869), Andrew Jackson Downing's *A Treatise on the Theory and Practice of Landscape Gardening* (likely the seventh edition, 1865), Frank J. Scott's *The Art of Beautifying Suburban Home Grounds of Small Extent* (1870), and the Board of Commissioners of Central Park's first *Annual Report* (1858). His extensive, judicious, and ultimately convincing use of diverse sources in this memorandum suggests he had quickly become acquainted with the large literature available.[23]

It is not possible to establish if Hall was a romantic theorist before he was appointed chief superintendent, since few documents remain from this period and no evidence indicates he had reflected much upon parks or scenic nature before Golden Gate Park. If, however, Hall did not incline toward a romantic view of nature when he took on the Outside Lands survey, he quickly became one as the park's executive head. As mentioned previously, he cited a range of romantic landscape design literature in his July 1871 report and then went on to recapitulate the history of landscape gardening outlined in Downing's *A Treatise* in the *First Biennial Report* of 1872. "The art of improving grounds," Hall declared,

> has undergone great changes in modern times. It was formerly the practice to make everything assume an artificial appearance, after fixed and regular forms, a seeming attempt to apply the rules of architecture to landscape gardening. Of late years, however, it has become the practice to leave nature as nearly in her normal state as possible, and only to endeavor to hide that which is unsightly, while still concealing the means applied.

Of course, this statement is highly ironic, because Hall did not intend to leave the sand dunes in their "normal state" but to transform them to fit a resource-consumptive model more appropriate to the humid east than the arid west.[24]

The year after the publication of the *First Biennial Report,* Hall's romantic notions were more developed still. The December 1873 *Overland Monthly* includes a lengthy article by Hall titled "The Influence of Parks and Pleasure-Grounds" in which he quotes "the lamented Downing," recites the history of Central Park in detail, and argues at length about how "the broad and simple lines of natural scenery [influence] the mental and moral condition of humanity." In the same way that the public was embracing universal education to improve minds, Hall urges, so it needed to embrace parks because of their value "in guiding the emotions, and regulating the habits of members of society." Writing in his later years, a solidly romantic Hall elaborated further.

> The foremost and most forcefully used argument in favor of the proposition [for a park] has been an urging of necessity for that which can possibly be provided only by a tract of land having an attractive country-like character.
>
> The argument has been made upon the humanitarian basis of necessity for fresh air, bright sunshine, cool shade, for gentle exercise for quieting and reposeful rest, for pleasurable mind-diverting recreation, and for peaceful though enlivening landscape upon which to rest the eye while within an environment free from distracting influence.
>
> The space within a city, fully meeting these specifications—affording these reliefs and opportunities—can by no possibility be other than that which constitutes a woodland park. . . . They are grounds so formed and grown and verdure-clad that

they are and on first sight seem to be just adapted for human occupancy in the pursuit of relief from urban hard-line surroundings and disturbing city-like influences. Such a place is recognized by an *intuition* (emphasis added) when one comes into it.

These quotes reveal the strength with which Hall embraced many of his romantic predecessors' beliefs. Like Downing, Olmsted, and Vaux, Hall felt certain that the quiet contemplation of natural scenery refreshed and that a true park was green and its impact transcultural. No one had to explain a park to the visitor; he responded to it "intuitively."[25]

Hall also implied that an urban park elicited the same spontaneous response in a visitor as the natural world. Neither he nor his predecessors claimed that every element from a truly natural scene could be or should be in a park; rather he believed that the trees, shrubs, grass, rocks, and water that were artistically arranged as a park became "natural" despite the tension between art and nature.

> When man undertakes to make a woodland park, his object and sustained endeavor must be to cause the result to seem to be a work of nature. . . . [As a result] the most artistically and practically successful woodland park making may not challenge the widest praise, simply because those who see it do not realize that it is the work of man. They *instinctively* take it for granted that *nature made it* (emphases added).

Thus, the proper urban park, which was a work of critical, theoretically informed art, was also a natural object, satisfying the innate desire of individuals for country.

> A woodland park is of value in a city in proportion to its practical effectiveness as country. To be practically effective as country it must be spacious and not be broken into by artificialities. Such a place appeals to that sense, and, in beneficial measure, satisfies that craving in those who can not get away from the city, which is appealed to and satisfied in those who have taken themselves far away, by the influence of the real country into which they have come.[26]

In the *Second Biennial Report* (1874), Hall spelled out exactly for whom the park was designed.

> First—The eminently respectable and well-behaved portion of the adult community who demand a first-class reception.
>
> Second—Ladies with their families, children in [the] charge of nurses or guardians, boys and girls, and ladies who may wish to enjoy themselves in a homelike manner.

Just as sociologist Galen Cranz concluded in her analysis of women and parks in this era, Hall did not judge women to be truly "adults" who could reasonably "demand" that the park work as designed but instead defined them by their roles as mothers or as the full-time occupants of domestic space.[27]

## IMPLEMENTING HALL'S ROMANTIC PLAN
### The Sand Dunes

The initial construction problem facing William Hammond Hall and the Park Commission was the vast expanse of sand dunes. Under the prevailing westerly winds, they regularly moved from the west onto the 270 acres of immediately developable land at the park's eastern end, threatening to overwhelm them. In Hall's account of the project,

> the unique problems were: first, to economically stop the inroad of fresh sands from the sea . . . ; second, to stop the sands of the wide-spread dunes from drifting over and about the park space . . . ; third, to start and maintain vegetation of some sorts upon them so that park making might go forward; and, finally, to create luxuriant park growths upon deep, seemingly dry and barren sands as the only soil.

As it turned out, Hall's engineering background prepared him well for this tremendous environmental transformation. Having been previously engaged in coastal work, he knew to import, and learned to adapt, several useful if imperfect sand dune reclamation technologies that biotically addressed the first three issues, making the fourth possible.[28]

Both supporters and opponents of the Outside Lands site realized that the dunes had to be fixed before a romantic park could emerge, but the latter presumed the cost would be a princely sum of "at least several hundred thousand dollars." Critics felt the expense would be great because they thought the only technological solution to the first of Hall's problems—stopping the inroads of fresh sand—was to build sea walls along the western shore of the site. This price tag was far greater than the Park Commission could afford and was politically untenable, but Hall knew of an "economical" alternative. As a coastal engineer he had learned of successful and relatively inexpensive efforts to stem the advance of coastal sands in Europe, especially those begun in 1787 by Nicolas Brémontier between the mouths of France's Gironde and Adour Rivers. Hall, along with Paul Rousset, who was French and an Outside Land holder, Eugene Lies, also French, and Eugene Sullivan, a park commissioner, felt certain that these European methods could be applied to San Francisco.[29]

The Europeans had discovered that fresh sand brought up by the waves could be restrained by planting mat, or marram, grass (*Ammophila arenaria*) and sea lyme grass (*Elymus arenarius*) on the dunes nearest the ocean. Their powerful roots held this spreading carpet even as the large blades captured the flying grains. As sands accumulated, the plants simply grew upward through them. The Europeans also had stopped inland dunes from drifting and started vegetation upon them by simultaneously depositing the seeds of a shrub and a tree species so that first the shrub and then later the tree would hold the dune in place and divert winds above loose sand. This technique employs a natural process—plant succession—where first the "pioneer" shrubs germinate and grow, creating conditions favorable for the ensuing growth of secondary trees. Alone, neither species would thrive without a tremendous amount of human labor, but the Europeans had demonstrated that the correct pair of plants eliminated the need for human intervention. As it turned out, the San Franciscans had to modify the technique to fit the local environment.[30]

When an initial experiment using the French combination of maritime pines (*Pinus nigra*) and yellow broom (*Cytisus* spp.) failed to hold the San Francisco sands, Hall and his associates reconfigured their mixture. They had noticed on dunes farther inland that several species of native lupines (*Lupinus arboreus* and *L. albifrons,* in particular) were naturally functioning like the imported broom, so they gathered seeds, soaked them in water, and then scattered a blend of broom, maritime pine, and lupine seeds. This trial was more successful than the first attempt, but problems continued. Every species germinated well, records Hall, "but the tiny pines died as seedlings, and the broom was being choked by the lupin when the advance of the sand drift completely covered the little plantation during the second winter after sowing." At this point, an accident provided the key to open the door of success. While Hall and his associates were encamped on the dunes for a month, one of their saddle horses was corralled on a small area of bare sand. Frequently, while eating, it scattered its feed of whole soaked barley seeds. As luck would have it, the rains came, the barley "quickly sprouted and clothed several yards of loose sand with a vigorous green growth, [and] an idea was thereby suggested." In a casting of mixed seeds, the barley would sprout very quickly and hold the sands during the initial winter and spring until the lupine could sprout and grow large

**TABLE 3.1** Woody Plant Species Used to Reclaim Golden Gate Park's Sand Dunes

| Species | Site of Previous Reclamation Use |
| --- | --- |
| *Pinus maritima* [*Pinus nigra*] (maritime pine [Austrian pine]) | France |
| *Pinus pinaster* (cluster pine) | Mediterranean |
| *Pinus sylvestris* (Scotch fir) | Prussia |
| *Pinus larix* [*Larix decidua*] (larch [European larch]) | France and Prussia |
| *Tamarix gallica* (French tamarisk) | Mediterranean and England |
| *Tamarix germanica* [*Myricaria germanica*] (German tamarisk [false tamarisk]) | Mediterranean and England |
| *Ailanthus glandulosa* [*Ailanthus altissima*] (Japan varnish tree [tree-of-heaven]) | Europe |
| *Alnus glandulosa*[a] (common alder) | Prussia |
| *Alnus incana* (northern alder [white alder]) | Prussia |
| *Salix argentea*[a] (seaside willow) | France |
| *Salix arenaria*[a] (sand willow) | Europe |
| *Casuarina quadrivalvis* [*Casuarina stricta*] (coast she oak [coast beefwood]) | Australia |
| *Casuarina glauca* (desert she oak) | Australia |
| *Leptospermum laevigatum* (sandstay [Australian tea tree]) | Australia |
| *Leptospermum gladiatum*[a] (sword sedge) | Australia |
| *Spartium scoparium* [*Cytisus scoparius*] (common broom [Scotch broom]) | France |
| *Spartium monospermum* [*Genista monosperma*] (Spanish broom [bridal-veil broom]) | Southern Europe |
| *Ulex europaeus* (common furze) | France |
| *Prunus maritima*[b] (beach plum) | North American Atlantic coast |
| *Erica communis*[ab] (common heath) | Unknown |
| *Phormium tenax*[b] (New Zealand flax) | New Zealand |
| *Genista* (unnamed spp.)[b] (brooms) | Probably Eurasia |
| *Pinus insignis* [*Pinus radiata*][b] (Monterey pine) | California |
| *Pinus contorta*[b] (shore pine) | California |

*Source: Second Biennial Report of the San Francisco Board of Park Commissioners* (1874), pp. 35–38.
   *Notes:* Both botanical nomenclature and common names are as given in the report; current terms are provided in brackets when they differ from the historic ones. Species are listed in order of importance in the park as indicated by the park commissioners.
   [a]Unable to confirm this botanical name.
   [b]Usage in Golden Gate Park less certain, but mentioned in the report.

enough to continue holding the dunes through the summer and the following winter. By that time a plant such as a broom would be mature enough to sustain itself and make the fix permanent.[31]

In December 1872 and January 1873 a further refined mixture of barley, lupines, maritime pine, and *Albizia distachya* was scattered over 100 acres. This trial succeeded and "the work of sand dune reclamation was vigorously prosecuted." Hall and his colleagues decided that the reclamation process would proceed more rapidly and successfully if the pines were not simply scattered as seed but intentionally germinated, grown for a year or two in a nursery, and then planted out. Additionally, they diversified their palette of woody species to find the best possible combinations. This inexpensive, biological approach gave the commission some financial breathing room and a valuable public success, one they touted loudly in their *Biennial Report* of 1874. Instead of the hundreds of thousands of dollars that the detractors had claimed dune fixing would cost, the modified European methods could be applied for approximately $30,000, Hall estimated. During the next two years the vast majority of the 700 acres of drift sands were thus brought to a standstill, making it possible to build roads and concentrate on Hall's fourth problem—creating luxuriant park growths.[32]

### The Horticultural Expertise of Frederick William Poppey

Even as Golden Gate Park's administrators were attacking the problem of the drift sands, they began to plant the park's eastern end. According to the *Second Biennial Report*, the park employed a head gardener to have "exclusive management of the details of the horticultural works." The raising and planting of the park's ornamental trees and shrubs was the expertise of the landscape gardener rather than the landscape architect. The latter prepared a plan for the entire park, arranging water, rock, topography, and vegetation into appealing scenes; but the former had to fill in the details with plants whose colors, shapes, and habits would produce the correct effects while thriving in the diverse microenvironments present across any stretch of 1,000 acres. When Frederick Law Olmsted warned William Hammond Hall that the San Francisco park would require "invention, not adaptation," he was probably thinking about ornamental horticulture as much as design, because the relationship between sand dunes and plants was poorly understood in the 1870s. Only a handful of today's ornamental species had been introduced to the San Fran-

cisco Bay area and few of those had been planted on the dunes. Hall engaged a series of individuals to oversee the responsibility for landscape gardening in the park, but none proved satisfactory until Frederick William Poppey. More than simply competent, Poppey stands out. A close look at his California journey and his romantic views exposes the intimate relationship between Hall's landscape design for Golden Gate Park and the vegetation that came to clothe it.[33]

The sequence of events that led to Poppey's California odyssey began when William Hammond Hall wrote to Olmsted on January 15, 1872, detailing the "very unfavorable circumstances" of Golden Gate Park's development. "Hardly any money—Commissioners with no taste and no appreciation of taste—Outside influence brought to bear upon the every motion of the person in charge. . . . [Consequently,] a decided plan for this work *must be fixed upon immediately*" (his emphasis). Hall hoped for Olmsted's assistance and asked him for a critique of the Golden Gate Park plan. By then Hall had read widely through the landscape literature, but his plan had been created approximately a year earlier, when he had known much less and had been under the impression that the plan would be officially reviewed by Olmsted and Calvert Vaux. In addition to admitting that he was not an experienced park designer, Hall confessed that he was poorly qualified to hire a horticulturist. A prospective employee was claiming to being an expert in ornamental horticulture, but Hall was unsure. Did Olmsted know anything of "F.A. Miller—A landscape gardener—who claims to have been employed upon Central Park in 1858?" If not, did Olmsted know a "landscape architect, or gardener more properly, who would come out to this country with the prospect of a couple or three years of employment . . . on this work?" If Olmsted could develop a critique of the Golden Gate Park plan, explain it to a landscape gardener, and then send him to San Francisco, this person "would . . . be doubly qualified." Olmsted's February 20 reply brought little relief. He would develop a critique of the Golden Gate Park plan but warned that "no more difficult problem has probably ever been

FACING PAGE:
Beginning in 1873, pine trees were grown for a year or two in the park nursery before being planted in the semistabilized sand dunes near the coast. Like the trees in the upper photograph, they were arranged in close, repetitive lines. In a decade or two, they matured to form breaks, like the one shown in the lower photograph, which lifted the wind off the surface and kept the immediately eastward sand from moving. Reproduced by permission of the San Francisco Museum and Historical Society.

presented in our profession than that involved in the San Francisco park under-taking." He set his consultation fee at $1,500, a figure that discouraged further dis-cussions with the commissioners. Nor could Olmsted assist Hall with his labor sit-uation. He did not know F. A. Miller and could not suggest a useful alternative. The only expert Olmsted could recommend as Hall's assistant was an engineer, Hall's area of expertise, not the needed landscape gardener.[34]

Two years later, William Hammond Hall still lacked a reliable gardening expert. Corresponding with Olmsted in January 1874, he once again asked him to recom-mend a landscape gardener "skilled in the handling of large grounds and thor-oughly conversant with the details of his profession," and this time Olmsted could help. Responding in February, the landscape architect recommended Frederick William Poppey, a Prussian who had trained at the Royal Educational College in Berlin and had thirty-six years experience as a landscape gardener. He had been employed as a gardener in San Antonio, Texas, when he had first arrived in the United States, was currently in his sixth year of employment at the Hudson River State Hospital in Poughkeepsie, New York, and had been a consultant for Olmsted and Calvert Vaux on Brooklyn's Prospect Park. His current supervisor, the state hos-pital's superintendent, described Poppey as a gardener whose "taste in landscape gardening is very correct and natural. . . . under a good manager who had a mind of his own . . . Mr. P. would be *most valuable*. I do not know any one whom I would recommend in preference to him." Olmsted himself added, "I think Poppey as likely to serve you satisfactorily as any one I have had. His special inclinations in land-scape work I should think well adapted to your design." Approximately one year later, in the late winter or early spring of 1876, Poppey arrived in San Francisco.[35]

Frederick William Poppey shared many romantic landscape ideas with Andrew Jackson Downing and his contemporaries. For instance, when once asked whether he thought landscape gardening was an art or a science, Poppey described it as an "art founded on science" because a landscape gardener had to know and refer ex-tensively to the natural world. A scientific knowledge of plants and their natural distributions taught a landscape gardener how to arrange them into a piece of art. Like most romantic painters, Poppey saw no reason to refer to landscape paintings for guidance on how to make new landscapes of any kind. Landscape gardeners and landscape painters, he argued, were "supposed to copy from nature, and I do not see why we should go at it in a round-about way, and take, as our models, the mere daubings of a painter, when we can go directly to nature." The landscape gardener should observe nature, repeating and revising its patterns for maximum aesthetic impact. Poppey also knew the history behind these landscape theories and their contemporary use, testifying before a California Assembly committee that Golden Gate Park was laid out in the "free or English style" advocated by Downing, Olmsted, and Vaux, and which was "the present style of all the parks we are laying out." Poppey relied on a tree typology quite similar to the one enunciated by Downing in his *Treatise on the Theory and Practice of Landscape Gardening*. Downing had focused primarily on gross morphology rather than ecology, leaf or flower color, family origin, or leaf shape, referring to trees as round-headed, oblong, and spiry-topped. In a similar fashion, Poppey divided trees into "the conical, the globula, and the drooping," demonstrating that he was as much a romantic park maker as Hall, who became his supervisor.[36]

## THE ORNAMENTAL PLANTINGS

Shortly after William Hammond Hall became superintendent in August 1871, he ordered trees planted in the Avenue and eastern end of the park so that it would begin to appear more like a humid-environment park. According to the *Third Biennial Report of the San Francisco Park Commissioners*, the park purchased more than half of these first plantings, but popular historians Guy and Helen Giffen report that most deteriorated if they were planted in exposed and sandy conditions. Although no official list of these purchases remains, the Giffens reconstructed it, providing us with an insight into Hall's vision for the park and the sources for his mental picture. According to the Giffens, the first trees planted were Norway maple (*Acer platanoides*), sycamore (*Platanus racemosa*), maritime pine (*Pinus maritima*), English yew (*Taxus baccata*), Austrian pine (*Pinus nigra*), elder (*Acer negundo*), Monterey cypress (*Cupressus macrocarpa*), alders (*Alnus* spp.), cottonwood (*Populus* spp.), acacia (*Acacia* spp.), blue gum eucalyptus (*Eucalyptus globulus*), and several varieties of oak (*Quercus* spp.). Four additional sources corroborate the Giffens' list. For one, *Pinus maritima* was part of the initial sand dune reclamation project, as previously mentioned. The *Second Biennial Report* (1874) mentioned a sizable list of plants known to be useful in such dune reclamation, and although it is not clear which of these species were employed in Golden Gate Park, included among them, as named, were "Common Alder" (listed as *Alnus glandulosa*), "Northern Alder" (*Alnus incana*), "Common Elder," "Monterey Cypress, several of the Euca-

**TABLE 3.2** Trees and Shrubs Planted in Golden Gate Park, 1871–1875

| | In the Avenue and Eastern Park | In the Western Park |
|---|---|---|
| 1871–72 | 8,430* | 0 |
| 1872–73 | 16,745 | 0 |
| 1873–74 | 15,470 | 300 |
| 1874–75 | 7,934 | 17,504 |
| Totals | 48,579 | 17,804 |

Source: Third Biennial Report of the San Francisco Board of Park Commissioners (1875), p. 40.

*Of these, the park purchased 6,630 while 1,800 were raised in its nursery.

lyptus, and Acacias." The *Third Biennial Report* (1875) noted that the *Cupressus macrocarpa* planted in the park were 10–12 feet in height, while the *Eucalyptus globulus* were almost 18 feet. The height of these trees in late 1875 suggests they were planted in the first year or two of the park's construction. Additionally, as Table 3.3 illustrates, species of *Acacia* and *Pinus* were raised, along with *Cupressus* and *Eucalyptus*, in the park nursery during 1870–71. If the last two genera had been planted before 1875, then it seems likely that the former two had also been planted. At least some of these were probably *Pinus nigra*. Finally, according to *The California Horticulturist*, the Park Commission purchased elms, maples, and poplars in 1871–72. Although Giffen and Giffen do not mention elms (*Ulmus*), they do note the maples (and their close *Acer* relative, the elder) and the poplars (both cottonwood and poplars are in the genus *Populus*). It is therefore reasonable to conclude that the tree species detailed in Giffen and Giffen were purchased rather than grown in the park nursery and that their list is reasonably accurate. But if so many of the trees were going to languish or die, why were they planted? One could surmise that these trees were planted because they were all that was available or that they died because they were treated poorly, but there is no evidence to support either of these suppositions. There were several nurseries in the area with more species than those selected. The latter possibility seems unlikely because large sums were spent to provide fertilizer and water to the plants. To solve the mystery, we must consider the man in charge of the plantings, William Hammond Hall, and explore the link between his ignorance and his method for developing expertise.[37]

Golden Gate Park was without a fully qualified landscape gardener from 1870 to 1875, leaving Hall to direct the selecting and planting of trees. An engineer rather than a horticulturist, Hall may have referred to the park reports and books he had amassed but they would have been of small use, because they contained little specific information on trees. The park reports generally included a comprehensive plan, budgets, and incidental information but few planting particulars at a more detailed scale. Nor were gardening books of much assistance, because they were aimed at a geographically dispersed audience and concentrated on general design issues and plant *forms* rather than *species*. Hall could have asked the local nursery people for suggestions; he certainly had the opportunity. Unfortunately, as a series of articles in their monthly publication, *The California Horticulturist and Floral Magazine,* reveals, the nursery establishment lined up against Hall and his planting of the Avenue and other eastern park areas prior to fixing the western dunes. They wanted the sand treated immediately, because they thought fixation would protect the eastern park from the ongoing problem of encroachment and would attract property owners to the area around the park. Apparently, the nursery people were, at least initially, unaware of the novel dune-fixing approach being tried.[38]

If Hall had sought a nurseryman's advice, the selection probably would have been somewhat different but it would not necessarily have been any more successful. Although this area was not completely a horticultural *terra incognita,* it was a poorly known, difficult site, leading even Frederick Law Olmsted to hold serious doubts about the probable success of its planting. Furthermore, since no nurseries were located in the immediate vicinity and most ornamental planting projects were occurring farther east, the nurserymen in the region would also have been

**TABLE 3.3** Tree Species Raised in the Golden Gate Park
Nursery, 1870–71

| | |
|---|---|
| *Acacia* spp. (acacias) | 1,200 of 10 varieties |
| *Chamaecyparis lawsoniana* (Port Orford cedar) | 500 |
| *Cupressus* spp. (cypresses) | 3,500 of various varieties |
| *Eucalyptus* spp. (Australian gums) | 1,500 of 15 varieties |
| *Pinus* spp. (pines) | 6,500 of various varieties |
| *Pittosporum* spp. | 500 (probably *undulatum*) |
| *Schinus molle* (pepper tree) | 350 |
| *Sequoia gigantea* (big tree) | 400 |
| *Sequoia sempervirens* (redwood) | 500 |

Source: *First Biennial Report of the San Francisco Board of Park Commissioners* (1872).
    Note: The botanical names are current nomenclature; the common names are as shown in the report.

guessing about which species would be best, albeit in a more informed fashion than Hall. Horticultural ignorance was common in San Francisco and elsewhere in America, making solid information difficult to obtain. Henry Winthrop Sargent, a horticultural experimenter and author noted that "'What shall I plant?'" was one of the principal inquiries he was addressing in his supplement to the 1859 edition of Downing's *A Treatise on the Theory and Practice of Landscape Gardening*. The information available on the "habits and character" of horticultural species, he regretted to say, was "very meagre." For example, he included everything he knew and could glean from others to produce a hardiness table for U.S. evergreens, but it still ran for only six pages and included no discussion of soil, water, or nutrient requirements (the major concerns in Golden Gate Park), only responses to frost.[39]

Given William Hammond Hall's prior effort to develop landscape design expertise by reading and adapting the published works of others, it seems reasonable to suggest that he adapted the plant list as reconstructed by the Giffens from Andrew Jackson Downing's *Treatise,* which was in its seventh edition and widely available in the early 1870s. Hall owned a copy, and if it was a sixth or seventh edition, published in 1859 and 1865 respectively, then it not only included Downing's thoughts but also Henry Winthrop Sargent's horticultural information and a plan with description of New York's Central Park. It is clear in Hall's writings and can be surmised from his reading that he, like many Americans, respected Downing as a master landscape gardener. For example, when Hall first wrote to Frederick Law Olmsted in February 1871, Downing was the only landscape designer he mentioned, referring to him as a "gentleman of great taste." A few months later, Hall legitimated the reputation of a landscape gardener he cited in his unpublished memorandum of July 1871 by simply noting that the man was "a pupil of Mr. Downing." Alternately, the Central Park report Hall had been reading before he sketched out a plan for Golden Gate Park praised Downing and his writing and editing of a garden journal, *The Horticulturist, a Journal of Rural Art and Rural Taste.* Although there is no direct evidence, these citations suggest that Hall's positive opinion of Downing either initially arose from or was later reinforced by his reading of the latter's *Treatise.*[40]

Written for amateurs and professional alike, Downing's *Treatise* was a comprehensive guide to landscape gardening, embracing horticultural issues when other writers were confining their discussions to design alone. In the early chapters, Downing put forward a set of landscape principles that were drawn from various British designers and were similar to those used in Central and succeeding parks. In the latter chapters Downing offered a tree typology to be used when creating a park-like landscape and, to fulfill the book's usefulness, made the unusual move of promulgating a list of specific trees and tree genera that fit into the typology, making it possible for a reader to develop a romantic landscape. With the exceptions of the acacias, the eucalyptus, and the Monterey cypress, Downing recommended all the other trees subsequently listed by the Giffens, often at the species level, for their ability to create a romantic landscape design. He used such terms as *grand, majestic, symmetry, irregularity, bold, smooth,* and *round* to connect specific plants to the concepts of the Beautiful and the Picturesque, indicating to which genre or genres a species best contributed. For example, of the oaks, he wrote:

> We are fully disposed to concede it the first rank among the denizens of the forest. . . .
> As an ornamental object we consider the oak the most varied in expression, the most *beautiful, grand, majestic,* and *picturesque* [emphases added here and below] of all deciduous trees. . . . there is no tree, when forming a wood entirely by itself, which affords so great a variety of form and disposition, light and shade, *symmetry and irregularity,* as this king of the forests.[41]

And of the various pines he said:

> As ornamental trees, the Pines are peculiarly valuable for the deep verdure of their foliage, which unchanged by the severity of the seasons, is *beautiful* at all periods, and especially so in winter; for the *picturesque* forms which many of them assume when fully grown; and for the effectual shelter and protection which they afford in cold, bleak, and exposed situations.[42]

The comment on pines was especially appropriate to the coastal areas of Golden Gate Park, where the wind was cold and steady. It must have caught Hall's eye.

This coincidence between the trees initially planted in Golden Gate Park and those named by Andrew Jackson Downing suggests that an inexperienced and pressured Hall saw Downing as *the* expert, and he was indeed one of America's best-known gardeners and landscape designers. Unfortunately for Hall, the natural environment is not uniform, and landscape plants are less transferable than landscape theories.

The deterioration of the first scenic trees prompted Hall to continue his search for an experienced landscape gardener and to alter his planting strategy. Until

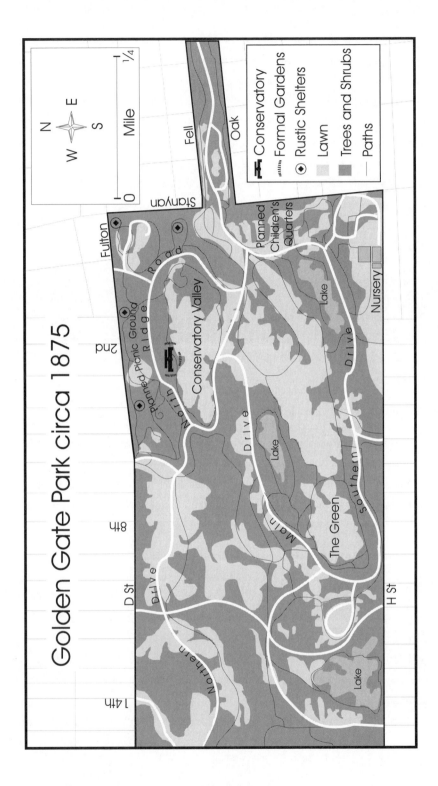

# Golden Gate Park circa 1875

**Legend:**
- Conservatory
- Formal Gardens
- Rustic Shelters
- Lawn
- Trees and Shrubs
- Paths

Poppey arrived in early 1876, Hall maintained the pace of plantings for environmental modification but slowed his efforts to create scenery. In the *Second Biennial Report* (1874), Hall emphasized wind rather than art in his account of the recent plantings. He knew that the species selection, now reduced, and the choices of site and arrangement for the plantings were not in keeping with design theory, but declared nonetheless,

> a sacrifice of much that is in good taste . . . is not only justifiable, but necessary, in the endeavor to overcome [the] evil effects [of the wind]. Thus, the planting at Golden Gate Park has nearly all been done with this view. The trees selected were chosen for their well-known rapid growth and hardy disposition under existing circumstances, and it is expected that many of them will be supplanted by specimens of other varieties as the primary end is attained.

Hall tried to explain the planting shift pragmatically, but it is clear that he had also been chastened by his horticultural failures.[43]

Only after Poppey's arrival did the engineer's report once again stress the effort to create scenery. In the *Third Biennial Report,* published in late 1875, months after Poppey's appearance, Hall boasted,

> Now a portion of the grounds within the Golden Gate Park Reservation, is in a condition to receive such finishing touches as will make it much more attractive than it hitherto has been. All the work which is now being undertaken and which will be carried forward during the present season, is of a character calculated to produce this finished appearance. The area of turf is being greatly increased; shrubs, flowering and foliage plants, creeping vines and spreading undergrowth, are being introduced; the grouping of trees finished and perfected; ornamental and rustic structures built for the convenience and comfort of visitors, as well as the addition to landscape effect which they afford; and a considerable length of walk and ramble put in a finished state for use during the coming Spring and Summer.[44]

Within its first six years, Golden Gate Park's fundamentals were complete. Just as William Hammond Hall's plan remained the guide for future designs, so his and Frederick William Poppey's horticultural plantings remained the framework for nearly all additional vegetation.

# THE PUBLIC REACTS
# TO ITS NEW PARK

Every metropolis of consequence now boasts its public pleasure grounds, which even the poorest are privileged to enter.
Paris has its Bois de Boulogne and its Garden of Plants;
Berlin has its "Under the Lindens" and other great drives
and walks; London has its St. James' and Regent's parks,
New York city its Central Park, Chicago its Lincoln Park,
boulevards and public squares; Philadelphia its Fairmount
Park, St. Louis and other cities are not deficient in this
respect, and San Francisco has its GOLDEN GATE PARK.

> *Daily Morning Call*, December 12, 1875

## VISITORS, REPORTERS, AND HORTICULTURISTS

Golden Gate Park generated expansive, sometimes flamboyant, comparisons. The
*Daily Morning Call* situated it within a pantheon of the best-known parks in
America and abroad, yet Golden Gate Park was only five years old and consisted
mostly of undeveloped sands. Characterizations like the *Call*'s, whether resplen-
dent with praise, quietly supportive, skeptically distant, or bitingly cynical, expressed the new park's reception by three segments of the public—the park users,
the newspapers, and the local ornamental horticulturists—well illustrating San
Francisco's response to its new amenity. Each group represented an important side
of the populace that generally supported, but sometimes opposed, Golden Gate
Park during the romantic period that stretched into the 1880s.

From the reaction of San Francisco's residents, one can easily conclude that the new park satisfied a well-developed but limited desire to come in contact with the sort of eastern, humid nature it represented. Frederick Law Olmsted had been concerned about the inappropriateness of an eastern-style park in San Francisco, but apparently few users shared his trepidations. People flocked to Golden Gate Park. "From the numerous visitors who continually resort to those grounds, we have received the most gratifying marks of approval and interest," beamed an 1872 Park Commission report to the Board of Supervisors. More than 250,000 visitors passed through the main entrance at the Baker Street (eastern) end of the Avenue (now called the Panhandle) during the park's first full year of operation, and visitations quickly rose to over 500,000 by 1875. Since several other, unmonitored entry points existed, the official counts were undoubtedly conservative.[1]

A detailed examination of the visitor numbers for these years reveals that Golden Gate Park's first users were similar to the park advocates, relatively well off. Of the 254,956 visitors recorded in 1873, only a slim proportion, 15,033, entered on foot, the remainder being wealthy enough to arrive in a carriage or on horseback. The situation was even more lopsided two years later, when only 13,494 of 516,170 visitors arrived on foot. The low number of pedestrians can be explained by two factors. First, few people owned any form of personal transportation in 1873, because a horse, and more certainly a horse and carriage, represented a major capital investment as well as a continuing maintenance cost. Only a minority could afford the expense of keeping a horse or of periodically hiring one to carry themselves and their families to the park. The rest of the public had to walk and rely on public transportation—or, in the case of San Francisco, suffer from the lack of it.[2]

A shortage of convenient public transport is the second factor explaining the low number of pedestrian park visitors. As a local historian, Raymond Clary, deftly stated it, "if you were too poor to own a horse and carriage, the task of getting to the park was almost insurmountable." The city's public transport network was equal to most elsewhere in America, having begun with a horse-drawn omnibus in 1852, expanded to include many horse-drawn street railways and a few steam-powered street railways during the 1860s, and then embraced cable-car railways as well in 1873. The Golden Gate Park site, unlike the location Olmsted had proposed, was poorly accessible using these modes of transport, leading one wag to remark, "In the matter of convenience, it will be at once admitted, that [Golden Gate Park] has none to offer." For nearly a decade after work began on the park, no

Carriages gather along Portsmouth Square around 1870. Their $1.50 to $4.00 fare each way from the square to Golden Gate Park was prohibitively expensive for the average San Franciscan, whose weekly income was approximately $3.50 at the time. Reproduced by permission of the Holt-Atherton Special Collections, University of the Pacific Libraries, Stockton, California.

mass conveyance was available to any point along its boundary. Instead, the four closest transportation lines ended approximately three-quarters of a mile away. Writing in the *Third Biennial Report,* William Hammond Hall, then the park's superintendent, attributed the lack of public transport to a combination of topographical and technological causes. He credited the "retarded . . . development of the portion of the city in the direction of the Park, and the consequent construction of street railways between it and the settled portion of the city" to "the existence of the range of hills extending in a southeasterly direction from Laurel Hill and Lone Mountain Cemeteries." Today this ridge runs from the edge of the Presidio, near the Julius Kahn Playground, through Presidio Heights, along Laurel Hill, and then declines toward and through Alamo Square. Most of the city's development had occurred to its east and south, between sea level and 100 feet, because the ridge's elevation generally exceeds 200 feet, not dropping below 100 feet until it approaches the intersection of Market and Guerrero Streets. According to Hall, "street railways must necessarily be operated to disadvantage" if they took a direct line from downtown over the ridge to Golden Gate Park, "and thus improvements have been forced southward upon the prolongation of the easier lines of travel, to a distance much greater than that which the Park is from any central point in the city." The situation, observed the superintendent, was "unfortunate," and, he urged, "there must be some popular means of communication by rail between the city and these grounds" in the near future.[3]

Hall's concern for the street railways' "disadvantage" reflects the limits of the period's public transport technology. Horse cars could not ascend many San Francisco streets because of the steep grades. Amy Bridges, a tourist from New England, described California Street as "so steep that grass grows in it on some parts of it as carriages cannot drive there." And even those streets that a horse car could scale were often unattractive to the era's private transportation companies because they could not be served without the company's costs exceeding revenues. The original, site-insensitive, gridded street plan sent cars directly up and down the faces of many excessively steep hills, some with grades surpassing 20 percent. Hall described how "'booster' teams of one to three horses per car, were used on the steep-grade parts of several lines. Passengers used to step off and walk up the hills along side of the car and get on again at the top." If the roads had been laid out like railroad tracks so that their grades were constant, instead of as a real-estate development tool where the separation and the direction were uniform, then horse car routes might have arrived at the park shortly after it opened. Unimaginative planning, whose goal was the quick sale of property, and sharp topography combined to stymie the horse car. Cable cars, by contrast, could ascend these hills without assistance; but the presence of the loose sand, especially west of the Presidio–Alamo Square ridge, limited their use to the built portion of the city. Potential investors in an extension of the cable cars feared that the blowing sand near the park would enter the cable slots and the abrasive grit would clog them, leading to excessive maintenance costs, unreliable service, or both.[4]

The result of this technological-topographical collision was inadequate public transportation to Golden Gate Park. A variety of horsecar or cable car lines running along Bush, Sutter, Post, and Geary Streets terminated at Cemetery Avenue (now Presidio Avenue), but from there it was a trying, lengthy trudge through sand dunes and about the Calvary and Masonic Cemeteries to where the park began at Fulton and Stanyan Streets. Alternatively, if one disembarked at the horsecar line's terminus at Eddy and Pierce Streets, it was a ten-block walk to the park's main

A steep California Street west of Kearney Street in 1875. The cable car system is new, having been installed during the previous year. Reproduced by permission of the Bancroft Library, University of California, Berkeley.

entrance at Oak and Baker Streets. As described by Raymond Clary, "the streets were unpaved, and the walk was either dusty or muddy, depending on conditions. . . . that district was inhabited by many undesirable characters. . . . Indeed, the area was so disreputable that the sheriff authorized early park workers to carry guns on their way to and from the new park." These conditions so discouraged pedestrian park visitors that the *Daily Morning Call* railed against the situation in December 1875. The splendors of the park, pointed out the newspaper, "are for the rich alone, and are, at present, entirely beyond the convenient reach of the mass of our population. This is a most serious defect. There is no way a poor man can reach Golden Gate Park except at a ruinous outlay. He must employ a cab at a price that is wholly beyond his means, or be content to remain at home."[5]

The poor transportation conditions were supposed to improve when a horse-car line was extended to the park in July 1876, but despite the *Call*'s assurances and William Hammond Hall's plea, the line did not materialize and no direct public transport reached Golden Gate Park until February 1880. At that time, the Geary

Horsecars, like this one at Market, Post, and Montgomery Streets, functioned well on level ground but were inefficient and dangerous when forced to climb straight up steep hills. Photograph by Carleton E. Watkins, reproduced by permission of the Society of California Pioneers.

Street, Park and Ocean Railroad Company extended its cable car service, which had terminated at Geary and Cemetery Streets, to the park with a steam-powered line traveling west along Point Lobos Avenue (now Geary Street) and south down First Avenue (now Arguello Boulevard) to the park's perimeter at Fulton Street. This railroad was successful from its first day, and the park's visitation figures jumped immediately, especially on Saturdays, Sundays, and holidays. More than 625,000 additional people visited the park in 1881 than had in 1880 (an approximately 60% increase), and the park commissioners attributed the swelling visitor counts to the new connection created by the street railway. The Market Street Cable Railway Company, which was owned by the Southern Pacific Company, soon followed suit, perhaps because of their competitor's enormous success, and connected its Haight Street line to the park at Stanyan Street in 1883. With the two lines in place, the park became easily accessible.[6]

The newspapers's reactions provide another vehicle for comprehending the park's initial reception. Solid support for a large, rural-like park had emerged

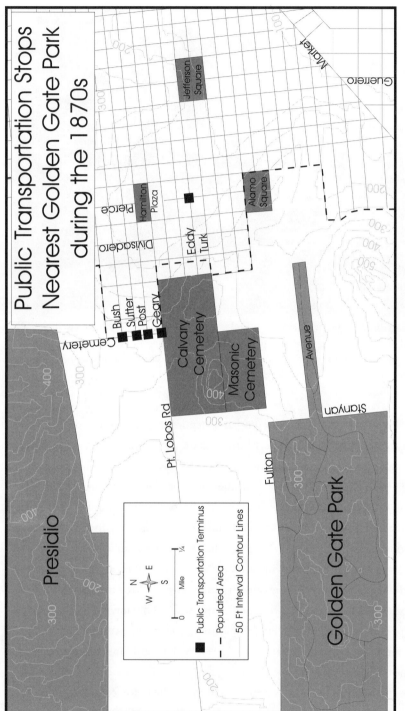

Public Transportation Stops Nearest Golden Gate Park during the 1870s

San Francisco's public transportation lines ended well east of Golden Gate Park because of the steep ridge lying between it and the city's populated area. Furthermore, blowing sand, which clogged cable slots, was common west of the ridge. Passengers who disembarked along Cemetery Avenue had to slog through these sands and around the high ground in Calvary Cemetery and Masonic Cemetery.

The Geary Street, Park and Ocean Railroad became the first mass transit line to Golden Gate Park in February 1880. This steam-powered train carried passengers between the railroad's cable car terminus at Geary and Cemetery (now Presidio) Streets to the park at First (now Arguello) Avenue and Fulton Street. Reproduced by permission of the San Francisco Museum and Historical Society.

among San Francisco's residents, select members of the municipal government, and several local newspapers during the 1860s. Although there had also been journalistic criticism at the time, it was generally directed at the location of the park rather than at the idea of one. Once the site had been selected and Golden Gate Park's physical development began in 1871, the newspapers' response, in the words of William Hammond Hall, "was about equivalent to—'O, give them a chance, and let's see what they can do.'" As time passed, their enthusiasm intensified, with a handful becoming keen supporters by the end of the first year of work.[7]

The construction work that first caught a newspaper's attention was the grading and macadamizing (paving), which began in May 1871 with the Avenue and in August extended into the park proper. These labors commenced shortly after Hall had given his unofficial, unsolicited design plan to the Park Commission in

The Market Street Cable Railway Company began running this, the second, mass transit line to Golden Gate Park, from Market Street to Haight and Stanyan Streets in 1883. Reproduced by permission of the San Francisco Museum and Historical Society.

February or March and were expanded into the park about the time he became superintendent and initiated the tree plantings. Approximately one year later, in the summer of 1872, the *Daily Morning Call* carried an editorial encouraging the public to visit their new Golden Gate Park. "Those persons who have not paid a visit to the park grounds for some time past will be surprised to learn that drives have been laid out and improved for six or seven miles in length. . . . Seven or eight thousand trees have been planted. . . . Enough can be seen to convince the most skeptical that, eventually San Francisco will have one of the finest parks on the continent." This praise and support was a sharp reversal of the position the paper had taken three to four years earlier, when it had predicted failure for any improvement attempts. Declaring all efforts foolish, if not plainly criminal, the *Call* had editorialized in 1869, "The people's money is to be thrown away." The pace of planting, road building, and trail construction had so dramatically transformed the site from its native "sand waste" to a Central Park–style landscape that the paper revised its stance and announced that the public's funds had been well spent on this "finest" of parks.[8]

The *Daily Evening Bulletin* was even more liberal in its support. Despite criticisms of the site by others, the author of an October 1872 *Bulletin* article found that "the natural topography is peculiarly adapted to the [park's] purpose: presenting in its undulating and broken surface . . . a pleasing rural aspect." The rolling, shifting sands were in the process of being fixed through seedings of rye and lupine; but to the reporter, the relief clearly offered "suitable localities for lawns and lakes, rambles and rockeries, pleasure grounds for old, and play grounds for the young; with extended drives, sheltered rides, and all the requisites of a popular place of resort." The newspaper also demonstrated knowledge of park making elsewhere, by noting that San Francisco's park was more accessible (at least in direct, linear distance if not in cost, safety, or travel time) than similar parks in New York, Philadelphia, Brooklyn, Baltimore, and Chicago. Three months later, in January 1873, the *Bulletin* once again returned to the subject, praising in particular the picturesque and sublime views available in all directions as one rode through the park itself.

> The drives through the avenue and winding among the shrubbery knolls are finely macadamized, and at every turn reveal new aspects of scenery. The sandy wastes and grand ocean on the west; the Golden Gate and the long strait leading from it through high cliffs to the Bay on the north; the city and Bay and the Oakland hills on the east; the Miguel range on the south; all are noble outlooks. No wonder people who can afford to ride and drive go there in increasing numbers.[9]

The plaudits from newspapers were not limited to the aesthetics of the park, for they also became supporters of the management. The San Francisco *Chronicle* had declared itself "bitterly opposed" to the park during its earliest years, but by 1875 the paper was waxing lyrical on numerous positive points. Under the caption "Coaxing the Barren Lands to Blossom as the Rose," an October article noted that over a thousand visitors were enjoying the park on an average Sunday, finding there many "judiciously" laid out drives and picnic grounds with "lovely rustic buildings and dancing pavilions." The most outstanding feature, in the *Chronicle*'s opinion, however, was the "reclamation of the sand and establishing thereon a young growth of forest trees. . . . A great portion of the Park at first consisted of verdureless sand dunes, which have been almost wholly reclaimed. The surface is rolling knolls and valleys, while here and there a picturesque peak enhances the beauty of the whole." Of course, the beauty sought was foreign to the location, so while the knolls were currently covered in "coarse native shrubbery and dwarf trees," the management was transforming the native environment by "eradicating them as fast as practicable," in order to replace them with "green slopes and handsome [ornamental] shrubs." As far as the editor was concerned, the natural environment was without value and since it was being supplanted rapidly, the management of the park was "in excellent hands." Not only were the results commendable, but the *Chronicle* approved of the management's methods also. "Everything is done according to routine and the discipline of the force is admirable."[10]

While the newspapers initially displayed a circumspect attitude, the local nursery people, landscape gardeners, and their public organ, *The California Horticulturist and Floral Magazine,* condemned the park resoundingly. They found the site unacceptable, having been obtained for the wrong reasons. "The Supervisors," scolded the *Horticulturist* of February 1871, "went so far as to secure a site for a Park, but we doubt very much whether they had the interests of the city at heart, when they accomplished the deed." Expressing the biases of an industry dedicated to artistically arranged rather than natural landscapes, the editor questioned the site's suitability for ornamental plant species, since only the eastern end of it was immediately developable into a Central Park–style landscape. "Three-fourths of the ground consists of hills of drifting sand, destitute of any vegetation, while a small portion near the city is better adapted to park purposes." The article hinted at the political origins of the site and condemned the lack of expert consultation in its selection. "We do not say that the projectors of the scheme have acted in bad faith towards the city; but, although that may not have been the case, they certainly depended too much upon their insufficient judgment, and should be severely censured for not consulting the public, and such men as are qualified to give an opinion as to the practicability of the scheme." William Hammond Hall found this vehement opposition "an embarrassing circumstance. . . . At the very outset of the project and before any work of development was undertaken, the local horticulturists . . . to all appearances *en masse,* arrayed themselves against the sand-waste park site; and . . . the Commission." Nor could these criticisms be ignored. The *California Horticulturist* was affiliated with two of the state's largest, most influential journals, *California Farmer* and *Pacific Rural Press,* so it found its way onto the desks and into the homes of most influential San Franciscans and Bay Area residents.[11]

Nor was the *California Horticulturist*'s condemnation limited to the site's selection; the February piece was only the first in a two-year-long series of articles denouncing the park's management. Why, the journal would repeatedly ask, were the commissioners and their superintendent building roads and planting vegetation in the Avenue prior to reclaiming the drift sands that covered most of the park property? The Avenue was to be the entrance, but to what? Golden Gate Park would never become a site that the public would want to enter until the property was properly clothed in shrubs and trees. In addition, "checking" the drift sands would be doubly beneficial. First, it would protect that portion of the park nearest the city from sand encroachment and so lower the costs of grading and maintaining roads both inside and outside the park. Second, and more importantly, fixed dunes would increase the value of the park itself and, in a cascade effect, stimulate nearby owners to stabilize the dunes on their property and raise values farther out. Continuing with this theme, the next month's issue suggested that "some experiments in [dune fixing] would be very desirable." Unknown to the *California Horticulturist*, such experiments were in progress. Superintendent Hall and his staff had already developed their grass-shrub-tree method on the dunes just east of the ocean but had been careful to keep any word of the experiment out of the papers. They had said nothing to the press because they feared raising and then dashing public expectations should the experiments fail. The wisdom of choosing the Golden Gate Park site was being steadily second guessed, and a failure might have swung public opinion strongly against it and the park management. However, once Hall's "economical" method for controlling the dunes with a succession of plant species brought public praise, such as that from the *Bulletin*, the horticulturists ceased this reproach.[12]

Finally, the horticulturists also complained about the failure of the Park Commission to purchase plants from local suppliers. According to Hall, the nursery people felt they "could raise [the necessary plants] . . . better and cheaper than the Commission's employees could" and that "their local industry should be encouraged" by these publicly financed purchases, but he rejected the horticulturists' demands with what now seems a rather weak argument. His reasonable premise was that the site was something of a horticultural *terra incognita* on which little if any planting had been done. One of his conclusions follows sensibly from the premise: "The park horticulture . . . development must necessarily, be largely tentative, requiring much to be done by way of experiment." His principal conclusion, however, is less defensible—that "workable contracts for nursery stock under such conditions" were impossible, so the park would grow its own plants. But if limited horticultural understanding called for tentativeness, then purchasing a few each of a wide array of plant species rather than raising them would have made more sense. There was no shortage of ornamental species available through local nurseries; at least a dozen businesses, including the European Nursery on Jessie Street, Collie and Stuart Nursery on Lone Mountain, and Commercial Nurseries near Mission Dolores were located nearby and stocked such plants. It would have been wiser to experiment with a range of purchased, scattered plantings before committing limited resources to the production of various species and especially before the large-scale production of a few species. As his development of a dune-fixing technique demonstrated, Hall was an experimenter who knew how to approach a planting problem, but his explanation smacks of a desire to retain control over as many park elements as possible rather than a rational analysis. In addition, it may have been an effort to take some revenge upon the park management's loudest critics.[13]

When recounting his relationship with the private nurseries in an unpublished memoir of his park experiences, Hall painted a picture of the nursery people as unreasonable and himself as a pragmatist who bore them no personal animosity. One phrase in particular implied that he had bent over backwards to protect the park's interests and yet be magnanimous with the nurseries. "To meet immediate wants, . . . between 6000 and 7000 trees and shrubs were purchased . . . in the spring of 1872," but what he failed to mention was that at least some of the plants, perhaps a majority, came not from *local* nurseries but distant ones. He was neither as practical nor as unbiased as he wished to appear. "The Commissioners are purchasing trees in San Jose," complained the *California Horticulturist* in March 1872, "which could have been had for the same price in this city." And, to rub salt in the wound, it was not as if all nurseries had had an equal chance to be suppliers. "The Committee of the Horticultural Society," continued the magazine, "is of [the] opinion that the Commissioners should have made out a list of such trees and shrubs as were needed, and advertised for proposals, whereby deriving benefit from the consequent competition." It seems that Superintendent Hall or someone else in the park's management had arranged for the plants without a public announcement.[14]

This unannounced, nonlocal purchasing deeply irritated the San Francisco horticulturists, driving the *California Horticulturist* to attack the Park Commission and its management during the remainder of 1872. In April, for instance, the magazine suggested that readers needed to remove their Pollyanna glasses and take a hard look at the park. "Good-natured people may feel disposed, after reading the last report of the Park Commissioners, to credit them with good deeds, and place confidence in their promises of future action, but practical and scientific men must necessarily look upon the present system of improving the Park as a failure." Four months later, the magazine again hammered the management about its failure to conduct experiments with sand-fixing grasses, but sometime before January 1873, the journal lost its interest in pursuing the Park Commission. Perhaps the successful and highly visible demonstration of the sand-dune fixing method just east of

Strawberry Hill during the 1872–73 season, the wide acceptance of the park, plus the lack of any subsequent out-of-town plant purchases left the journal feeling there were no further benefits to be gained by their criticisms. For whatever reason, Golden Gate Park was absent from the pages of the *California Horticulturist* during 1873.[15]

When the park was once again noted in the pages of the magazine, in May 1874, the tone was entirely new. The sneering and carping had been replaced by high praise.

> Few of our citizens who have not visited this Park during the winter have any idea of the improvements which have been made. A fine road has been run down through the sand-dunes. . . . The hitherto barren hills of white sand have been covered with a rich green mantle of hardy Lupines. . . . The drives have been extended, new flower beds laid out, a great number of trees and shrubs planted, and now exertions are being made to improve the approaches to the Park. . . . we have a really beautiful Park, which is a credit to the city, and gives good promise of being, at no very distant day, one of the finest in the land.

It would seem from the accounts of visitors, newspapers, and horticulturists that, although Golden Gate Park's beginning was rocky, by the end of 1875 there was general support for it, the Park Commission, and its experts. Nonetheless, before 1876 was over, the park's administration would change dramatically.[16]

## DISRUPTION AND PERSISTENCE AFTER 1875

In late 1875, even as the park was becoming a popular resort, forces gathering outside the Park Commission and its staff were precipitating a turnover in its management. William Hammond Hall blamed the change on a personal vendetta against himself and an effort by municipal officials to distract the public from their malfeasance elsewhere, but an economic panic and a shift in political parties in both San Francisco and Sacramento also contributed to resignations by the superintendent and the entire Park Commission. The years 1870 to 1875 had been ones of economic expansion and wealth in San Francisco, because the booming Nevada silver mines, which were owned largely by San Franciscans, had combined with a business depression in the East and the completion of the transcontinental railroad to greatly stimulate immigration and the local economy. At the same time, the

A party of six enjoys Golden Gate Park during the 1870s. Reproduced by permission of the Bancroft Library, University of California, Berkeley.

situation was precarious, because stock in the Nevada silver mines, like any stock, was subject to speculation and volatility. For example, between January and May 1872 the aggregate value of mining stocks on the local market rose from $17,000,000 to $81,000,000. Businesses of all sorts flourished as those who were succeeding in the mines and making money on stock investments spent liberally. Real estate sales skyrocketed, construction expanded rapidly, giving employment to a large force of laborers, many of whom had recently arrived, and retail sales jumped on the quick wealth being spent easily on luxury goods. In June, however, came a crash. The value of stocks had been rising on the basis of legitimate silver strikes but also because a small coterie of mine owners and investors had been spreading false reports about new veins and covering up the waning production in older ones for their own benefit. When the bubble burst, the stocks' value dropped abruptly to around $21,000,000 in ten days. Nevertheless, as historians Lewis F. Byington and Oscar Lewis relate, "public confidence was only temporarily shaken; the undoubted richness of the mines and the constant announcement of new discoveries again aroused the public's taste for speculation." The situation, of course, was untenable in the longer run.[17]

On September 18, 1873, Jay Cooke and Company failed in New York and precipitated the most devastating U.S. business panic to date. The depression that followed was severe and lasted well into 1877, but California's isolation insulated it from the worst effects. In the blithe words of historian John P. Young, "during the most exciting period of this financial storm San Francisco serenely pursued her way, scarcely affected by the disasters of the East." The insouciance of San Franciscans, rather than distant economic failures, brought disaster down on the city. By 1874, less than two years after the June 1872 crash in mining stocks, San Francisco was riding another, albeit brief, wave of affluence, driven by the success of several mines but most especially the Consolidated Virginia. Writing in 1878, the historian John S. Hittell described the situation:

> The Gold Hill bonanza had now reached the height of its splendor, and the Crown Point and Belcher were paying immense dividends. In three years and a half the two mines had taken out more than forty million dollars, a result previously unapproached. . . . While they were still at the flood tide of their prosperity, the still greater bonanza of the Consolidated Virginia was found near the northern end of the lode, and in May [1872] it began monthly dividends of three hundred thousand dollars. Every week brought news from the advancing drifts, cross-cuts, and winzes, and proved the ore body to be larger and richer. Experienced miners, who were represented as trustworthy experts, expressed the belief that the ore in sight would yield fifteen hundred million dollars. The excitement was intense; the aggregate value of the Comstock shares, as indicated by the quotations of the market, rose at the rate of a million dollars a day for nearly two months, and the year closed when the fever or frenzy of speculation was near its culmination.

On paper, the value of the Consolidated Virginia mine rose from around $100,000 in 1871 to $150,000,000 by the end of 1873 as it produced unprecedented amounts of silver. Nevertheless, even a rich yield could not always keep up with the market value of a mine's stock. By the middle of 1875, the paper value of the Consolidated and other mining stocks had been run up to heights bearing little relation to their intrinsic worth. They were wildly overvalued, and when the decline came, it was sharp and savage. The aggregate value of stocks rapidly fell by $100,000,000. Of

that amount, $42,000,000 was lost in a week; and by 1878, the value of the two lead-
ing mines had declined by $140,000,000. Since most of the shares were owned in
San Francisco, the descent, according to Byington and Lewis, was a loss of "$1000
on average for every . . . adult in the city; and though a large majority had never
owned any of these shares, all were affected." The crash caught nearly everyone
flatfooted because the yield from the mines was near its peak. "Not only did thousands of small speculators suffer, but several of the large financial houses were
thrown into difficulties and scores of [investors] faced bankruptcy."[18]

This shaky economic situation was further aggravated when one of the most
important, and supposedly solid, financial institutions of San Francisco, the Bank
of California, became insolvent on August 25, 1875. Its president had overspent his
own and the bank's funds on the development of San Francisco's broader economic base. The bank had, for example, invested in a woolen mill, a sugar refinery,
a furniture factory, and a watch manufacturer. Economic diversification was a
valuable goal and the bank might have survived the run that led to its failure but
for the tremendous shrinkage of the mining stocks it owned and the loans it had
made to borrowers possessing these stocks. The combination of a stock crash and
the Bank of California's failure pitched San Francisco into a depression in 1876
that, distinct from the rest of the United States, lasted through the remainder of the
decade. During these years there was a severe drop in the city's economic activity.
Port landings, for instance, fell 26 percent between 1875 and 1879, while the real
value of manufactured goods declined 27 percent between 1877 and 1880. Real
estate transactions plummeted 48 percent before the end of the decade, and employment in the manufacturing sector dropped 6 percent between 1877 and 1880.[19]

Partly as a result of the economic collapse, Democratic mayor Andrew Jackson
Bryant (1832–1882) and nine Democratic supervisors were swept into office in San
Francisco in 1875 even as the Democrat William Irwin (1827–1886) was elected governor of California. The San Francisco Democrats had run on a platform of fiscal
conservatism and "pay as you go" direct taxation instead of long-term bonds.
Their antibond position threatened the development of Golden Gate Park, because
bonds had been the primary method used to finance construction since the park's
beginning. If bond funds were reduced or eliminated, then either a tax increase
would be needed to offset the loss of income or a decline in spending on the park
would be necessary. It was upon this stage of rapidly changing economic and political circumstances that a vendetta was carried out against Hall.[20]

As soon as the Democrats were sworn into state office, the Assembly announced an investigation into two charges of mismanagement at Golden Gate Park. The assemblyman who initiated and led this inquiry was D. C. Sullivan, a newly elected Democrat from San Francisco and a former Golden Gate Park blacksmith who sought revenge against William Hammond Hall because the superintendent had fired Sullivan for padding his bill by more than 100 percent. First the state alleged that Hall had used park funds and materials for personal gain, but the charges were dropped and the whole affair had little to do with Golden Gate Park. However, the state also contended that Hall and his staff had damaged Golden Gate Park by unnecessarily cutting trees, leaving the park in a terrible condition. The trees had been removed because they had been planted closely together when young and needed thinning as they matured. Following a standard horticultural practice, groups of young trees had been planted near each other, rather than being individually staked, to provide mutual support, especially in wind. As the trees aged, they would shade out and crowd each other unless they were thinned repeatedly over the years to achieve optimum health and ideal form. According to the horticultural adage, it was best to "plant thickly and thin quickly." Nevertheless, many nonhorticulturists were ignorant of the practice and condemned it. Of the forty-one witnesses who testified at the hearing, the most reproving critics of the tree thinning turned out to be former Golden Gate Park laborers, not horticulturists, and the investigators sharply depreciated their testimonies. However, the committee did take testimonies from a number of local gardeners and nursery people. Although some of these horticultural experts felt the trees should have been retained, most supported the practice, conceding that the cutting of trees was necessary for the long term development of the park even if it was not immediately appealing.[21]

In order to protect the park, sympathetic forces suppressed the investigating committee's report, but sufficient damage had been done to seriously cripple further development. The Assembly hearings had been widely reported in the press and led to doubts about the competence of the park's management. As a result of the hearings, the economic depression, the Democrats' opposition to bonds, and a local political fight, the state legislature voted to abolish the sale of San Francisco park bonds and to base Golden Gate Park's future income on a local property tax that turned out to be woefully inadequate. At the new, reduced income level thus available to the park, much less could be accomplished in terms of labor, capital improvements, and maintenance. Between 1875 and 1876, for example, park expenditures dropped from approximately $98,000 to $62,000, but even this decline does not reveal the immediate severity of the reduction. The new tax was calculated to provide approximately $125,000 per year but actually yielded less than $36,000 for 1876 and 1877 combined because of the economic downturn. All but about $800 of 1876's expenditures were made possible by using nearly all of the remaining cash from bond sales, with expenditures slipping below $39,000 in 1877 because no cash remained. The commissioners became so strapped for revenue they even took to reporting the money they received from "the sale of Park horses used up in service." Hall called the period 1876 to 1889 "The Dark Years"; park expenditures averaged less than $54,000 annually and did not approach their 1875 level until 1889. Romantic principles continued to direct park development but, maintenance was minimal, the reclamation of the sand dunes effectively halted during 1877, and everyone's salaries, including the superintendent's, as well as the size of the work force were cut and then cut again. The only expansions in the work force were temporary, coming in the fiscal years 1878 and 1880 when private gifts were made to the park board in order for it to employ "persons in needy circumstances," and the only structures built were the restaurant, known as the Casino, and the Conservatory. The latter has become one of the best-known and most frequently photographed features in Golden Gate Park, but it would probably not exist except that it came as a gift. The large, steel-framed glasshouse, modeled on one at Kew Gardens in London, had been imported from England by a wealthy San Jose resident, James Lick, who died before it could be assembled on his property. Still in the crates, it was purchased from Lick's estate by a group of rich and influential San Franciscans, including Leland Stanford, Charles Crocker, Claus Spreckels, and park commissioner William Alvord, and given to the Park Commission in 1877 with only one stipulation—that it be assembled within eighteen months. The commissioners were so short of funds they would not have been able to erect the structure during the allotted time period except for a special release by the California Legislature to sell bonds for that purpose.[22]

It was the end of Hall's superintendence. A proud man, he took the actions of the state as a personal insult and resigned in 1876. The entire Board of Park Commissioners resigned in sympathy with him, but the governor was able to convince them to rescind their resignations and to hire a new superintendent, William Bond Pritchard (1842–1915). The former assistant superintendent and an engineer of military training, Pritchard was honest, competent, and respected by Hall and the com-

The Conservatory, seen here shortly after its erection in 1879, was imported from England by James Lick, who intended to use it on his estate but died before it could be assembled. It came to Golden Gate Park as a gift from some wealthy city residents, who purchased it from Lick's estate. Photograph by Carleton E. Watkins, reproduced by permission of the Society of California Pioneers.

missioners. He would remain superintendent until 1881, but the period was difficult, with funding at the lowest in the park's history. Nonetheless, he achieved notable accomplishments. While most of the budget went to maintaining the first five years' plantings and roads, both were expanded slightly and the Conservatory and Casino erected. According to Hall, Pritchard's "training and aptitude as a disciplinarian and administrator, with his quietly persistent optimism" carried Golden Gate Park through these difficult years. He carefully managed his limited budgets and kept employee morale high, but he nevertheless left in disgust in 1881 to become a civil engineer in Los Angeles.[23]

After a one-year hiatus without a superintendent, F. P. Hennessey succeeded Pritchard. The search for a replacement had been difficult and extended because the commissioners, who were hamstrung by inadequate funding, had set the salary for Golden Gate Park's new superintendent unreasonably low. They might have been forced to accept an untested head but felt lucky to hire Hennessey, a "quick-tempered Irishman" who had years of experience in Golden Gate and Central Parks.

William Hammond Hall, however, distrusted the man; and another of Hennessey's influential and former employers, Frederick Law Olmsted, referred to him as "a sly, intriguing and untruthful man." Hennessey ended up holding the post of superintendent for less than one year, being let go and replaced in 1882 by John J. McEwen, of whom little is known. McEwen, like Hennessey and Pritchard before him, had a pitiably small budget; but his work earned praise from Hall. Maintenance work was becoming more demanding as park use increased and the plantings aged, requiring planting and replanting of the sand binders marram grass (*Ammophila arenaria*) and sea lyme grass (*Elymus arenarius*) near the Ocean Beach. McEwen retained the superintendent's post until 1886 when John McLaren, who headed the park for a phenomenal fifty-seven years, succeeded him. McLaren is discussed in the next chapter.[24]

During the remainder of the romantic period, while Superintendents Pritchard, Hennessey, and McEwen were in charge of the park, the public's use of and positive attitude toward Golden Gate Park never waned. It was frequently included in tourist and other promotional drawings of San Francisco, newspapers continued to write upbeat commentaries, and little criticism came from other quarters. The *Daily Alta California* of August 17, 1879, favorably reviewed the steady, if slow, development of trees, roads, and views, saying, "while nature has done much, art has not been idle." Another paper, the *Daily Evening Bulletin* of May 2, 1879, praised the commissioners for doing a good job of reclaiming the drifting sands and for "improving and beautifying the grounds." The *Bulletin* found attractive the flowers on both the lupines used to control the drift sands and the ornamentals planted in the more developed parts of the park. "As it was designed to be, the Park is a popular place of resort."

Unfortunately, the park's floral successes were also causing an increase in crime, prompting one of the rare instances when romantic-period women were mentioned as visitors to Golden Gate Park. The same *Bulletin* article reported that the park commissioners had been compelled to adopt "regulations prohibiting visitors from plucking flowers or handling shrubbery," but that the regulations were frequently violated. "Women visiting the Park are represented to be the chief offenders. Valuable plants have been mutilated, and in some instances destroyed or carried away bodily from the conservatories and the grounds by vandal hands." The commissioners intended to be stricter in the future and to make examples of a few offenders who were "detected plucking either wild or cultivated flowers . . . the one being just as necessary for the work of relamation as the other is for that of orna-mentation." The newspaper was especially incensed because the park was widely popular and "the efforts of the Commissioners to make the Park attractive ought to be seconded instead of impeded by those who frequent that place."[25]

## ROMANTIC GOLDEN GATE PARK AND THE VIRTUES

The beginning of Golden Gate Park can be viewed as a local and historical issue rather than a generic and theoretical one, because the events leading up to its cre-ation were unlikely to be repeated elsewhere. For instance, the park became a novel means of settling what had been a difficult struggle over the Outside Lands as well as a battleground between the superintendent and the local horticulturists. On the other hand, San Francisco's experience is like that of other cities because of its links to the pursuit of the good society. San Francisco's park advocates, like their coun-terparts elsewhere, expected their park to cultivate the four virtues, but they ex-pressed this sentiment less often than they had during the initial park-development period. Once Golden Gate Park had legal standing, a budget, and a staff, advocates could relax their efforts to persuade and justify. However, the newspapers and other publications in romantic-era San Francisco continued to link the park to the vir-tues, and the material ones—public health and prosperity—clearly took precedence over the behavioral concerns about social coherence and democratic equality.

In the 1860s and 1870s, the residents of San Francisco did not suffer from dis-eases as badly as people in eastern cities did, so they treated parks and public health differently. East of the Mississippi River, parks typically were regarded as mecha-nisms for preventing common epidemics, because many Americans, including a substantial number of health professionals, subscribed to the miasmatic theory rather than the germ theory of disease. Parks were therefore considered a health enhancement measure because they were open spaces where tainted air was diluted by clean breezes. The *Califronia Horticulturist* poetically declared, "Here invalids and convalescents feebly [recuperate] their wasted forces." In San Francisco, how-ever, Golden Gate Park was only occasionally referred to as "the lungs of the city," where people could enjoy fresh air. It was believed that San Francisco's climate, especially the gusty winds, kept the likelihood of accumulating miasmas low. "It should be a source of gratification to the community to know," wrote San Fran-cisco's public health office in 1867, "that owing to our invigorating climate, the death record will compare favorably with any city in the Union, of comparative population, notwithstanding the well-known fact that San Francisco is the City of Refuge for the halt, the lame, and the blind of the Pacific coast."[26]

The more important public health issue for San Francisco's park advocates was the relationship they perceived between urban life and enervation, or a lack of individual energy. Park supporters argued that the hectic pace of the city's burgeoning commercial activity was exhausting, particularly to the city's adult males. A visit to Golden Gate or another public park would refresh tired businessmen by offering them opportunities for escape from the race. "They can afford not only the opportunity for breathing freely an improved and purified atmosphere [that is, one without miasmas] but the space and incitements to exercise and relaxation, promoting pleasurable reunions while feasting the eyes with their fresh verdure . . . exhilarating the mind, giving buoyancy to the spirits, and a new and healthy impulse to the circulation." With bodies and minds refreshed and energized, people were healthier, more vital, and could more easily continue the struggle toward financial success. According to Frederick Law Olmsted, enervation was much too common in San Francisco, and he insisted the municipal government was responsible for providing means for personal improvement.

> The more important part of [San Francisco's population] is wearing itself out with constant labor, study, and business anxieties, at a rate which is unknown elsewhere. This is to a great extent, perhaps, a natural and necessary result of the present circumstances of its commerce; but that there should be so little opportunity and incitement to relief—to intervals of harmless and healthy recreation, as is the case at present—is not necessary, and is not wise or economical. Cases of death, or of unwilling withdrawal from active business, compelled by premature failure of the vigor of the brain, are more common in San Francisco than anywhere else, and cause losses of capital in the general business of the city, as much as fires or shipwrecks. Such losses may be controlled by the [municipal government] to a much greater degree than losses by fires, and it is as much its duty to take measures to control them, as it is to employ means to control fires.

Enervation was a personal condition but it was also a public issue that could be addressed by a municipality, and to neglect it would be unconscionable. Moreover, the suppression and prevention of an individual's unwilling withdrawal from business was as much an economic issue as uncontrolled fire and thus a municipality's responsibility.[27]

Other San Francisco park campaigners claimed that the presence of Golden Gate Park would contribute to local prosperity in at least three other ways as well. First, according to the editor of the *Daily Alta California,* a large urban park was part of all the "great" cities, like New York, Paris, and London. These metropolises drew crowds of tourists who spent freely on food in local restaurants, merchandise in local stores, local lodgings, and local transportation while they were in town to visit the park and other "cultural" features. San Francisco's merchants supported Golden Gate Park, of course, for these same reasons. "We must give our city," urged the pro-business *Alta,* "the attractions of the chief watering place, as well as the great commercial and manufacturing centre of Pacific America." This argument, which continues to resonate today, was frequently noted and widely repeated during the romantic era. The *Daily Morning Call* noted in 1875 that many of Golden Gate Park's visitors were strangers drawn from out of town to tour and view this amenity. A great park attracted great wealth.[28]

The park also helped San Francisco retain wealth. According to local lore, migrants usually came to the city to "make their fortunes." They might become involved in mining, shipping, warehousing, retail, finance, or manufacturing; but once they succeeded, many were thought to depart for distant cities with cultural attractions. At least one travel writer decided that Golden Gate Park countered this trend. According to B. E. Lloyd, the park was so attractive that the rich remained in San Francisco to display the material benefits of success in the park.

> On pleasant holidays, and Sundays in particular, the Park presents a lively scene. Gold-mounted carriages of every approved pattern, drawn by richly caparisoned steeds, driven by uniformed livery-men, whose brilliant buttons are conspicuously numerous, and containing beautiful belles and gallant beaux, are seen whirling swiftly over the open road, now lost behind a curve, now penetrating a thicket—appearing and re-appearing, rivaling each other in display, as well as emulating each other in merry-making and jollity.

Such descriptions might seem crass and elitist in the twenty-first century, but the wealthy wanted to "see and be seen" and riding in a conspicuously rich carriage through Golden Gate Park expressed achievement in the clearest terms in 1876.[29]

Second, the experience with New York's Central Park had demonstrated early on that once a park's location was identified and construction begun, the property values around it did increase. Historians Roy Rosenzweig and Elizabeth Blackmar estimate that the value of lots fronting on Central Park increased by a factor of ten or more between the late 1840s, before the park site was decided, and the late 1850s, after work had been initiated. This relationship between a park and property values was noted in San Francisco as early as Frederick Law Olmsted's 1865 letter to the *Daily Evening Bulletin*. It is "the experience of other cities, both in Europe and the United States, . . . that [an] increase in value of the public resources . . . result[s] from the construction of a park." Expectation of this increase in property values accounts for how the park received its initial funding. Six-percent bonds issued by the City and County of San Francisco were to support the park, but the city usually sold this sort of bond at an 8 percent discount and could not in this case because the legislation enabling the park also forbade bond discounting. Under such conditions, the bonds would typically have fetched no offers, yet the park was able to sell $75,000 in bonds at full price. Abraham Seligman, an Outside Land holder, was the only purchaser at the first sale, on August 1, 1870, and again at the second, on May 12, 1871. According to the *First Biennial Report*, Seligman bought the bonds because he "expected to reap an indirect benefit in the improvement of the Park, and the consequent appreciation in the value of [his] property adjoining." The park bonds were a dual-pronged investment for Seligman, who apparently knew about parks and property value increases elsewhere. The tendency for property near a park to increase in value was not forgotten in the following years either. "It is a well-known fact," touted P. J. Sullivan's 1880 real estate brochure, "Homes For All," "that REAL ESTATE ADJOINING LARGE PUBLIC PARKS always becomes the most valuable for residences, and what was true of the surroundings of Central Park in New York will be equally demonstrated in the neighborhood of Golden Gate Park in San Francisco." Increased real estate values had also been noted repeatedly by many Outside Land homesteaders and helped persuade them to reach a settlement with the city.[30]

Last, increased property values meant an increased property tax base for the city. The new, higher tax base would be more than sufficient to pay off the park's indebtedness. The *Second Biennial Report* trumpeted this point on its first page,

It would be a waste of time to advert to the hygienic and esthetic influences of pleasure grounds. These were known to a remote antiquity. It was reserved for modern experience to demonstrate that outlays of this nature constitute a profitable invest-ment; it has been thoroughly proved in all other cities where Public Parks have been made that the increase in the amount received from taxation, on the enhanced value of property resulting from Park improvements is largely in excess of the interest on the money expended.

The increased taxes, most of which would be derived from lands near the park, first paid off the park bonds sold to Abraham Seligman and other investors while the remainder could be used either to pay for such municipal services as police and fire or to lower the rates on properties distant from the park. In either case, everyone assumed wealthier residents would be paying the taxes, since they would be the owners of the attractive sites near Golden Gate or another park.[31]

Park activists discussed both of the behavioral virtues, but social coherence was more frequently mentioned than democratic equality. They mentioned social co-herence, or in the language of the day, "morality," more often because its most identifiable antithesis, crime, was more commonplace and distinguishable than was a lack of democracy. Golden Gate Park, its backers claimed, would help to overcome the undesirable rise of social divisions within the city's populace by, for example, operating as an arena for numerous "healthful recreations," such as stroll-ing, picnicking, and croquet playing. Superintendent William Hammond Hall maintained that these recreations appealed to multiple segments of the popula-tion, from the wealthiest to the poorest. In the pleasant and uplifting setting of the park, Hall claimed, the various groups came to appreciate each other's recreations, take part in them, grow socially homogeneous and thus promote greater demo-cratic equality.[32]

Many of San Francisco's elite accepted the argument for social homogeneity through parks because they feared the vice they thought could arise with hetero-geneity. Activists reasoned that crime would be reduced and public spiritedness promoted if residents from all the city's groups could mingle in Golden Gate Park, and they supported their argument by noting the low crime rates in the area of the park. The *Daily Morning Call* was so impressed with Golden Gate Park's crime record it compared safety there to that on a busy downtown street. "The visitor is as safe in its secluded haunts as on Montgomery or Kearny Streets." In the haven of the park San Francisco's residents were "uplifted" through social intercourse and progressed toward a mutual, "higher" state of civilization.[33]

At the same time, it is important to recognize that one finds a connection between all four virtues and the park only at a collective, abstract level. No individual San Franciscan consistently expressed a belief in the capacity of the park to foster all the virtues, although on occasion, a single source, such as the *Daily Evening Bulletin,* would express two, or even three. "The steady improvement of the Park, and the furnishing of easy and economical means of reaching that resort and the ocean side, will largely further the prosperity of the city, while their sanitary and moral influence can hardly be overrated. We need something near at home that will tempt our hard-working population to break off in the daytime and seek a bit of nature." But the *Bulletin's* pronouncement was the exception, and it is possible to identify all four virtues in strength in San Francisco only in the context of the writings of many park backers. The virtues are a constellation of moral qualities attached to a park, but the perceived arrangement varied by individual, with the specific order of importance and degree of support unpredictable in advance.[34]

In contrast to the park's supporters, at least one observer felt that some of the arguments in favor of the park served purposes other than the purported ones. "The Park Commissioners have been rather overdoing the business of praising the advantages which are to flow from [Golden Gate Park]," protested one cynic.

> We are told that it will exert a potent influence upon the moral condition of society and prove a great moral reformer, all of which is "flabbergast" pure and simple. The Park is, of course, a great benefit, and it will pay well as an aid to increase of real-estate values; beyond that it is for the rich few, and it is used almost entirely by them. . . . When the object is to secure a large appropriation from the legislature, calling the Park a great influence in the direction of moral reform is dust that may be thrown in the eyes of our lawmakers at Sacramento, but it would not be tolerated at any other time.

In one sense, this critic was very perceptive. He seems to doubt that enhanced public health, social coherence, or democratic equality would ever prevail in San Francisco, and as history demonstrates, they have yet to triumph. Nonetheless, he misunderstood the power and continuity of culture, for as we shall see, when a romantic vision failed to succeed, San Franciscans did not dispense with the goal but instead redefined nature as something rationalistic and, in so doing, reinvigorated their pursuit of the virtues.[35]

Many visitors arrived and departed Golden Gate Park by cable car. The gateway that marked the park's main entrance is on the left in this 1887 scene at Stanyan and Haight Streets. Vendors often sold flowers and other goods near the gate, especially on Sundays. Note the patrolman in the foreground. Reproduced by permission of the San Francisco History Center, San Francisco Public Library, and the Union Pacific Railroad.

The Stanyan and Haight Streets entrance to Golden Gate Park in 1886. Walking through the gateway and down the slope beyond it took a visitor to Alvord Lake. The depot for the Park and Ocean Railroad, which was built in the park without the Park Commission's approval, is on the left. A fruit stand sits between the two structures, and a Haight Street cable car is visible in the left foreground. Reproduced by permission of the San Francisco Museum and Historical Society.

Alvord Lake was created in 1882 and improved in 1894, just before this photograph was taken. Alvord Bridge went up in 1889. They were named for former San Francisco mayor and park commissioner William Alvord and formed a popular spot for quiet contempla-tion. Through Alvord Tunnel, under the bridge, lay the children's playground, whose Sharon Building is just visible above the tunnel. Reproduced by permission of the Library of Congress, Prints and Photographs Division (LC-USZ62-104782).

The park was especially popular on Sundays, when large numbers would bike, ride, walk, and rest. Here people gather at the intersection of Middle Drive (*at right*) and Main Drive (now John F. Kennedy Drive). The Conservatory is off camera at left. Reproduced by permission of the Bancroft Library, University of California, Berkeley.

The tunnel to the Conservatory, visible beyond it, running under Main (now John F. Kennedy) Drive, had a rustic stone entry planted in a lush, "tropical" style. The intersection with Middle Drive is off camera to the right. Reproduced by permission of the San Francisco Museum and Historical Society.

The Conservatory as seen from the southwest corner of Conservatory Valley. The carpet beds of flowers are in exuberant bloom—in December, testament to the mild San Francisco winters that inspired the Midwinter Fair of 1894. The Terrace is to the right and slightly beyond the Conservatory itself. Reproduced by permission of the San Francisco Museum and Historical Society.

The James Garfield monument from the Terrace northeast of the Conservatory. The Arizona Garden sits in the foreground and the Children's Playground can be glimpsed in the distance on the right. The Francis Scott Key monument is faintly visible through a gap in the trees, to the right of the Garfield monument. Reproduced by permission of the California History Room, California State Library, Sacramento.

Lawn bowling, one of the many sports that came with the rationalistic era of park design, became a highly popular game at the beginning of the twentieth century. The hedge on the right blocks any view of the sport from the Sharon Meadow, a romantic, contemplative space beyond. From the San Francisco Board of Park Commission's 1910 *Annual Report*, opposite p. 72; reproduced by permission of the Bancroft Library, University of California, Berkeley.

A view of the stream and pond in rustic De Laveaga Dell. This rocky feature included numerous ferns, mosses, irises, and native reeds and grasses, as well as the covering oaks. From the San Francisco Board of Park Commissioners' 1902 *Annual Report,* opposite p. 12; reproduced by permission of the Bancroft Library, University of California, Berkeley.

The Buffalo Paddock, reminding visitors of the American expansion across the plains and prairies, was popular, especially with children. Reproduced by permission of the California History Room, California State Library, Sacramento.

FACING PAGE:
*Top:* Huntington Falls cascades 110 feet down the eastern side of Strawberry Hill into Stow Lake. Constructed in 1894 with a donation from Collis P. Huntington, it is topped by a rustic bridge, straddled by ferns, arched by tree branches, and concludes in a trout pool. Reproduced by permission of the San Francisco Museum and Historical Society.

*Bottom:* Stow Lake from Strawberry Hill. The rustic boathouse (*center*), where rowboats could be rented, sat on the northwest corner of the lake; it was torn down in 1937 but rebuilt in 1946. The 64-foot Prayer Book Cross, celebrating the Book of Common Prayer, can be seen in the distance, where it still stands. Reproduced by permission of the California History Room, California State Library, Sacramento.

The Temple of Music in Concert Valley held popular outdoor band concerts every Sunday afternoon throughout the year. It was badly damaged in the 1906 earthquake but was rebuilt and continues to be used today. The road in the foreground leads to the museum (*off left*) and the Japanese Gardens (*off right*). Reproduced by permission of the California History Room, California State Library, Sacramento.

# RATIONALISTIC GOLDEN GATE PARK

There are efficient parks, many of them, and the splendid
spirit that in the past has prompted the acquisition of
embryonic parks is now interesting itself more and more in
their development to meet the needs for which such areas
were acquired. With the new possessions there is becoming
apparent a more painstaking study to find just the park
chord that responds most harmoniously to the delight and
benefit of the greatest number of adults and children. . . .
The new conception of the usableness of parks is to develop
. . . practical aids to the general satisfaction in parks.

George Burnap
*Parks: Their Design, Equipment, and Use*

I t is difficult to establish a precise beginning for a rationalistic attitude toward
parks, since it was a process rather than an event. The rationalistic era began at
different times around the United States. The 1880s can be identified as the broad
period of transition in San Francisco because the most important characteristics
of a rationalistic viewpoint were present after 1890 but only a few were identifiable
before 1880. Within this decade, one year, 1886, emerges as most important, because a wholesale change in the park administration occurred that year as rationalistic park advocates came to its fore. William Hammond Hall, the former superintendent, reappeared, in a new post, and the governor appointed an entirely new
Board of Park Commissioners and park superintendent.

The state law creating Golden Gate Park required the governor of California to appoint a San Francisco Board of Park Commissioners every four years. It could be a simple, uncontested reappointment, selective substitution, or a radical replacement of the entire board. The last was difficult and occurred only under the sort of extraordinary circumstances that developed during the 1880s. At the time, the Southern Pacific Railroad was a powerful economic and political force throughout California, involving itself in seemingly every niche, no matter how unimportant it might appear. The 1886 appointment of the San Francisco Park Commissioners became another, if minor, battleground in the ongoing political struggle to break that corporation's strangle hold on the state. In the 1882 and 1884 elections, Governor George Stoneman and a number of other Democrats had been elected to Sacramento on an antirailroad ticket, with most of their support coming from rural voters, that is, those outside San Francisco. The state's farmers felt that the railroads were taking advantage of them by providing transportation selectively and by charging excessively high shipping rates. Conversely, San Franciscans, who in the same elections had chosen a Democratic mayor and several other officials, selected Christopher Augustine Buckley, the city's "Blind Boss." Buckley, a railroad-supported politician, had enraged Stoneman by opposing the governor's electoral slate at the state 1884 convention; so Stoneman was prepared to go against Buckley wherever possible, but especially on the boss's home ground. Dismantling San Francisco's then pro-railroad park board and reorganizing it with men sympathetic to Stoneman's position was an option the governor relished exercising in 1886.[1]

Governor George C. Perkins, Stoneman's predecessor, had appointed William Alvord, John Rosenfeld, and Frank Pixley to San Francisco's park board in May 1882. Alvord, unlike the other commissioners, originally had been elected to the board in 1873 by the seated commissioners and then twice reappointed by governors before Perkins. A supporter of Superintendent William Hammond Hall, Alvord had steadfastly defended the spatial integrity of Golden Gate Park during the ten years before his third appointment to the commission. John Rosenfeld and Frank Pixley, by contrast, were under the influence of the "Big Four" owners of the Central Pacific Railroad—Mark Hopkins, Leland Stanford, Collis P. Huntington, and Charles Crocker—and this pair orchestrated Alvord's resignation from the board in July 1882, only shortly after his reappointment. The Big Four had been proposing since 1880 to build a steam railroad line *in* Golden Gate Park. The Southern Pacific Railroad, which would merge with the Central Pacific in 1885, owned the Market Street

Cable Railway Company, whose line terminated at Haight and Stanyan Streets, across from the entrance to Golden Gate Park. The Central Pacific wanted to create a four-mile line, the Park and Ocean Railroad, that also would have a station near Haight and Stanyan Streets. Here passengers could easily transfer from the Market Street cable car and then take the new line through Golden Gate Park along H Street (now Lincoln Way), turn north along Ocean Beach, and finish their trip near Sutro Heights. Alvord, to the railroad's irritation, had continuously opposed the proposal, so Rosenfeld and Pixley hatched their plan to remove him. Earlier in Alvord's stretch as a park commissioner, he had donated money to improve the small lake that now bears his name, near the western end of the park. At the time of the donation he had insisted that it be called simply "the Lakelet." The other commissioners had acquiesced to his wish, but when Alvord left San Francisco shortly after his third reappointment, Pixley, who was president of the board, and Rosenfeld held a ceremony renaming the lake after their absent colleague. When Alvord returned to the find the change he was incensed; he resigned when Rosenfeld and Pixley refused to rescind the name. Once Alvord was gone, the remaining, pro-railroad park commissioners quickly elected Leland Stanford to replace Alvord, clearing the way for the Park and Ocean Railway to build its line. The new commissioner, however, was sensitive to possible legal action, so he never attended a board meeting and did not vote in favor of his railroad's request, because to do so would have been a clear conflict of interest. Nonetheless, he resigned from the park board in June 1883 once the building of the line was assured and was replaced in September by Irwin McDowell, another of the railway's supporters.[2]

Stanford's confidence was such that construction of the line began in August 1883, even before the Park Commission had officially given its permission. When a *Chronicle* reporter, who was suspicious of the construction, asked a foreman at the site when the railroad had obtained approval to build, he found out it had not. He was told, "Mr. Stanford wanted the road. That's all." This legal "oversight" was soon rectified, however, when on October 12, 1883, Rosenfeld, Pixley, and McDowell voted to officially allow Stanford, Huntington, Crocker, and "their successors or assigns" the right to build the railroad line. Soon the line was finished, carrying first railroad and then trolley car traffic. It was this Board of Park Commissioners that Governor Stoneman wanted to replace with his own men when the regular round of four-year appointments were to be made in spring 1886. However, the

The Park and Ocean Railroad once ran through Golden Gate Park. This 1886 illustration shows the steam engine pulling closed and open cars near Ocean Beach at the western edge of the park. In only sixteen years, the blowing sand dunes had been largely transformed into a stable greenspace, albeit requiring much additional irrigation. From Margaret Sidney, *The Golden West, as Seen by the Ridgway Club* (Boston, 1886), p. 330.

governor needed to maneuver cautiously because of the political power of the railroads, so Stoneman enlisted the aid of a knowledgeable San Franciscan—William Hammond Hall—for the project.[3]

In 1878, two years after Hall had resigned as superintendent of Golden Gate Park, he obtained a job in the state engineer's office of California. Skilled, determined, and savvy, he advanced to the top of this department. As its head, Hall had responsibility for much of the on-going effort to contain the annual flooding of the Sacramento and San Joaquin Rivers as well as the development of a number of irrigation systems around the state. In May 1884, he was reappointed state engineer by Stoneman and became, in his own words, "a member of the official family . . . initiating a close personal as well as official association." The basis for this close association was their mutual support for irrigation and flood control.[4]

Knowing of William Hammond Hall's experience with and continuing interest in Golden Gate Park, and aware that appointments would be made the following spring, Stoneman asked Hall during 1885 to help him identify some new park board members. Hall agreed, but the task turned out to be difficult because of personal jealousies and the demand for adroit political maneuvering. Early in the process Hall obtained the governor's support to appoint former park commissioner and mayor William Alvord, William T. Coleman, and Creed Haymond. Coleman was a retired merchant and sugar refiner who had come to San Francisco in 1849 and, in his early San Francisco days, had acted as a leader in the Committees of Vigilance. Haymond worked as a lobbyist and the general solicitor for the Southern Pacific Railroad but was included because he was a park advocate, willing to publicly champion Golden Gate Park, and had the political clout to get the park's financial support increased by the state legislature. According to Hall, these three would have been "a first-rate Board . . . all men with real interest in and understanding of the subject." However, Frank Pixley fought Haymond's appointment through their mutual supporter, Leland Stanford. When Haymond withdrew his name from consideration so did Alvord and Coleman. Nevertheless, Hall fought Pixley's reappointment by transferring support from his original three candidates to Joseph Austin and Richard P. Hammond. The former was a successful local merchant, port warden, veteran fireman, and a claims adjudicator for a steamship company who had lived in San Francisco for thirty years. Hammond held the post of U.S. surveyor general for California and was a cousin of Hall, but he had obtained the governor's support through his own Democratic Party connections. The governor added to the list retired General William H. Dimond, a former member of the U.S. Sanitary Commission (predecessor to the Red Cross) and a successful ocean shipper. Austin, Hammond, and Dimond were appointed the new Board of Park Commissioners, with Hall as a "consulting engineer."[5]

On May 12, 1886, the new board held its first meeting, taking note of their accounts and requesting that Hall officially present them with a report outlining his recommendations at the earliest opportunity. Turning to Superintendent John J. McEwen, the board informed him that he was now accountable for the actions of every park employee, and they furthermore demanded a list of "inefficient"— that is patronage—employees, to be discharged. Shortly, "an extensive exodus of men from the park payroll began." Subsequently that same year, Superintendent McEwen himself resigned and Hall, "on loan" from the state, temporarily reassumed the mantle of superintendent. As it was never intended to be a permanent position for Hall, the park commissioners asked him to locate and hire a "competent" replacement superintendent when he was ready. He soon found his successor in a Scottish-born gardener.[6]

In 1873, John McLaren (1846–1943) had arrived at San Francisco from his homeland to begin a prearranged tenure as the head gardener on a San Mateo County estate. Only twenty-seven years of age, McLaren nevertheless had extensive experience, having begun his "calling" as a gardener's apprentice at the age of fourteen. Born into a farming family, McLaren had developed an "intense passion" to learn the more formal aspects of landscape gardening after working on several Scottish estates. By his late teens, he understood the practical aspects of gardening but wished to know more about botany, taxonomy, and design; so he traveled to Edinburgh and obtained a job at the Royal Botanic Garden, where he attended classes and gained experience with more elaborate styles of gardening. Although he never graduated, he "acquired a great deal of horticultural knowledge . . . worked and read voraciously and seems to have acquitted himself with some merit."[7]

John McLaren accepted successive positions on several more Scottish estates after ending his formal education, but in 1872 he was hired away to America by George Henry Howard, a trustee of the Bank of California, who owned 6,500 acres on the peninsula south of San Francisco. Howard had been developing these grounds for many years—Frederick Law Olmsted had prepared a plan for the estate in 1865—but now he wanted gardener McLaren to enlarge the estate's ornamental landscape. McLaren busily labored for Howard over the next fourteen years until he was hired away by Hall in 1887.[8]

A strong-willed, independent-minded man, Superintendent McLaren was described by one of his foremen, Roy L. Hudson, as "gruff," "dour," and "a plucky Scotsman of boundless energy." Hudson felt that McLaren had been an excellent choice for superintendent because he had local experience, was a "superb plantsman," and had the gardening "confidence born of good training." Only someone like McLaren "would attempt the monumental task of taming several hundred acres of rapidly shifting sands." His confidence extended to other arenas. According to Hudson, McLaren "was never afraid of anyone whether he be an influential politician or a powerful gardener." Raymond Clary offered a similar analysis— "politicians hated him because he did not take orders. He gave orders, and they were obeyed." More importantly, McLaren was politically astute, knowing how to manipulate the city's constituencies and agencies to defend the park from intrusions. For example, when the city decided to extend Sunset Boulevard north through Golden Gate Park to Lincoln Park, McLaren shrewdly offered park land in the line of this route to the Police Department for an academy. "The Police Department jumped at the offer, and soon a Police Academy stood in the way." He was also an astute judge of San Francisco society. The position of park superintendent controlled the employment of hundreds of workers and large budgets, so people actively pursued it. Only a politically astute superintendent could have kept his position for 56 years while the city's demographic, social, and political environment changed rapidly about him. An expertly trained, experienced, powerful bureaucrat, John McLaren oversaw the rationalistic period of parks in San Francisco. Under his direction, Golden Gate Park's generic, romantic landscape was segmented into specialized functions, and San Francisco came to have small parks in many of its neighborhoods.[9]

## THE SEGMENTATION AND SPECIALIZATION OF GOLDEN GATE PARK

A defining characteristic for the early rationalistic period was the appearance and multiplication of new, special-use areas within Golden Gate Park. Advocates of a romantic park had campaigned for an extensive, scenic landscape with only a handful of features—water, grass, shrubs, and trees—but the later campaigners rallied to have specific locations in the park designated for each of a wide range of intensive activities. Numerous specialized spaces appeared, each with its own promoters and users; but a few—the park's horticultural elements, museums, playgrounds, and athletic facilities—stand out because each one, rather than the park as a whole, allegedly fostered at least one of the four virtues. In addition, all garnered wide support among the populace, generated great controversy, and substantially transformed Golden Gate Park. As each new use appeared, the amount of romantic landscape, which continued to have its own supporters, shrank. The source for this increasing spatial segmentation was, of course, the urban society that surrounded the park. San Francisco was experiencing a growth in the number of social segments that used and supported the park. It was no longer designed primarily for adult men. "Your Commissioners have always borne in mind," insisted the park report for 1895, "that the public is made up of separate human beings with separate tastes, whose comfort and convenience demand regard." Rationalistic park proponents expressed their belief that many of these "separate tastes" needed encouragement, as they overtly tied new activities and spaces to the virtues, and to women, children, and adolescents as well as men.[10]

*Ornamental Horticulture*

Attitudes toward the horticultural definition of nature in Golden Gate Park had begun to change even before the 1886 appointment of a new commission and superintendent. The romantic period's definition of a park had largely begun and ended with grass and trees, requiring only a few of the latter, probably less than 100 species. From the beginning of the rationalistic period, the number of species planted was much higher. For example, a June 1882 inventory of the park nursery listed a total of 134,006 individual plants representing a minimum of 184 species, and a planting register at the back of the same source noted that 171,576 individual plants of a minimum of 107 species had been put out into the park during the preceding year. Of the 107 species, only 9 were considered by the enumerator to be trees or shrubs: *Acacia latifolia, Grevillea robusta* (silk oak), and an unknown number of species and cultivars of the genera *Salix* (willows), *Cupressus* (cypresses), *Eucalyptus, Pinus* (pines), *Pittosporum, Syringa* (lilacs), and *Platycladus* or *Thuja* (arborvitaes). Of this list a total of 57,344 were planted. The enumerator categorized the remaining 98 species as "Shrubs and Herbaceous Plants" and noted that gardeners had planted 114,232 individuals in the park, including such herbaceous flowering annual species as *Antirrhinum* (snapdragons) and *Lobelia*, herbaceous flowering perennial species like *Dahlia* and *Pelargonium* (geraniums), and numerous woody shrubs that flowered either conspicuously (e.g., *Escallonia rosea*) or inconspicuously (e.g., *Mahonia* spp. [Oregon holly]).[11]

The appearance of shrubs and herbaceous plants in great diversity and quantity presaged three permanent changes to the park's horticultural elements. First, the park's plant diversity steadily increased. The 1888–89 *Annual Report* listed 768 species and cultivars living in the park grounds, but by 1899, the number had swollen to 1,421, and in 1924 it reached a staggering 2,273. Much of the diversity was likely the result of purchases. William Hammond Hall's policy of growing nearly all of the park's plants in its own nursery had fallen by the wayside, perhaps as early as 1880 and likely no later than 1882. Sometime during those three years the management realized that the park's one-quarter-acre nursery was too small for their needs. Even though the management had yet to dramatically expand the palette of plant species in the park, they had already determined that "it would take 25 years to raise plants enough to complete the park," so they increased the size of the nurs-

Many plant species first appeared in Golden Gate Park during the rationalistic period of park design. New, flowering varieties had recently been planted on both sides of this path along the road. Strawberry Hill rises in the background, with its Sweeney Observatory, built in 1891 and destroyed in the 1906 earthquake. Reproduced by permission of the San Francisco Museum and Historical Society.

ery to 1.35 acres during 1882 and at about the same time began to purchase plant materials from outside. A bill from a Parisian seed company, Vilmorin-Andrieux, and letters from Superintendent John McLaren to the Santa Barbara nurseryman Francesco Franchesci indicate that McLaren was purchasing an array of plants not just locally but internationally. The park's nursery received the seeds of nearly one hundred species from the Parisian company on one occasion alone, and over the years, McLaren may have ordered as many as several hundred species from Franchesci's well-known nursery, the Southern California Acclimatizing Association. The superintendent's support for plant diversity may have originated in the fact that he was chiefly a gardener, and so interested in the horticultural aspects of parks, rather than a landscape architect drawn by a park's scenery. Superintendents with backgrounds like McLaren's were unexceptional in his day; in the view of a contemporary landscape architect, George Burnap, "highly competent as such" but too interested in "the aspect of the individual plant. . . . Their influence has resulted in plant

Representational, fanciful, and sometimes even functional "carpet beds" of flowering annuals gained popularity during the rationalistic period. In this picture from approximately 1893, they grace the bank and grounds before the Conservatory. This floral sundial kept accurate time. Photograph by Isaiah West Taber ("The Sun Dial, Golden Gate Park"); reproduced by permission of the Society of California Pioneers.

collection rather than plant composition,—interesting horticulturally but rarely so pictorially." The brisk increase in horticultural diversity was also likely abetted by increasing budgets, with the Park Commission's total expenditures for 1889 at $94,608 but up to $222,178 in 1899 and $1,022,384 in 1924.[12]

A second change in Golden Gate Park's horticulture was the use of thousands of colorful flowering herbaceous plants in large designs. Geometric and fanciful plantings, such as fleurs-de-lis, were installed year-round about the Conservatory, where they heightened the drama of the approach, as well as elsewhere in the park. This style of planting, known variously as "carpet-bedding" or "bedding out" and relying on large masses of bright, energetic colors rather than shades of green, was a clear move away from the romantic period's naturalistic, tranquil plantings.[13]

Finally, an increase in the number of woody shrubs suggests a maturing park with expanded hedges. As its trees matured, Golden Gate Park's rising canopy needed additional shrubby growth below to maintain the "clumps" and "masses" of green vegetation that had been planted in the 1870s. According to William Hammond Hall, by 1886 "the forestation of Golden Gate Park was made up of large clumps of trees ten to thirteen years in the ground, whose prime for shrub-like effect was past." Shrubs for hedges reflected the park advocates' desire to isolate and highlight the new park segments with specialized purposes, creating a need for visual and physical separation within the park. Hedges along the edge of a lawn bowling area or a children's playground prevented the sight of them from intruding upon the more contemplative portions of Golden Gate Park.[14]

It is possible to link the first two of Golden Gate Park's three horticultural changes to the virtues. The commissioners and other rationalistic park supporters believed that a diverse collection of plants would develop among San Franciscans a sense of equality and tolerance, especially if they were exposed to it at a young age. If "trees and plants indigenous to the soil of many countries" could go together to be a park, then why could not many nationalities work together to be San Francisco? Furthermore, the novelty of the plant diversity attracted tourists, thus promoting prosperity, even as the increasing use of colorful plants refreshed people through beauty and pleasure. "The park is full of delightful surprises; exquisite bits of color that suddenly and unexpectedly come into view to charm the eye and elevate the mind," the commissioners declared.[15]

## Museums

William Hammond Hall, like Frederick Law Olmsted, felt that museums and athletics each had their role in life, but not in a park. A museum, they argued, was an urban amenity best located elsewhere because it was untypical of the rural landscape represented by a park. Nonetheless, museums built in various "revivalist" styles sprang up in parks across America during the rationalistic era. Romantic park structures had generally been small, irregular, and rustic so that they would inconspicuously blend into a scene; but during the rationalistic period, these older buildings were eclipsed by large, geometric, neoclassical edifices whose architecture commanded attention. The orderliness and history of these new exteriors were revered because they recalled Western cultural progress. Neoclassical in particular was, as landscape architect and critic Christopher Tunnard explained, "a

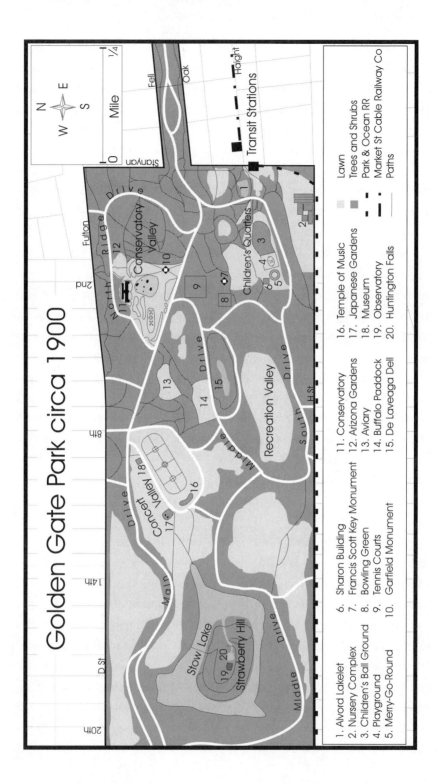

# Golden Gate Park circa 1900

1. Alvord Lakelet
2. Nursery Complex
3. Children's Ball Ground
4. Playground
5. Merry-Go-Round
6. Sharon Building
7. Francis Scott Key Monument
8. Bowling Green
9. Tennis Courts
10. Garfield Monument
11. Conservatory
12. Arizona Gardens
13. Aviary
14. Buffalo Paddock
15. De Laveaga Dell
16. Temple of Music
17. Japanese Gardens
18. Museum
19. Observatory
20. Huntington Falls

Lawn
Trees and Shrubs
Park & Ocean RR
Market St Cable Railway Co
Paths

Transit Stations

flexible style which could make a unity of a building by combining boldness of plan with refinement of detail. It made possible the handling of entirely new building types, frequently of great scale."[16]

Despite Hall's early opposition, Golden Gate Park's first museum was opened in 1895. From the perspective of the early twenty-first century, one can see that this museum was a mechanism for praising and teaching the dominant cultural order to San Franciscans of all ages and backgrounds. Like the earlier museum at Woodward's Garden, it included a display of the "wonders" of nature, the artifacts of non-Western peoples, and the material wealth and artistic creations of the cultural tradition that had produced the museum. One of the park's most popular attractions, the museum drew over 3,000,000 visitors before 1903, at which point it was the third largest museum in America.[17]

Although having a museum in Golden Gate Park had been proposed as early as 1887, none developed before the closing of the Midwinter Fair of 1894. The 1894 California Midwinter International Exposition (as the Midwinter Fair was officially known) was a local version of the 1893 Columbian Exposition in Chicago. The large crowds and the profits reaped by the Chicago fair struck Michael H. de Young (1849–1925), commissioner of California's exhibit there, as something that could be of value to San Francisco. In 1893, San Francisco was suffering through as severe an economic depression as the rest of the United States. De Young, the owner of the *San Francisco Chronicle* and an outspoken advocate for the San Francisco business community, thought that a San Francisco fair similar to Chicago's exhibition would rapidly bring outside wealth to the area, create jobs, and generally boost the sagging local economy. According to historians Arthur Chandler and Marvin Nathan, de Young "gathered together the San Francisco businessmen at the Columbian Exposition and set forth his dreams. Though there were skeptics among them, the majority liked what they heard and immediately pledged over $40,000 for the enterprise, the largest single contribution of $10,000 given by financier and future San Francisco mayor James Duvall Phelan." The emphasis on financial return among the fair's organizers was so pronounced that its first working title was "The Commercial World's Fair." Moreover, de Young sought to demonstrate the benign qualities of the local climate to the rest of America by holding a novel midwinter fair rather than the traditional summer fair. In the 1890s, few Americans knew how much the winter climate of San Francisco was milder than that of most eastern locations. In particular, de Young hoped to entice wealthier tourists west, convert

The new Golden Gate Park museum was tightly fitted with displays of natural history, such as animal skeletons, the artifacts of non-Western peoples, and Western art. From the San Francisco Board of Park Commissioners' 1910 *Annual Report*, opposite p. 80.

them into permanent residents, and thus expand San Francisco's general wealth. This rationalistic argument for increased general wealth recalls those made by various progressives in favor of the use of public facilities by the greatest number for the greatest good.[18]

Back home in San Francisco, de Young found it easy to drum up extensive support for an exposition. His newspaper editorialized in favor of the fair, with features beginning as early as June 1, 1893. That headline read, "WE MAY HAVE A FAIR. Scheme of Californians at Chicago. A Commercial Show in San Francisco. Foreign Exhibitors Willing to Come After the Great Exposition." He personally solicited patronage from influential individuals such as Republican governor of California, Henry Markham (1840–1923), and then-Independent but formerly Republican mayor of San Francisco, Levi Ellert (1857–1901). Both supported the fair, and the latter, the first native-born mayor of San Francisco, presided over it from opening to close. In addition, the idea of a midwinter fair attracted hundreds of private contributors who believed it would revitalize business then and in the future. The business community proper, local artists, some trade workers, and even the newspaper boys contributed money to the venture.[19]

At the same time, however, the opposition to de Young's scheme was vocal and loud. One critic labeled the exposition "the Midwinter Fake," others said it could not be prepared in the short time allotted, and the largest contingent resisted because the fair was to be held in Golden Gate Park. De Young was unconcerned about holding an exposition in the park because he considered it vacant land, and when he and the other organizers proposed to locate the fair on a 60-acre site at the park's east end, opponents arose to resist this "destruction." Superintendent McLaren and Park Commissioner William W. Stow were both dead set against an exposition in the park. McLaren argued that the fair would despoil the park's fresh and maturing flora as well as set an unacceptable precedent for holding large, commercial ventures in the park. People would come to think of the park not as a retreat from the city but as an empty space awaiting public exhibitions. Commissioner Stow, the former head of the railroad lobby and a millionaire conservationist, denounced the plan in front of de Young at a park board meeting: "You come in here and destroy a tree that has been growing for twenty years. The fair will be here for six months. Trees will be here for a thousand years." De Young was unimpressed and determined. "What is a tree?" he asked Stow rhetorically. "What are a thousand trees compared to the benefits of the exposition?"[20]

In the end, the complaints of Commissioner Stow and others were dismissed collectively by Park Commissioners Richard P. Hammond and Joseph Austin and other fair promoters as protests of "the usual objectors to all great projects" and "ultra conservatives." There were, they argued, precedents for an exposition in a park. For one, San Francisco had granted permission to use public greenspaces for fairs as early as 1868. In January of that year, the Mechanics' Institute was given permission to hold their fair in Union Square, delaying the "planting and sowing of the square as a small park for two years." For another, the 1893 Columbian Exposition had been held in Chicago's Jackson Park, also a large, urban park, making it difficult to argue that a Midwinter Fair in Golden Gate Park was inappropriate. Had not the grounds of the Chicago exposition, fair supporters asked, been designed by none other than Frederick Law Olmsted? Was his involvement not an endorsement of the basic proposal? Besides, declared the official organ of the fair, "just as the Columbian Exposition had transformed a disease-breeding marsh into a beautiful park (the Jackson Park site was largely undeveloped at the time), so should the Midwinter Exposition make the comparative wilderness of Concert Valley [the proposed site] to blossom like the rose." This rationalistic comparison

The 1894 California Midwinter International Exposition, or simply the Midwinter Fair, filled the eastern end of Golden Gate Park. Strawberry Hill, surrounded by Stow Lake, can be seen on the left, while the undeveloped Richmond District's sands, San Francisco Bay, and the Marin Headlands fill the background. The Court of Honor and the Bonet Electrical Tower sat at the center of the fair. The Fine Arts Building, which would become the Memorial Museum, is immediately right of the tower. Reproduced by permission of the Society of California Pioneers.

was clearly disingenuous, since Golden Gate Park's Concert Valley sat in an area already fully developed.[21]

In the face of powerful support, precedence, and the compelling example of Chicago, effective resistance failed to materialize. On July 10, 1893, Golden Gate Park was designated the official location for the Midwinter Fair. Ground-breaking ceremonies were held on August 24th, and the fair opened on January 27, 1894. Ironically, despite the protests generated by a proposed 60-acre site, the fair covered almost 200 acres. Centered on Concert Valley, it stretched from Fifth Avenue to Fifteenth Avenue on the east and west and from the northern to southern edges of the park. When it closed on September 1, 1894, the exposition had attracted more than 2,000,000 visitors and earned $66,851.49, or approximately 5 percent of the total receipts. This tidy profit made it possible for the fair's Board of Directors to fulfill their promise to clear away the event's structures by the end of November 1894, but instead they walked away, leaving the skeletons behind. Superintendent John McLaren repeatedly requested that the board follow through on their promise. Finally, in January 1896, he lost his patience and began dynamiting the deteriorating edifices, taking "great delight in watching the gaudy architectural fantasies blow apart in showers of multicolored debris." Soon nearly all fair structures were removed, but McLaren and the Park Commissioners retained two features, the Japanese Village, because it blended well with the natural beauty of Golden Gate Park, and the Fine Arts Building, to be used as a museum.[22]

The Japanese Village, popularly known as the Japanese Tea Garden, was inspired, like the Midwinter Fair itself, by a similar feature, the "Hoo-den," at the Columbian Exposition in Chicago. A concession envisaged and run by Asian art dealer and real estate developer George Turner Marsh, the Japanese Village included a magnificent gateway, tea room, and theater for dancers and acrobats. To produce an authentic

The Midwinter Fair's Court of Honor centered on the Bonet Electrical Tower and was surrounded by exhibit halls, including the Southern California Building, the Horticultural and Agricultural Building, and the large Mechanical Arts Building on the right. Reproduced by permission of the California History Room, California State Library, Sacramento.

air, Marsh had hired Japanese craftsmen to construct the buildings and Japanese landscape gardeners to surround the structures with a traditional garden containing bonsai, ponds, falls, bridges, paths, and stone lanterns. The village was popular with the public, and because its garden was an acceptable feature for a park, the San Francisco park board purchased it from Marsh at the fair's end. It remains a popular feature today.[23]

The Fine Arts Building displayed a solidly conservative collection of romantic and Victorian sculptures, watercolors, oil paintings, engravings, etchings, drawings, and carved gemstones throughout the fair. The edifice itself was a two-story, 8,000-square-foot structure designed in an Egyptian revival style by C. C. McDougal, a lesser-known among the exposition architects. McDougal's choice of an Egyptian mode was odd because it was unfashionable. Egyptian motifs had been common from the 1830s until the 1850s, but almost no one used them in the 1890s. Furthermore, an Egyptian arts building was particularly peculiar because when the style had been used in earlier decades, it had most often appeared on funerary structures and prisons. There was no tradition of designing museums or art galleries in this style. As the Midwinter Fair wound to a conclusion, its board of

Sixteen months after the Midwinter Fair closed, Park Superintendent John McLaren finally had nearly all the structures razed, because the fair organizers had failed to clear the site as promised. The Fine Arts Building, in the background, was not destroyed but continued as the Memorial Museum. Reproduced by permission of the California History Room, California State Library, Sacramento.

One of two constructions retained after the fair, the Japanese Tea Garden displayed the people, culture, and landscape of Japan, which was relatively unknown in the United States in 1894. The interior of the Tea House is shown in this illustration from *Scientific American*. This fair element was retained because its garden fit into the park and was popular with the public.

directors decided to place the disposition of the structures, in particular the Fine Arts Building, and of the remaining funds into the hands of the director-general, Michael H. de Young. All structures were scheduled for immediate destruction and removal at fair's end, but de Young approached William W. Stow, the President of the San Francisco park board, with the idea of retaining the Fine Arts Building and its donated contents for a museum, and using the final fair funds to purchase new collections. Stow rejected the notion. No fair buildings should remain in the park, he told de Young; but more importantly, he went on, a museum did not "belong in a park." "That," admitted de Young, "made me angry."[24]

As with the proposal for the Midwinter Fair itself, the campaign for keeping the museum in the park quickly drew on examples from elsewhere, especially New York. According to a somewhat apocryphal history of the museum, de Young told Stow, "Every great museum in the world is in a park. In Central Park in New York,

The Midwinter Fair's Fine Arts Building was not razed but became the first of several memorial museums in Golden Gate Park. It appears here around 1900. Reproduced by permission of the California History Room, California State Library, Sacramento.

the great Metropolitan Museum is on one side and the Museum of Natural History on the other." Stow, said de Young, acknowledged the strength of the reasoning and reversed himself. "Your argument is good," acquiesced the park board president, "Put your museum in the Park." Whether this story is true or not, the park board formally accepted the structure, renamed the Memorial Museum, and the collections that filled it to "utmost capacity," on March 23, 1895, for the people of San Francisco, "who derive great pleasure and instruction from examination of its interesting contents." In his acceptance speech, new park board president Joseph Austin made no mention of the building's unusual, Egyptian revival design but described the interior and its collections at length. The structure, however, would have a relatively brief, if eventful, history. It was damaged during the 1906 earthquake and repaired. As the collections swelled, a Spanish revival annex was added, in 1918, and then another Spanish revival building and tower were completed in 1920. Immediately after this third building was constructed, the collections were transferred into it. In 1928, the new building was renamed the M. H. de Young

Memorial Museum, honoring the former director, who had died three years earlier, and the original building, which had always been prone to leaking, was razed without comment.[25]

Describing the new museum in their 1924 report, the park commissioners reiterated their rationalistic predecessors' view that San Franciscans would learn and be entertained in a museum located appropriately in Golden Gate Park.

In the sense that it is devoted exclusively to education and information in painting, sculpture, antiques and historical relics, together with exhibitions of the applied arts of all countries, the M. H. de Young Memorial Museum is a notable addition to the other instructive and entertaining features of Golden Gate Park. . . . de Young conceived the philanthropic idea of adding to it a building or group of buildings that

The M. H. de Young Memorial Museum shortly after its completion in 1920. This structure replaced the original museum, which had sat to the right, just off camera. Reproduced by permission of the San Francisco Maritime National Historical Park (A12.29.974 GL).

would contain sufficient space for as complete a collection of art, history and examples of constructive labor as might prove adequate for the future economic and intellectual growths of a great city.

Rationalistic park advocates considered Golden Gate Park a good location for the M. H. de Young Memorial Museum and the Academy of Sciences Buildings that joined it because they believed that these features and the park's vegetation would promote prosperity by attracting tourists. Additionally, the contrast between the high arts and primitive arts, both found in the M. H. de Young Memorial Museum, would develop social coherence by representing San Franciscans as a uniform, civilized group in contrast to the world's traditional populations. Thus, the mission of the museums, like that of the plants, was to foster the same virtues that, since 1865, park proponents had claimed were associated with places of nature.[26]

### The Playground

Early in the rationalistic period, the commissioners built a playground in Golden Gate Park to encourage the virtues through organized play. It is thought to be the oldest established playground in the United States. The money for the facility had been bequeathed to the park in 1885 by a U.S. senator from Nevada, William Sharon. Sharon considered himself a San Franciscan, but he had also been the manager of the Virginia City, Nevada, office of William Ralston's Bank of California during the silver boom of the 1860s. Both he and Ralston amassed fortunes. With his, Ralston built the Palace Hotel, the Metropolitan Theater, and other impressive structures in Virginia City. Sharon spent his, as historian Oscar Lewis says, "by having himself elected to the U.S. Senate." Since Sharon had not designated in advance how his bequest to Golden Gate Park was to be spent, a struggle for its use ensued. Suggestions were made by various groups to build a beer garden, a music pavilion, a marble entry gate, or a playground. Eventually, the issue was resolved after Governor Stoneman in 1886 appointed the new park commissioners, who, along with Hall, ultimately supported the playground idea.[27]

To create a level setting for the grounds, a hill near the junction of the Avenue and the park proper was removed and used to fill a small, fresh-water lake in the southeast corner of the park. The Children's Quarters, as the playground was called, were erected on the filled site. When complete and dedicated on December 22, 1888,

The Children's Quarters consisted of the Sharon Building (*center*), a merry-go-round, and a play area with benches, swings, teeter-totters, and more. This playground was formed in the rationalistic period, when park advocates believed childhood was an important stage in the development of adults. From the San Francisco Board of Park Commissioners' 1910 *Annual Report*, between pp. 48 and 49.

the quarters included a merry-go-round with canvas awning, an area for directed play, and the Sharon Building, a monumental San Jose sandstone structure of an uncertain revivalist style offering a refreshments concession and shelter during inclement weather. Soon new features were added, starting with donkey and goat-cart rides in 1889. During 1891, a permanent roof was built over the merry-go-round, new walks and a skating and bicycling rink was constructed, while benches, swings, teeter-totters, May poles, and a rustic house were arrayed east of the Sharon Building. Over the years, the rides were discontinued and the equipment has been regularly replaced, but the area remains the only playground in Golden Gate Park.[28]

San Franciscans associated at least two virtues, public health and democratic equality, with the children's area. For example, the printed program for its opening day festivities clearly joined the new area to public health. "It is believed and earnestly hoped, by the Commissioners, that many hundreds of children will be taken from our streets, and with the facilities now afforded them for . . . healthful recreations, will grow up to be better men and women than had not the munificence of the late Senator Sharon provided them with these play-grounds." In this view, streets were dirty, polluted, disease-ridden, and dangerous because of traffic. In the clean, pure, safe environment of the park, children could play and mature into healthy Americans. Additionally, in discourse similar to psychologist G. Stanley Hall's (see Chapter 1), the play area was said to promote democratic equality amongst the various segments of society. The rich and poor, native and foreign-born, whites and children of color would learn to treat each other equally during play in such a natural setting. This ideal was most clearly caught in a poem written for the festivities opening the Sharon Building and playground.

> Bright-eyed lass with tattered gown,
> No one dares to scoff or frown
> Just because you are less fortunate than they;
> 'Tis no castle for the rich
> But for you, my little witch;
> There must be no aristocracy in play.

> Welcome, olive Española,
> With your merry Farandola,
> Here no line of caste or color may be drawn;
> Welcome, sun-brown Italiano.
> And the swarthy Africano
> With his hair as short as grass upon the lawn.

> Whether black or brown or yellow,
> You are welcome, little fellow!
> No policeman here to eye you as you pass,
> Or to chase you with a club
> If you breathe upon a shrub,
> Or abuse that ancient sign—"Keep off the grass."

According to its proponents, the playground remained "the most popular and beneficial of the many spaces devoted exclusively to [juvenile] recreation" for many years.[29]

At least one writer, however, thought the commissioners had made a mistake with the Sharon Building. As he saw it, they had been too insensitive to the needs of poorer San Franciscans. "Now it seems to me," complained author Charles S. Greene in an article about San Francisco's parks, "that one of the gravest mistakes in all the Park management is this building. It is pretty, it is enduring, it is a fine monument to the donor, but the children get but little benefit from it, and the poor children, who should have been most considered, get no benefit from it at all." The park management was numb to the limits poverty placed on the poor, continued Greene.

> It is not often that poor parents can give their little ones, for an afternoon's outing at the Park, more than the ten cents required for [trolley or cable] car fare, and unless they have money to spend they have no use for the Dairy [a restaurant]. When one considers what might have been done with fifty thousand dollars in the way of supplying a large, airy wooden building, full of appliances for amusement for all the children, where the poorest might find a game or gymnastic apparatus, and above all, welcome even without a five cent piece; and then notes how small a proportion of the persons who enter the House are children and how small a proportion of the children enter it, there cannot but be the feeling that some one has blundered.

Greene applauded the idea of a building but condemned the monumentality of it. Something built less "for the ages" would have allowed more funds to have been directed to a children's subsidy. This admirable goal was lost in the politics of creating a playground that also had to honor Senator Sharon.[30]

## Athletics

The ascendancy of rationalistic park supporters also led to a change in attitudes towards active sports in Golden Gate Park. For many of these park promoters, athletics contributed to the presence of the four virtues, especially public health. In their 1897 appraisal of Recreation Valley, the park's large, grassy field for baseball, football, cricket, lacrosse, and tennis, the commissioners reported that the area was well used and of great social value in densely populated San Francisco.

> In crowded cities, public recreation grounds are moral necessities for the physical development of the younger generation. From recent statistics it is shown that in large and populous cities where such places of recreation do not exist, the death rate is much higher than in cities possessed of such pleasure grounds.[31]

Recreation Valley was an invaluable addition to the park and in the eyes of the commission, it "more than fulfilled the purpose for which it was intended"—a doorway for nature-based athletics. "Here at the outskirts of a crowded city, within easy access from every point, the youth, more especially those athletically inclined, can escape from the city's close confinement, and each in his own way, engage in such sports of manly and vigorous exercise as their fancy dictates." It was important to San Francisco's park backers that the residents of a democratic city in an industrializing society learn to work together in an efficient and supportive manner. Games such as baseball and football encouraged an attitude of competition and cooperation among adolescents and young adults, especially males. Anything less would have been seen as irrational and counter to the spirit of progress. Thus, by 1901, baseball was commonplace in Golden Gate Park.[32]

By 1924, providing enough athletic space within Golden Gate Park became a trial, however. Ironically, the commissioners saw the challenge as resulting from their own earlier efforts to create athletic opportunities.

> The surprising growth of the athletic spirit during the past few years has been a source of much concern to several park commissions because of the obvious difficulty of providing sufficient space for games and meets without overcrowding. As this spirit spread through the years until it began to assume the importance of a great public necessity, to meet its demands became a problem difficult of solution because the more liberal the provisions for the allotment of spaces the greater the demands for more of them. The comparatively large area devoted to tennis, for example, was soon asserted to be almost totally inadequate; many acres had been prepared for football, baseball and other games, but it was urged that these were not sufficiently large.[33]

Not all sports facilities were intended for the exclusive use of men. Active pastimes, particularly bicycling and tennis, where women could participate and excel, began in the 1890s. For example, the opportunity to bicycle drew more than 5,000 male and female riders to Golden Gate Park on a single Sunday in August 1895. This enthusiastic embrace led to the immediately popular "bicycle road," which ran parallel to Main Drive.

> Cyclists of both sexes in large numbers frequent the park every day and night when the weather is favorable, and during the afternoons the large open space adjoining

Several athletic games, including baseball on the right, underway in Recreation Valley (also called "Big Rec") on a beautiful weekend around 1900. Games occurred in various locations; permanent facilities for particular sports did not appear for several decades after the park's opening. Reproduced by permission of the San Francisco Maritime National Historical Park, Muhlman Collection (A22.34.152 N).

the music grounds is filled with ladies learning to ride the wheel, most of them attired in knickerbockers or bloomers. Any day in the week a long line of bicyclists can be seen on the road specially constructed for their use, and on Sundays every drive in the park has its large quota.

Tennis courts came to Golden Gate Park slightly later than bicycling. The first were built atop the site of the old music stand in 1902. By that time demand for courts was so pent up that as soon as the initial ones were built they were inadequate to the pressure. In their first public report thereafter, the commissioners acknowledged this situation, stating that the tennis courts were "so popular as to warrant the construction of new ones from time to time to meet the demand of the players." Part of the reason they were exceedingly popular came from the early, strong acceptance of tennis by women, who flocked to this relatively acceptable sport. At the same time, the park commissioners wished to make their concern for women's needs clear, so the 1902 *Annual Report* noted a relatively new feature, the women's bath and changing rooms at the tennis club house.[34]

Despite increasing opportunities, San Francisco's women remained athletically disadvantaged relative to men. Although the number of women who actively participated appears to have stayed small and the press and official reports only rarely

Bicycling in Golden Gate Park became popular during the rationalistic period. Unlike other public forms of athletics, it was socially acceptable for women. This 1898 photograph showing more women than men, illustrates the enthusiasm of women for this recently available pastime. Reproduced by permission of the California Historical Society (FN-22639).

mentioned female athletics, public pressure against it was intense. When women were not being simply chided for "unseemly" strenuous outdoor activities, they were being denounced vehemently. As historian Raymond Clary recounts, "women were soon riding bicycles at all hours of the day and evening. Editorials and sermons from the pulpits howled over this practice." The democratic aspects of the bicycling women were observed by some with alarm: "As the sport grew in popularity, rich men were heard to grumble that one could not tell a rich man's daughter from a 'typewriter, or office girl.'" The uncertainty arose because a plain bicycle and outfit were the usual arrangement and financially accessible to many. Obviously, not every San Franciscan thought democratic equality was a virtue.[35]

## A TOUR OF GOLDEN GATE PARK'S RATIONALISTIC INTERIOR

The margins of Golden Gate Park remained as they had been during the romantic period—thick plantings of trees and shrubs that stood boldly apart from the surrounding landscape. However, the process of social and spatial segmentation permanently altered the internal geography of Golden Gate Park. Where the entire park had once been a relatively undifferentiated natural landscape, only the western two-thirds—the area beyond Strawberry Hill and Stow Lake—remained relatively undifferentiated between 1890 and the 1920s while the fixing and afforestation of the dunes continued. During much of this time it was obvious to visitors that the larger part of the park had been created upon moving sand. Roads were extended to the coast but just a few special uses, for example, the stadium where football, polo, bicycling, running, and other sports could be played, had been constructed. These additions occurred as Golden Gate Park's eastern end became more densely developed and the western end came to look more like a sylvan scene.[36]

In contrast to the western end of Golden Gate Park, the eastern range came to consist of a patchwork of special-use settings. A casual visitor no longer encountered the romantic park's enfolding, generic, nonurban nature when he or she

Popular demand finally brought tennis courts to Golden Gate Park in 1902. The game, like bicycling, was especially popular with women. From the San Francisco Board of Park Commissioners' 1910 *Annual Report,* between pp. 72 and 73.

entered the park. Instead visitors were greeted by a distinctive setting depending on where they entered. Take, for example, the case of a middle-class family who arrived at the terminus of the Market Street Cable Railway, or any of several other lines that also ended at Haight and Stanyan Streets, circa 1900. (See Gallery 1, "A Walk through Golden Gate Park circa 1900" and the map on page 148.) Walking from the terminus across the street into the park, they were greeted immediately by the flourishing Greenspace. Strolling past a charming Alvord Lakelet with its pom-pom trees, long stretches of benches for resting and quiet contemplation, calm waters, picturesque rocks, and lush, floriferous plantings, visitors passed into the stalactite laden tunnel under the elevated South Drive. Like Endale Arch in Brooklyn's Prospect Park, it framed the park beyond, so that as one came out of the "cave" the open and active area of the Children's Ball Ground was dramatically revealed. Straight ahead, beyond a tall, verdant hedge, lay the Children's Quarters with its swings, merry-go-round, donkey rides, and seasonal flowerbeds arrayed about the castlelike Sharon Building. These pleasures were middle class and much like the ones once available in privately owned Woodward's Gardens (see Chapter 2).

Turning north the family needed to wander only about one-third mile to enter Conservatory Valley. The approach took them past the Francis Scott Key Monument, which today sits in the Music Concourse, across Middle Drive, down a slope past thick, luxurious plantings, and into another tunnel that passed below Main Drive (now John F. Kennedy Drive) and whose mouth had been decorated to appear like rockery. Like the one near the entrance, this tunnel also framed a scene and heightened drama for exiting visitors, who reveled in the expansive, colorful carpet beds that signified wealth and spread out before the radiant white Conservatory. Modeled on one in London's Kew Gardens, the glass house enclosed palms, ferns, and other plants from tropical regions. Tourist Amy Bridges found the Conservatory to be "full of interesting plants and pretty flowers, especially orchids. I saw a pink passion flower." For most visitors, orchids suggested the exotic and lush that was so distant from San Francisco. Stepping out into the cooler, drier air and heading east, our family walked out onto a side of the Conservatory Valley and into the alluring Arizona Garden of unusual, southwestern U.S. plants, including *Agave*, *Yucca*, and other succulent species. From the Arizona Garden's heights, everyone could gaze south across the Conservatory Valley to the memorial for assassinated president James Garfield and the picturesque, rising hills beyond. Conservatory

Valley, a highly developed section in the 1900s, was one of the park's most popular and heavily visited features.[37]

About midway between the playgrounds of the Children's Quarters and Conservatory Valley lay an assortment of recently introduced athletic spaces. Clustered about what had once been the Music Grounds were situated the bowling green, a croquet field, and the tennis courts. The last, as we have seen, were immensely popular and would expand over the next decades. Croquet, a stately, almost passive game, had been played on lawns about the eastern end of Golden Gate Park for decades but had recently gained sufficiently in popularity to justify its own ground. Lawn bowling, in contrast to croquet, had only recently been introduced on the West Coast, and the 1902 commissioners had embraced it, hoping the game "would be beneficial to young and old alike."[38]

Immediately west of the tennis courts was a picturesque horticultural delight, De Laveaga Dell, which had been developed atop the former Deer Glen. The latter had been one of the first attempts to create a zoo or menagerie in the park and was begun during the 1880s. The 1902 commissioners' report described the Dell as abounding "in every natural beauty" and reminiscent of Central Park's Ramble. It rested "between two high sloping banks, along which a foot path has been laid leading to the west and where overhanging oaks form a leafy canopy, revealing from the eastern end of this little dell an interior worthy of the brush of any painter." Running down the center of the glade was a stream terminating in a pool, while about them rose rock ledges in whose pockets and crevices grew a variety of ferns, mosses, and other moisture-loving plants. In the Mediterranean climate of San Francisco, a display of lush moistness called to visitors. To the east of the pool, six large iris beds were planted, which in bloom put on a glorious, colorful display.[39]

Moving south out of the Dell, our family came to one of the oldest and most athletically oriented parts of the park—Recreation Valley, also known as "Big Rec." Here baseball, football, and other active sports were regularly played. Backstops, bases, goals, lines, and other equipment were brought out onto the fields just prior to a game. In succeeding decades, these informal grounds would be transformed into permanent fields; the transition began with the handball courts, constructed on Recreation Valley's northeast edge between 1900 and 1905. The commissioners, in a back-handed comment rich in ambivalence, felt that the handball courts had "proven an interesting feature." Perhaps none of them enjoyed the game.

Continuing in a northwesterly direction brought the family to the former site of the 1893 Midwinter Fair, which by the early 1900s had come to be known as Concert Valley and was the growing center of educational activities. On its northwestern perimeter lay the Egyptian revival Memorial Museum, which covered only a small portion of Concert Valley; its successor, the M. H. de Young Memorial Museum, would expand to include most of this side of the valley by the end of the 1920s. The Buffalo Paddock and the Aviary were located just beyond the eastern edge of Concert Valley so that families could easily move from the cultural collections in the museum to these natural ones. These live collections were relocated, however, when the California Academy of Sciences and the Steinhart Aquarium were constructed opposite the de Young Museum during the 1920s. Southwest of the Memorial Museum and separated from it by an open space of grass and flowerbeds sat the Japanese Village or Tea Garden. A few feet away from the village, commanding Concert Valley and giving it its functional name, rose the Spreckels Temple of Music. Seventy feet high, 160 feet wide, and with a stage capable of holding 100 musicians, the colonnaded, sculpted, neoclassical band shell had been dedicated on California Admission Day (September 9) in 1900 with a celebration of the fiftieth anniversary of the state's admission to the Union. The Temple of Music was the site of frequent free concerts, which often drew 10,000 to 20,000 listeners.[40]

Heading northwest from the Memorial Museum brought our visitors back to the wide Main Drive, and as they turned west, Strawberry Hill, the highest point in Golden Gate Park, drew them onward. Around the hill's base, the commissioners had created Stow Lake, and on the hill's eastern face they had constructed 110-foot Huntington Falls. These water features were described in the Midwinter Fair's official guide: "The water which fills the reservoir and surrounds the islands is pumped from the park water-works, which are in full view from the hill." Two bridges spanned the lake, one on the north "in the early Roman style and the other of a rustic device of red sandstone; both very charming features of the landscape." Here a visitor could rent a boat and row about, taking in the cool waters and rich vegetation of trees, shrubs, flowers, and lawn. Superintendent McLaren intentionally installed foliage that created a sense of eastern lushness to contrast with the surrounding area's distinct aridity. If one hiked to the top of the hill where the 300-foot, Roman-style, Sweeney amphitheater and observatory sat, the Golden Gate to the north, the hills to the south, and the park and ocean to the west were revealed.

Except where afforestation was occurring in the park, the vegetation was sparse, and even the new park forest stood out as only partially developed.[41]

From this point west there was a distinct shift in the park's vegetation. Natural vegetation had covered much of the eastern portions of the park when it was begun in 1870, but trees and shrubs had been carefully planted to supplement this richness. The result was openness framed and controlled by thick growths, with one special-use area often invisible from another. To the west, however, the natural vegetation had always been thinner. Virtually every tree from Strawberry Hill to the ocean had been planted, and these sand-dune-covered tracts were slowly being transformed into woods, lawns, and the occasional special-use space. It is only in recent years that the west end has begun to develop nearly as much as the east.[42]

Washington Square (*1.*) and Hamilton Square (*2.*) in 1901. The Parks Commission remodeled Washington Square just before this photograph was taken. Old walks were removed and sown to grass, and a 30-foot water basin was added. Hamilton Square also consisted largely of lawn and a few trees. It was popular as a neighborhood greenspace but increasingly became a developed recreation center during the 1910s. From the San Francisco Board of Park Commissioners' 1902 *Annual Report,* opposite p. 34; reproduced by permission of the Bancroft Library, University of California, Berkeley.

Portsmouth Square (1.) and Union Square (2.) in 1901. Portsmouth Square, the oldest public square in San Francisco, had been in terrible shape when the city embraced a new charter in 1900 and all city squares came under the control of the Park Commission. Old walks were promptly removed, the soil of the entire site spaded, shrubs planted, and much of the area sown to grass. Union Square was remodeled at the same time to include diagonal walks, thick shrubbery on the west (Powell Street), and flowering shrubs and annuals in a naturalistic style on all sides. From the San Francisco Board of Park Commissioners' 1902 *Annual Report*, between pp. 29 and 30; reproduced by permission of the Bancroft Library, University of California, Berkeley.

The remodel of Union Square also included a new, central monument to commemorate Admiral George Dewey's victory at Manila Bay in the Spanish-American War. The Hotel St. Francis (across Powell Street on the right) opened in 1904. Reproduced by permission of the California Historical Society, Bear Photo Service Collection (FN-33887).

The old city hall, destroyed in the 1906 earthquake, could be seen to the southeast from Jefferson Square, a space designed for contemplation and rest. Reproduced by permission of the California Historical Society (FN-33888).

Looking east in Jefferson Square on a busy day. Originally more than 11 acres and built on a slope, the southern, flatter half of the square was converted into the Hayward Playground when Turk Street was extended through the property. From the San Francisco Board of Park Commissioners' 1902 *Annual Report,* opposite p. 30; reproduced by permission of the Bancroft Library, University of California, Berkeley.

Lincoln Park, built on the site of a former city cemetery, was named after the president at the insistence of Civil War veterans. Many of its 150 acres became the grounds for a popular golf course, but the Palace of the Legion of Honor was built here too. From the San Francisco Board of Park Commissioners' 1924 *Annual Report,* p. 47; reproduced by permission of the Bancroft Library, University of California, Berkeley.

FACING PAGE:

*Top:* Alamo Square's nearly 13 acres were well developed by the 1910s, with some trees towering over a visitor. Reproduced by permission of the California Historical Society (FN-21267).

*Bottom:* The wind blew briskly through these recently planted shrubs and trees in the southeast corner of Alamo Square. Reproduced by permission of the San Francisco History Center, San Francisco Public Library.

Planted in pines, acacias, oaks, and the Monterey cypresses pictured here, Buena Vista Park's 578-foot peak commanded a superb view of the area's mountains, from Mount Hamilton to the south to Mount Tamalpais to the north and Mount Diablo to the east. From the San Francisco Board of Park Commissioners' 1912 *Annual Report,* opposite p. 30; reproduced by permission of the Bancroft Library, University of California, Berkeley.

The San Francisco Zoo covers the site of the former Herbert Fleishhacker Play Field, with its salt water swimming pool. A vast tank 1,000 feet long by 100–150 feet wide, the pool could hold 10,000 swimmers. Adjoining the pool was an athletic field with five baseball diamonds and ten tennis courts. A children's playground nearby included a merry-go-round, gymnastic equipment, and other games. From the San Francisco Board of Park Commissioners' 1924 *Annual Report,* p. 35; reproduced by permission of the Bancroft Library, University of California, Berkeley.

The vegetation in South Park's oval garden in 1910 was radically changed from the development's beginnings decades earlier (see illustration on page 35). The Park Commission had thinned plantings, laid walks, and sown lawn to attract neighborhood picnickers. Reproduced by permission of the California Historical Society, George A. Berton Collection (FN-33886).

# THE MANY SMALL PARKS
# OF SAN FRANCISCO

At the present time public spirited people . . . appreciate the
value of open spaces in town and cities. They realize that
such areas are not only desirable but increasingly necessary
in order that opportunity for exercise and for the enjoyment of outdoor beauty may be more generally provided.
. . . they approve of a large increase in the number of playgrounds and parks. But few . . . seem yet to understand
that these open spaces are of great variety, that they are or
should be selected and designed to serve radically different
purposes.

Frederick Law Olmsted, Jr., and John Nolen
"The Normal Requirements of American Towns and Cities
in Respect to Public Open Spaces"

## THE CHARTER OF 1900

Both the municipal charter of 1851 and the 1870 state legislation enabling Golden
Gate Park had restricted the ability of San Francisco to acquire and develop new
parkland during the nineteenth century, but these limitations evaporated on January 8, 1900, when the revised charter of the City and County of San Francisco
went into effect. The new charter, part of the progressivism that was sweeping California, gave San Francisco home rule in an increased range of local matters, much
reducing the control of the state legislature and impacting the city's parks in three
ways. It lifted the forty-year ban on municipal indebtedness, making it possible for

the city to obtain new park property without a vote by the state legislature or the municipal electorate. Under the new charter, the Board of Park Commissioners could purchase land anytime they could convince the Board of Supervisors to appropriate the money for it. Additionally, the city's small parks, public squares, and grounds came under the control of the Board of Park Commissioners. Prior to the new charter, most of San Francisco's small parks and squares were the responsibility of the Department of Streets, Sewers, and Squares, an overburdened department that ranked parks last in its responsibilities. The physical conditions in the city's parks and squares, even the ones in the neighborhoods of the rich and powerful, reflected their third-class status in the department. For example, Lafayette Square (now park) in the Western Addition was surrounded by very expensive homes in 1890. Nonetheless, it was described by the *San Francisco Chronicle* as "mostly an unimproved sand hill." Alamo Square to the south was in no better shape. According to the *Chronicle,* "its sole adornment was a rough board fence." The squares and parks were such in name only until the park commissioners gained responsibility for them. Finally, the new charter expanded the Park Commission from three to five members and converted it into a municipal department instead of a state-chartered, independent board. Now the mayor instead of the governor would appoint its members, and although the superintendent would continue to answer to the board, he and his staff would remain largely independent in practice.[1]

The new charter had been a key issue for the leading mayoral candidate of 1896, James Duvall Phelan (1861–1930). Phelan stands out in the period because he was a Democrat and a reformer at a time when some Republicans were bolting their party to form the Progressive Party in California. To understand how Phelan came to be mayor, it is necessary to examine the immediately preceding period. Christopher Augustine Buckley had been the Democratic boss of San Francisco during the 1880s. In the 1890 election, after a particularly dirty campaign, Republican boss Martin Kelly was able to have the mayor and seven supervisors elected. As a result of the overt corruption of the election, a grand jury was called to investigate; and ironically, its sweeping condemnations led Buckley, not Martin, to flee the United States. On the heels of his departure, a group of reformers gained control of the Democratic Party from 1892 until 1901. Suspicious of both parties and with the Democrats undergoing reorganization following Buckley's departure, San Franciscans proceeded to elect "independent" mayors in 1892 and 1894. However, the first of these, Levi R. Ellert, was hamstrung by Republican opponents while the latter, Adolph Sutro (1830–1898) was at the time in failing physical and mental health. As a result, Sutro was an ineffectual mayor who, according to the San Francisco *Examiner,* "passed his term in a state of exasperation."[2]

In the wake of these two unimpressive independents, the Democrats put forward wealthy J. D. Phelan for mayor in 1896, even though he had no previous political experience. The son of an Irish-Catholic gold rush migrant, merchant, and banker, Phelan had been raised in a rich, cultured home, graduated from the University of San Francisco, and studied law at the University of California. When Phelan's father died in 1892, the son inherited numerous properties in New York City, San Francisco, San Jose, elsewhere throughout California, and over a million acres in Oregon, as well as a fortune estimated at $11.5 million. Like his father, J. D. Phelan had become a banker; in 1896 he was "a thirty-five-year old attorney who was dashing, honest, and enormously wealthy. . . . He was undoubtedly the most well-connected Democrat to that point in San Francisco history." As a candidate he closed the labor-capital gap by being Irish-American and one of the city's wealthy elite. Running against the Republican boss's candidate and for "The New San Francisco," Phelan ran on the longest platform in the city's history; it contained twenty-two planks, including a proposal for new taxes to spend on parks and squares. In particular, Phelan was pursuing the support of the local improvement associations, which wanted many new and better parks in their neighborhoods. During the campaign, Phelan argued that he was the most honest candidate as well as the one who as mayor could get things done, and many voters had little trouble accepting his assertions, because Phelan's achievements in banking and real estate had made him a millionaire. On election day he won, but with only 46 percent of the votes cast.[3]

Despite a shaky beginning, Mayor Phelan got himself reelected and the new city charter passed during the election of 1898. He was personally gratified to see the municipality gather greater control over the local environment, because he believed its character had a substantial impact on urban residents' lives and therefore the social order. In a speech in support of the new charter Phelan declared that, since

"life, liberty and the pursuit of happiness" must be sought by so many in the great cities, municipal charters take their place by the constitution itself in their importance as instruments for the accomplishment of these great purposes. It is hardly flippant to say that without sanitation life is in greater danger than from the dreaded tyrant: "War kills her thousand peace her ten thousands"; without well paved and clean streets, parks and libraries; without order and security and all that flows from good government, that is, the government with which we are in close daily contact, liberty becomes other people's license, and happiness consists in a day out of town![4]

James D. Phelan is an excellent example of the influential, elite rationalistic park proponent. A founder of the Merchants' Association and the Association for the Improvement and Adornment of San Francisco (both of which were City Beautiful organizations), Phelan ran in favor of new municipal services, such as streetside tree planting, plus the extension of these and other services into the city's newer neighborhoods. While mayor, he put his ideas into practice and began San Francisco's multidecade beautification campaign by adding numerous public fountains, monuments, playgrounds, and parks. Then, in 1908, when he was no longer in government, Phelan was appointed by Democratic Mayor Edward Taylor (1838–1923) to the Board of Park Commissioners, where he was active for four years. Despite being a Democrat, Phelan was cut from much the same mold as many of the early members of California's Progressive Party. He was an outspoken critic of graft and waste, supported conservation and efficiency, and to this end favored and helped mastermind San Francisco's reservoir in the Hetch Hetchy Valley of Yosemite National Park. These positions made him well-liked by other reformers, including President Theodore Roosevelt.[5]

## DISTRIBUTING NATURE ACROSS SAN FRANCISCO

Once the revised charter was enacted, coordinated development began on the city's existing squares and small parks and the park commissioners received numerous requests to purchase and develop new sites. Almost immediately after responsibility for all parks and squares was transferred to the Board of Park Commissioners, Superintendent John McLaren began to landscape the board's twelve new properties, many of which had been left virtually unimproved, some since 1855. Transforming these neglected spaces alone would have been a major challenge, but the difficulty was compounded because they represented a 10 percent increase in the acreage managed by the Park Commission yet its budget rose only 6.7 percent. Nevertheless, a workforce of ten gardeners and seventeen laborers was assigned the task, with improvements becoming obvious. By fall 1900, Union Square, for example, had been relandscaped and Portsmouth Square was receiving attention. The *San Francisco Post* described the progress: "Work of an intelligent and painstaking character is also being done in many outside parks which for a long time have barely existed."[6]

The two most common sources requesting new parks were the park commissioners themselves or the city's proliferating local associations. According to historian Terrence McDonald, there was a sharp growth in the number of associations and groups demanding municipal services during the 1880s, 1890s, and 1900s; and one of the most powerful of these, the Association for the Improvement and Adornment of San Francisco (AIASF), included former Mayor James D. Phelan as a member. Formed in 1904, this City Beautiful group asked the Chicago-based city planner Daniel Burnham to redesign San Francisco, and he included a proposal for twelve small parks and playgrounds in his 1905 report. In addition to the AIASF, ethnic brotherhoods, fraternal organizations, labor unions, and neighborhood groups attempted to obtain concessions from the municipality. For instance, in the early 1890s, representatives from San Francisco neighborhoods beyond the boundaries of the 1851 charter began to attend the annual allocation meeting of the Board of Supervisors' Finance Committee. They demanded various improvements, including neighborhood parks, for their locales. Early in 1903, more than 1,000 property owners from the southern reaches of the city banded together as the Mission Park Association to work for the passage of bonds for a local park. They succeeded in adding to the September 1903 ballot a measure to purchase a piece of land that had been the site of two Jewish cemeteries, bounded by Dolores, Church, Eighteenth, and Twentieth Streets. It passed with 73.9 percent of the vote to become Mission (now Mission Dolores) Park. Fourteen acres in extent, the rationalistic grounds included elaborate plantings, terraces, two tennis courts, a wading pool, and an athletic field by 1924.[7]

However, the park commissioners themselves, rather than the local residents, had the greatest impact upon the creation of parks. With the new charter in place, the commissioners began almost immediately to petition the Board of Supervisors for money for new parks. The report of the park commissioners for 1902 recom-

Following the election of September 1903, the San Francisco Park Commission purchased two decommissioned Jewish cemetery properties to create Mission Park (now Mission Dolores Park). Taken around 1910, this photograph looks to the northeast from the park's southwest corner. The edge of the wading pool can be seen on the right, just beyond the palm trees. Reproduced by permission of the San Francisco History Center, San Francisco Public Library.

mended that the mayor and the Board of Supervisors establish at least a one-acre "recreation ground" for children in the "South of Market" district, referring to the crowded area south of Market Street.

> Again would this Board most respectfully urge upon the Honorable Mayor and Board of Supervisors the great necessity of establishing a piece of ground at least 800 by 500 or 600 feet, for a recreation ground for the use of boys and young people south of Market Street. . . . This district is now crowded with tenements, in all of which are troops of children with no place to recreate themselves except on the public streets, where . . . danger exists from passing cars and vehicles.

The board justified this proposed park by reference to its ability to promote the virtue of public health among children primarily, but also among adults.

> Hence, as a simple matter of protection, not to speak of sanitary reasons, we make this plea for the little ones of that section. . . . Parks are a priceless boon to the weak and the invalid of all classes, and particularly to the poor to be able to go from

cramped rooms and close atmospheres to regions of sunlight. Fresh air and green lawns are an indescribable pleasure and bring renewed hope as well as health.

At the same time the commissioners pointed out, "San Francisco has added practically no additions to its park area for over 30 years."[8]

The Board of Supervisors and the electorate bent with the prevailing political winds in favor of parks. In addition to the Mission Park bonds already mentioned, the September 1903 ballot included bonds funding a parkway linking Golden Gate Park and the Presidio, the transformation of Dolores Street into a palm-lined boulevard, an expansion of Pioneer Park on Telegraph Hill, and the purchase of land on Twin Peaks and St. Mary's Square. All but the last two measures passed, but it was only the beginning of the park board's expansion. Their 1910 report listed

Mission Park was heartily embraced by the neighborhood, but the wading pool did not have many takers on this overcast day. The pool later became the large sand-filled play area of today. From the San Francisco Board of Park Commissioners' 1912 *Annual Report*, following p. 82; reproduced by permission of the Bancroft Library, University of California, Berkeley.

In 1899, the area south of Market Street along Third Street was a densely packed amalgam of residences, churches, warehouses, offices, and factories. It had only two parks—.75-acre South Park (near the water and just to the left of Third Street) and 2.5-acre Columbia Square (well off camera to the right, but now gone). Neither of these sites could be used for active pastimes, so in 1902 the park commissioners recommended establishment of a recreation ground of at least one acre for children. Reproduced by permission of the San Francisco Maritime National Historical Park, R. E. Duggan Collection (A11.14.632 N).

thirty-four holdings, most of which had existed as squares or plazas before the new charter made them the responsibility of the Park Commission; but four were relatively new and notable—Presidio Parkway, Balboa Park, Mission Park, and Lincoln Park.[9]

The Presidio Parkway (today's Park Presidio Boulevard) was the first parkway in San Francisco, but parkways soon would be a well-established element of many municipal park systems. It extended .8 miles, from Golden Gate Park through Mountain Lake Park into the immediately adjacent Presidio, a landscaped, U.S. military reservation of approximately 1,500 acres. With "wonderfully enchanting views of the Golden Gate, and the range of mountains in Marin county," the Presidio was available to the public for scenic contemplation and active recreation. The parkway consisted of seven blocks of land, each 600 feet long by 240 feet wide, which were purchased for a total cost of approximately $360,000, and were justified in the park commissioners' 1910 report as a means to increase the amount of park land in San Francisco by making the Presidio available to more users. Streetcar lines to the Presidio were so indirect and inadequate that visitors in 1900 tended to travel first to Golden Gate Park, which had convenient public transportation connections, and then on to the Presidio, even though it was a nearly one-mile hike over sand dunes. The new parkway made that travel easier and purportedly refreshed travelers as they moved through its naturalistic setting.[10]

The Presidio Parkway was likely a descendant of the parkways designed by Frederick Law Olmsted and the firm of Olmsted and Calvert Vaux, even though the Park Commission reports identify no specific influences. On the one hand, San Francisco's 240-foot-wide parkway had romantic elements that recalled Olmsted and Vaux's work in Brooklyn and Buffalo: The main roadway was 50 feet wide—plenty of room for carriages, horses, bicycles, and early automobiles—and paralleling it on either side, but elevated 2 feet, lay a 15-foot-wide pedestrian path. Between the path and the roadway was a grassy, 10-foot-wide slope with shade trees clumped at intervals of 100 feet. On the other hand, the new parkway also had rationalistic elements, such as flowering shrubs planted between the shade trees and, on the outside of each footpath, a strip 70 feet wide, planted with still more clumps of flowering trees and shrubs.[11]

The three new parks noted in the commissioners' 1910 report were not as novel as the Presidio Parkway. The report related that Balboa Park (in today's Outer Mission District) contained approximately 9 acres, surrounded the House of Correction, and was in the process of becoming a rationalistic park. The park commissioners were especially pleased by the progress that had been made on a new ball field. Mission Park, to the north and east, was slightly larger at around 14 acres and also emphasized rationalistic concerns. Its vegetation was arranged in a formal, geometric fashion, rather that the flowing, naturalistic style of the romantic era, with terraces, grassy borders, shade trees, and groups of palms and flowering shrubs, all laid out in a visually rigid order. Mission Park also incorporated a number of areas for active recreation, including two tennis courts, a wading pool, and an athletic field. "The expectations of the founders of [Mission] Park," crowed the commissioners, "have been met." Lincoln Park, west of the Presidio around Land's End and formerly the City Cemetery, where largely the poor were buried, enclosed an expansive 150 acres and, like Golden Gate Park, combined romantic and rationalistic uses.

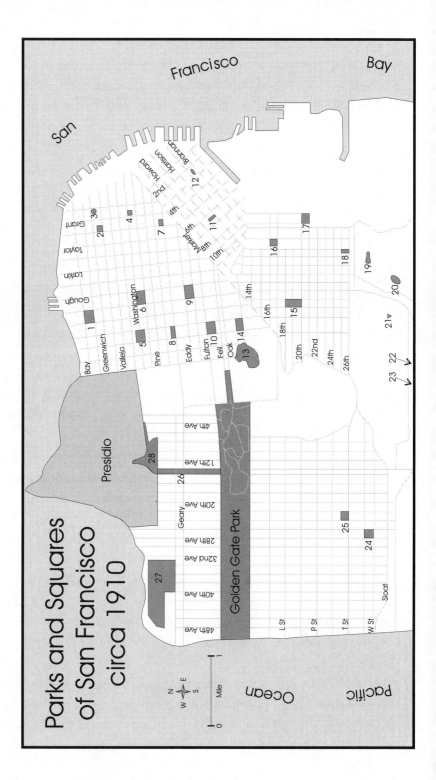

# Parks and Squares
# of San Francisco
# circa 1910

San Francisco Bay

Pacific Ocean

Presidio

Golden Gate Park

Mile

0    1

N
W    E
S

Bay
Greenwich
Vallejo
Washington
Pine
Eddy
Fulton
Fell
Oak

Gough
Larkin
Taylor
Grant

Market
4th
5th
6th
9th
10th
14th
16th
18th
20th
22nd
24th
26th

Howard
Harrison
Brannan
2nd

4th Ave
12th Ave
20th Ave
28th Ave
32nd Ave
40th Ave
48th Ave

Geary

L St
P St
T St
W St
Sloat

1  2  3  4  5  6  7  8  9  10  11  12  13  14  15  16  17  18  19  20  21  22  23  24  25  26  27  28

1 Lobos Square (now George R. Moscone Recreation Center)
2 Washington Square
3 Pioneer Park (Telegraph Hill)
4 Portsmouth Square
5 Alta Plaza
6 Lafayette Square (now Park)
7 Union Square
8 Hamilton Square (now Recreation Center)
9 Jefferson Square (included today's Hayward Playground)
10 Alamo Square
11 Columbia Square (now gone)
12 South Park
13 Buena Vista Park
14 Duboce Park
15 Mission Park (now Mission Dolores Park)
16 Franklin Square
17 McKinley Square (included part of today's Highway 101)
18 Garfield Square
19 Bernal Park (now Precita Park)
20 Holly Park
21 Fairmount Park
22 Balboa Park
23 Sunnyside Park (now Sunnyside Playground)
24 unimproved square (now Parkside Square)
25 unnamed square (now McCoppin Square)
26 Presidio Parkway (now Park Presidio Boulevard)
27 Lincoln Park
28 Mountain Lake Park

As a nod toward the former, John McLaren's "scheme of improvement" envisaged a scenic drive overlooking the Pacific Ocean at Baker's Beach with "magnificent views of the sea, the bay, islands and mountain ranges." At the same time, the commissioners sought the approval of rationalistic park supporters by spending $10,000 for a golf course and by accepting a gift from Adolph B. and Alma de Brettville Spreckels for the Palace of the Legion of Honor, a museum of French art that opened in 1924.[12]

Despite the 1910 report's enthusiasm for acquiring and developing new park land, the grasp of the park commissioners could not match their reach. San Francisco did not fill with parks, leaving the 1924 *Annual Report* to once again list thirty-four properties, the same number as in 1910. Oddly, nine of the small properties listed in the 1910 report were not mentioned in 1924's, and even though four were likely traded or sold to a private owner, one, Parkside Square, remained public property. Four other parcels (and half of another) were still owned by the city but had been transferred to another municipal department between 1910 and 1924 to become playgrounds or recreation centers. At the same time, nine new properties were added, including two parkways and seven parks ranging in size from less than .25 acres to 444 acres.[13]

One of the new parkways, Dolores Street, departed from the existing design traditions. About two miles in length, it extended north from Mission Park to Market Street and south from the park to Guerrero and San Jose Avenues. At 125 feet, Dolores Street was about half the width of the Presidio Parkway, and although the 1924 report describes it as a "splendid boulevard or parkway," neither vegetation nor foot paths for the unhurried traveler bracketed the roadway. Instead it was a simple thoroughfare bisected by "a palm shaded esplanade or alameda." The commissioners imagined Dolores Street would be an "arboreal and horticultural beauty," but more importantly, they wanted it also to be the location for the display of the many "memorial monuments" that were causing traffic congestion along Market Street. They thought the monuments should be moved to Dolores Street, making it the "great outdoor art exhibit of San Francisco."[14]

Conversely, the Harding-Lincoln Parkway (which is now known as Sunset Boulevard) followed San Francisco's older parkway pattern. It lay twenty-two blocks west of the Presidio Parkway and was under development at the time of the 1924 report. Two-hundred-forty feet wide, it was supposed to run somewhere between Thirty-Fifth and Thirty-Seventh Avenues for the approximately one-half

Dolores Street was transformed into a boulevard with street trees and a planted island intended to become the new "show place" for many of the monuments that had been erected along Market Street, but which were causing serious traffic congestion there. The monuments were never moved, however. Both of these images look north from the intersection with Seventeenth Street. The upper one was taken in the 1910s, shortly after the new plantings. The lower picture, taken in 2002, shows those plantings matured. Reproduced by permission of the California Historical Society (FN-12615).

mile from Lincoln Park in the north to Golden Gate Park. Passing through the latter as a transverse road, it would continue two and one-half miles south to the golf course in the new Harding Park. The commission envisioned a feature that had the "character of the Presidio Parkway" and would serve two functions. The roadway would provide drivers, bicyclists, and pedestrians with a parklike connection between the three parks and it would promote the virtue of prosperity. The Harding-Lincoln Parkway, pronounced the 1924 *Annual Report,* would be "valuable in an economic sense" because it, like park properties before, would generate wealth through "an increase of property values." However, parks superintendent John McLaren, who was opposed to the transverse road, scuttled the northern stretch by offering the Police Department land in Golden Gate Park at Thirty-Seventh Avenue and Fulton Street. A police academy arose on the site (today a Senior Center for the Richmond District), and neither the transverse road nor the Lincoln Park–Golden Gate Park stretch of the parkway was constructed.[15]

Like the parkways, the seven new parks and squares detailed in the 1924 report by the Park Commission served a range of needs. Two of the recent additions, Coso and St. Mary's Squares, were small and either relatively unimportant or underdeveloped at the time. They were simply listed in a financial statement rather than described like the other properties. Another small property, Huntington Square (today's Huntington Park), stood in sharp contrast because it was on prestigious Nob Hill adjacent to the Pacific Union Club, a private, very elite organization. Unsurprisingly, the square was arranged in a "stately formal way" with rationalistic displays of flowers, shrubs, and trees.[16]

Two other parks, Bay View and Sutro Heights, were larger than Coso, St. Mary's, and Huntington Squares and served romantic ends. Bay View Park, along the southeastern shore of the city, provided scenic views of San Francisco Bay and the Alameda shore; but a baseball stadium, Candlestick Park, subsequently imposed upon the views. Bay View's 30 acres were a gift from William H. Crocker and his Bay View Improvement Company. Sutro Heights to the northwest was also a gift. Sutro Heights, more an estate garden than a park, was bequeathed to the city by former mayor and park commissioner Adolph Sutro. Like Bay View Park, it overlooked water, in this case the Pacific Ocean. The 1924 *Annual Report* emphasized "the marine panorama of unexampled magnificence" available to a park visitor Sutro Heights.[17]

The final two parks, Harding and Sharp, were much larger than the others and emphasized rationalistic concerns. Harding Park, a 170-acre golf course between the two arms of Lake Merced, was situated near the southwest coast of the city and leased from a local water company. Golf was so popular in San Francisco that it prompted the creation of this park, which was a blend of romantic scenery and rationalistic activity. When the links at Lincoln Park opened they were soon so fashionable "as to be uncomfortably congested on Saturdays, Sundays, and holidays," leading to efforts "to secure sufficient acreage in a convenient location" for another course—Harding Park. Sharp Park was also a gift but an unusual one in that it sat outside of the City and County of San Francisco. Located well to the south along the Pacific Coast of San Mateo County, the property was accepted by the commissioners because of Superintendent McLaren's enthusiasm for the site. The 444-acre park had only recently become a part of the city's park system in 1924 and was barely developed. Nevertheless, the report correctly predicted a rationalistic park that would supply "the inevitable future needs for additional golf courses" and commented on "the mountainous character of . . . its rugged canyons and rocky summits, . . . [a] ground for ambitious hikers."[18]

## THE SEGMENTATION OF SAN FRANCISCO

Both the 1902 and the 1910 reports by the park commissioners expressed concern about the lack of neighborhood parks south of Market Street, which suggest they were becoming aware of the increased number of social-spatial segments within San Francisco. During the romantic period, from the 1860s to the 1880s, the city had been a single, relatively homogeneous (if chaotic) entity needing a single facility—ultimately Golden Gate Park but it could have been any of its rivals—to generate the virtues. The park commissioners' wish to create new parks reflected their growing recognition of the divergence of social districts within an increasingly heterogeneous San Francisco. In particular, the park board and other rationalistic park advocates perceived a major fissure at Market Street, one captured neatly and poetically by Jack London in 1914.

Old San Francisco, which is the San Francisco of only the other day, the day before the Earthquake, was divided midway by the Slot. The Slot was an iron crack that ran along the center of Market Street, and from the Slot arose the burr of the ceaseless, endless cable that was hitched at will to the cars it dragged up and down. . . . North of the Slot were the theaters, hotels, and shopping district, the banks and the staid, respectable business houses. South of the Slot were the factories, slums, laundries, machine shops, boiler works, and the abodes of the working class.[19]

By 1900, the Park Commission no longer saw a largely homogeneous if imperfect San Francisco from their side of Market Street, but instead beheld an urban landscape containing both the composed, narrow social order of an area like Nob Hill and the sort of varied, discordant sections referred to as "urban wilderness" by historian Sam Bass Warner. Between 1870 (the year Golden Gate Park was authorized) and 1900, San Francisco developed numerous, distinct districts identifiable by either their industrial, commercial, financial, residential, or ethnic compositions, or some combination thereof. In the spatially segmented society of rational-

Market Street, or "The Slot," was a social and spatial dividing line in 1900 San Francisco. The wealthy and middle classes lived, worked, shopped, and entertained themselves to the north (*left*), while industry, warehousing, and residences of the poor and working classes generally were confined to the south. Reproduced by permission of the Bancroft Library, University of California, Berkeley.

istic San Francisco, it was easier to identify and designate districts as particularly lacking in a virtue or virtues than it had been in the romantic period. Park activists thought the people living south of Market Street were especially, although not exclusively, living in vice-prone neighborhoods. In a novel move, the 1902 and 1910 reports openly advocated parks for this "tumultuous" district; and the commission's creation of parks, whether on existing or newly acquired properties, should be recognized as an effort to foster the virtues there. Although the South of Market area was foremost in the commissioners' minds, since then the district has lost rather than gained ground. Of the three properties held there in 1900, one, Mission Plaza, a triangle at Mission and 12th Streets, is completely gone; the largest at 2.5 acres, Columbia Square, has been reduced to a street name and replaced by diminutive South of Market Park; and only South Park remains intact.[20]

## A NEW TREE-THINNING CONTROVERSY

Although the city of San Francisco underwent social-spatial segmentation even as small to large parks were developed and created across its landscape during the rationalistic era, many romantic elements and practices nonetheless continued. For example, shortly after Governor Stoneman's May 1886 appointment of new park commissioners, a second forest-thinning controversy erupted, unfolding in a manner nearly identical to that of the one ten years earlier. Complaints were lodged by the *Daily Morning Call* and the *Evening Bulletin* newspapers against the removal of trees in Golden Gate Park. According to William Hammond Hall, the *Call* began the attack on August 15, 1886, under the title, "Woodman Spare that Tree."

> The manner in which the trees in Golden Gate Park are being thinned out by order of the Board of Park Commissioners, excites general amazement. A large number of the finest trees have been cut out. . . . Trees which were set out about 1869 or 1870 have within the past three days been hacked off, sawed up into lengths and carried off to the park wood yards. . . . If any fact is demonstrated easier than another it is that Golden Gate Park, with a scanty supply of trees, or with the trees unduly trimmed must cease to be a pleasure ground. . . . A general protest that the trees must be saved is gaining ground daily as the facts are becoming better known. Without them there can be no park.

The *Bulletin* shortly joined the attack and an outcry of alarm followed from the public.[21]

The park management quickly rallied experts to its defense. In an attempt to rebut the newspapers and to develop "sound public opinion and correct public taste," the new Park Commission took the unusual step of publishing and distributing an extensive explanation of their tree-cutting activities. The thirty-one-page pamphlet included statements of support from Frederick Law Olmsted, who at the time was near the peak of his landscape architecture career and by coincidence was in the San Francisco Bay area consulting on Leland Stanford's new college campus; from John McLaren, who was then supervisor of Henry Pike Bowie's peninsula estate; and from William Hammond Hall, the consulting engineer who had given the order to remove some of the trees. All three stated that it was necessary when developing park "plantations" to plant the saplings "thickly" (that is, close together) for mutual support but then to thin "quickly" (that is, as soon as necessary) so that the remaining trees would have enough light and space for proper development. They pointed out that thick initial plantings were especially necessary in Golden Gate Park because the young trees needed each other for mutual support against the severe westerly winds.[22]

Ironically, it was not thinning "quickly" enough that prompted the controversy. Golden Gate Park's trees were in severe need of thinning by 1886. As William Hammond Hall saw it, he had to order the cutting because the trees were "in an abominable condition, and, with a few notable exceptions," were "rapidly deteriorating for the purpose intended." These were the trees that had been planted in the early 1870s. Now they were 15 to 20 feet tall but only a few feet apart. Under such crowded conditions, tree branches, especially the lower ones, deteriorate from the lack of sunlight as they grow together. When a tree in this condition is freed, its lower branches are often dead and must be pruned off, leaving the trunk bare unusually high up and making the tree less attractive than it would have been had it grown under more open, that is thinned, conditions. Consequently, the thinning appeared radical when park employees began the removal of the usual "30 to 60 per cent. of trees planted."[23]

This incident demonstrates how committed the public remained to the protection of nature. Never mind that the trees were being removed as an accepted forest management practice. The initial reaction from the press and many residents was outrage at what they believed was desecration. William Hammond Hall claimed that the editors of the two papers began their attacks simply because they were a "prejudiced and hard-headed newspaper management." Despite this *ad hominem* explanation, the original criticism and the public reaction suggest that there was in the minds of these people an inchoate connection between the living elements of Golden Gate Park and the perceived ability of the park to promote prosperity through tourism, public health through the contemplation of beauty, and the other virtues. As the park managers learned during this episode, one basis for nature's ability to foster the virtues was its visual quality, which cannot be changed in a haphazard or high-handed manner without political consequences. In romantically designed parks, horticultural change had to be carefully managed.[24]

San Francisco was not the only city where a tree-thinning controversy erupted. Brooklyn, Boston, Washington, D.C., and New York each experienced similar debates. So serious were the late-1880s attacks upon the park management in New York City that Frederick Law Olmsted felt compelled to publish a general defense of the practice. His description of such confrontations brings to mind the more recent clashes over tree management in Golden Gate Park or between bird watchers and restorationists in Central Park.

> It has occurred repeatedly of late years that ladies and gentlemen, seeking their pleasure during the winter in public parks, have chanced to see men felling trees, and have been moved by the sight to take duties upon themselves that nothing else short of a startling public outrage would have led them to assume. Sometimes they have hastened to stand before a partly felled tree and have attempted to wrest the axe from the hand of the woodsman. Oftener they have resorted to the press and other means of rousing public feeling, and not unfrequently a considerable popular excitement has resulted. At the time of such excitements a strong tendency has appeared in many minds to assume that the act of tree-cutting marks those who are responsible for it as unsusceptible to the charm of sylvan scenery, and to class them with the old indiscriminately devastating pioneers.

Despite any horticultural justifications, Olmsted was astute enough to realize that the widespread misunderstanding of the future value of current tree thinning could affect park legislation. A park's tree plantations, the source of "the charm of sylvan scenery," could be compromised unless the public recognized the need for a judicious use of the axe.[25]

The Park Commission's pamphlet and the positive appearance of the park after the initial thinnings calmed the immediate furor in San Francisco. No further public protests occurred, and tree thinning became a regular aspect of Golden Gate Park in the following several years. Trees continued to be cut down, but many more instead were transplanted to other parks; this new practice may explain why there were no more protests. By the 1920s, only a few select trees remained at the site of the original controversy.

> Of the 800 or more trees . . . which in 1886 stood . . . on the south side of the Avenue leading up to the Park . . . and of which the cutting of about 80 was the chief act which stirred up the "public alarm" in that year, now scarce eighty remain, and these with a few others of more delicate habit since set out, afford all the forest growth that anyone could desire in that locality.[26]

## THE ENDORSEMENT OF ROMANTIC NOTIONS BY RATIONALISTS

Expert appreciation of contemplation in large parks is another example of the continuance of romantic notions into the rationalistic period. One of the best-known members of the City Beautiful movement, Charles Mulford Robinson, was an outspoken celebrant of segmented, rationalistic nature. A journalist turned planner, he felt that urban dwellers needed more than one type of park to satisfy their cravings for nature. At the same time, he defended large, romantic parks as quiet, contemplative retreats from the city, especially for the poor, who could not flee into the country.[27]

In Robinson's landmark work, *Modern Civic Art,* the differences between small public spaces, like squares, playgrounds, and neighborhood parks, and large urban parks are clearly set forth: "Smaller spaces can satisfy many of the desires of the crowded city people—can supply fresh air and ample play room, and shade of trees, and brightness of grass and flowers." Play and flowers, however, are the rationalist's concerns, and romantic nature, he recognized, was distinctly different. "The occasionally so pressing want of that quiet and peculiar refreshment which comes from contemplation of scenery—the want which the rich satisfy by fleeing from town at certain seasons, but which the poor (who are trespassers in the country) can seldom fill—is only to be met by the country park." Having made the distinction between the two major categories, Robinson proceeded to rank them.

The refreshment that the "park" as distinguished from the "square" is designed to give may be defined, then, as that of relief from the excessive artificiality of city life, and from its strain and striving. A large public park may serve, of course, a variety of purposes; but this one of them will be more prominent, more necessary, than the others. If there be ever a conflict in the requirements of the several purposes, the others must be sacrificed to this.

What would happen if scenery did not have precedence over recreation? None of the needs of urban dwellers, contended Robinson, "will be successfully realised and the result will be scrappy and confused." That is, there will be conflict between groups advocating different types of nature. Scenery had to precede recreation because only the former was an escape from the simulation and excess stimulation of an urban life. "The dominant *motif* [for a large park] must be that of change from the normal conditions of town life—from some of its unnatural pleasures as well as from its cares and its artificiality of outlook."[28]

The architect Daniel H. Burnham and the San Francisco Park Commission held opinions similar to those of Robinson. Burnham's 1905 plan for the city of San Francisco did not go into great detail on the style and value of parks, stating that "the important part which adequate park spaces may be made to play in civic life is now generally recognized and need not be dwelt on here," but Burnham's plan did presage Robinson's characterization of park types by distinguishing between "small parks and playgrounds" and "large parks." The former were supposed to furnish "plenty of shade and pleasant surroundings to those who resort to them" as well as "provide uniformly for the wants of all the people." In order that the small parks might be effective, their distribution had to be "governed by the density of the population in various sections of the city." The greater the density, the greater the number of small parks. Focusing more carefully, the plan noted that the internal arrangement of these spaces would include "a more formal disposition of tree-planting," which would "lend the . . . charm of contrast and color." In addition, Burnham pointed out to his elite supporters that the formality of the plantings was not lost on visitors; it amounted to "a lesson of order and system." He noted, "its influence on the masses cannot be overestimated." Large parks, such as Golden Gate Park, were distinguished from the small ones by their area, their inclusion of "natural beauty," and their grand open spaces laid out in a "romantic treatment." Burnham argued that Golden Gate Park would be inadequate to its task in the future, and he proposed ten additional large parks of more than 200 acres each.[29]

In their 1910 report, the park commissioners conceded that it was their responsibility to create and maintain romantic "public parks of vast dimensions." Large parks were supposed to be urban antitheses, "where the weary, whether weary of head work or hand work, may be refreshed by breathing pure air, gladdened by the sight of flowers and trees, and solaced by the sound of running waters." At the same time, the commissioners recognized that Golden Gate Park was an insufficient type and amount of nature. They knew it was their task to create and nurture many parks in San Francisco, in particular they needed to provide numerous rationalistic "parks and playgrounds of smaller areas." These smaller places, unlike a large park, had to be "at the door of the people, where the children may go for air and play . . . [and] accessible to men and women." One large park or just a handful of small parks would never satisfy the need; the city had to have many parks and squares. The commission's justification for both types of parks was similar to Robinson's defense, urban poverty. Although "the electric railway, the automobile, and perhaps the aeroplane of the future, may bring to the congested districts of the metropolis facilities for reaching the mountains and forests," even at "the cheapest basis imaginable this privilege would be denied to people having less than moderate means." In 1910, the park commissioners understood the issue of access, and it remains true in the twenty-first century that the urban poor lack easy, inexpensive connections to the countryside.[30]

## THE SAN FRANCISCO PARK SYSTEM AND THE VIRTUES

Chapter 5 recounted how rationalistic advocates linked various segments within Golden Gate Park itself to one or more of the virtues. Both Golden Gate Park as a whole and the many smaller San Francisco parks were praised by promoters for their ability to engender the virtues. For example, as San Francisco grew larger, public health remained an issue for park backers. Occasionally, a newspaper like the *Daily Morning Call* would refer to parks as "health-giving" places because of the "aromas" from trees. This imputed health benefit seems to have been either a continuation of the miasmatic theory of disease or merely an unspecific belief in the health-improving qualities of parks. Either way, the frequency of epidemic diseases in San Francisco did not approach those prevailing in other American cities, particularly the alarming situation in New York, despite the *Call's* epidemiological concern. Parks also continued to be seen as the rejuvenators of enervated individuals. Writer Richard M. Gibson characterized a San Franciscan who had just visited a small or large park as supremely ready for more work. "Relieved, he may jump on board a passing electric car and . . . be back again in the midst of the crush and hurry and confusion where the wild-eyed devotees of the god Money never cease throughout the livelong day from throwing themselves in front of his grinding Juggernaut." Hyperbole aside, the rationalistic park supporters' concern about a city dweller's loss of vitality seems to have been less self-directed than that of their romantic predecessors. The rationalists focused on the workers, upon whose labors the city's growing industrial sector depended.[31]

In addition to the virtue of public health, increased personal and taxable wealth continued to be attributed to parks of every size and in every neighborhood. The Park Commission envisioned new greenspaces south of Market Street, connected to Golden Gate and to the other parks by parkways and several tree-lined boulevards. The resulting system of linked, interconnected parks, they contended, would raise nearby property values and thus favor prosperity in an area inhabited by many impoverished, unhealthy people.

> The increased value of the land surrounding Golden Gate Park has paid for this reservation tenfold; and the same results would accrue in the event of a park system being adopted and carried out, for the southern portion of the city. . . . Improved parks encourage better building, and in consequence, more revenue to the city; besides a more healthful people and a decreased death rate.[32]

And finally, arguments pointing out the ability of these greenspaces to promote a democratically equal and coherent society continued to be made, albeit less frequently than during the romantic period. For example, E. French Strother of the San Francisco Playground Commission argued in 1909 that San Francisco's children needed playgrounds in the city's small and large parks. "Children denied the opportunity to work off their animal spirits in wholesome exercise," he warned, "pervert those spirits to mischievous uses." Alternately, if the city's many parks could be places for children to play, the advantages for society would be "incalculable." "Fewer child criminals, fewer probation officers, fewer juvenile courts, fewer reform schools. Fewer adult criminals, fewer policemen, fewer criminal courts, fewer jails. Less taxes for the machinery of hospitals and criminal law." In sum,

Strother claimed, if children could play in nearby parks, the results would be, "more happiness in youth and more health in manhood and womanhood."[33]

## RATIONALISTIC PARKS AND MORE

The Park Commission's goal of multiple, linked parks came to pass. By 1925, Golden Gate Park was linked into a system of more than two dozen small to large parks, squares, and parkways whose purpose, at least in the eyes of advocates, was to foster the four virtues. The 1,019-acre Golden Gate Park accommodated both romantic and rationalistic uses, albeit uncomfortably, while the smaller greenspaces were dedicated to rationalistic ends. Play areas, athletic fields, colorful plantings, and museums filled the majority of these smaller spaces; only a few coastal, bay, and hilltop locations aimed to provide stimulating romantic scenery. No longer were parks targeted primarily at adult men, as they had been in the romantic period; rationalistic park advocates wanted facilities that served boys, girls, and adolescent men and women as well. They wished their parks, both small and large, to foster the virtues in San Francisco. In one fashion or another, advocates claimed, all parks encouraged public health, prosperity, social coherence, and democratic equality among their users.

The rise of San Francisco's park system followed on the heels of three changes in the city. First was the tension that arose during the 1880s and 1890s between the romantic and rationalistic users and advocates of Golden Gate Park because the romantics' desire for contemplative views precluded rationalistic activities while the latter, in turn, interfered with romantic scenery. The two could coexist only if they were spatially separated. The demand to reconfigure Golden Gate Park grew, but since much of its western reaches remained loose sands even into the early twentieth century, romantic uses could not retreat westward as rationalistic ones filled the east end. The creation of small rationalistic parks and squares helped to satisfy some of this demand for rationalistic park facilities. Second, because San Francisco was increasing in population and becoming more complex as it underwent a process of social-spatial segmentation, it was no longer the relatively homogeneous society and space it had been when entering the 1880s. Rationalistic park advocates, many of whom lived in the emerging neighborhoods, wanted parks in the new areas rather than expecting everyone to rely on Golden Gate Park. All of romantic-era San Francisco was supposed to have been reformed by Golden Gate Park, but rationalistic-era San Francisco would be reformed neighborhood by neighborhood through a variety of small parks, squares, and parkways, as well as Golden Gate Park. Third, the reorganization of San Francisco's administrative and financial structure instituted by the Charter of 1900, which transferred a number of poorly developed small parks and squares from the ineffective Department of Streets, Sewers, and Squares to the newly municipalized Board of Park Commissioners, amplified the complexity of park administration, so that it, like the society, was increasingly segmented. Between 1900 and 1924, the board's budget more than quadrupled, providing it an increased ability to add features and properties. Superintendent John McLaren was able, for example, to purchase plants from outside sources and dramatically increase the horticultural complexity of San Francisco's parks. Colorful carpet beds, intriguing fern dells, and area-defining hedges came from the new money. The bond issues and numerous gifts allowed new properties to be added to the park system, and several units were linked by parkways.

In the decades after 1925, San Francisco did not rest on its park laurels. The city frequently added new locations, like tiny South of Market Park and expansive McLaren Park, most of them dedicated to rationalistic uses. Athletic fields, playgrounds, museums, and colorful plantings, rather than passive green spaces, remained the order of the day. Golden Gate Park also became increasingly oriented toward rationalistic ends after 1925. The Strybing Arboretum and Botanical Garden, Mary A. Kezar Stadium, the John McLaren Rhododendron Dell, and the Academy of Science, as well as many smaller features, like a fly-casting pool, joined existing ones. Large stretches of roads were periodically closed so that bicyclists and roller bladers could safely use them. Some exceptional and unwelcome additions, most notably a water reclamation plant and a sewage treatment plant, were forced upon the park. As in the nineteenth and early twentieth centuries, most new features were constructed in the eastern third of the park, so now it is effectively impossible to view passive, romantic scenes there.[34]

In 1998, a new master plan for Golden Gate Park was published, having been drafted and executed in stages for several years. A close reading of it suggests that the defenders of romantic views are gone but the backers of rationalistic facilities continue. According to the *Golden Gate Park Master Plan,* "the western edge . . . has lacked *activity centers* to draw people to use it. . . . most of the west end is little visited and is not an inviting area. . . . The goal of this plan is to increase . . . *activities* and transform this part of the park" (emphases added). The transformations

New rationalistic features, like the Mary A. Kezar Stadium (pictured here in the southeastern corner of the park), the Strybing Arboretum, and the fly-casting pool, continued to appear in Golden Gate Park through the 1980s. The stadium was built on the old site of the park nursery, which was moved to its present, expanded location between the Big Rec Ball Field and the lawn bowling green. From the San Francisco Board of Park Commissioners' 1924 *Annual Report,* p. 31; reproduced by permission of the Bancroft Library, University of California, Berkeley.

included, sensibly, the replacement of a sewage treatment plant with an additional soccer field. The plan also suggested refurbishing the Beach Chalet to include a restaurant, information center and museum, and retail area with gift shop, all of which was completed and the chalet reopened on New Year's Day 1997. Finally, the plan recommended renovating Murphy's Windmill, as had been done in 1981 to Dutch Windmill. The windmills, built in 1902 and 1905, had pumped ground water for irrigating the park, until the 1930s. Neither of these is now a functioning part of the park's water system; both are museum artifacts, connecting visitors to the park's history, which is part of San Francisco's heritage. The changes proposed in the plan are as yet incomplete.[35]

Strikingly, the master plan incorporates few strategies for protecting or restoring Golden Gate Park's romantic scenery. There are numerous designs for improving "landscape treatments" and replanting trees but no comprehensive program to reproduce contemplative landscapes. This absence is not surprising, since most romantic park advocates long ago shifted their focus to regional, state, and national parks. In a mobile, highly accessible world, it is easier for romantics to visit the truly natural scenes in Yosemite National Park than to defend a contrived one in Golden Gate Park. The struggle for San Francisco's parks did not, however, cease when the romantics largely withdrew their support. In recent decades, rationalistic believers have been engaged by a different opposition—advocates maintaining that the city's parks should be managed in an ecologically responsible fashion. For example, instead of giving more cars access to Golden Gate Park's museums or ball fields, these new park advocates argue for reduced individual but enlarged group access, in order to protect the environment. Visitors, they contend, should ride buses rather than drive their own cars. On another front, advocates from the Sierra Club recently asked why park trees should be cut to facilitate construction. They warned that, despite management's reassurances, a century-old grove of trees would not be replaced in Golden Gate Park soon. "Special care should be taken," they declared, "not to remove any trees unless it's essential." Increasingly the new advocates have suggested management strategies and actions that would make parks more "sustainable" and would encourage "ecotone diversity." In a particularly radical move, landscape architect Michael Laurie even suggested removing many of the exotic plants covering the west end of Golden Gate Park in order to restore the original dunes and vegetation.[36]

A history of the rise and impact of these latest park advocates is the topic for another study. They are mentioned here only because they demonstrate that parks remain at the center of America's debates about the relationship of the natural environment to society. Like the romantic and rationalistic advocates before them, the newest advocates link their arguments about organizing and managing parks to society. Their advocacy today exposes again the cultural concerns that underlay the arguments of San Francisco's park proponents in the past. San Francisco society, people were told, suffered from moral failings; so, from the perspective of the park advocates, the city did not function as it should. Normative concerns and a belief that society could be reformed by parks informed those advocates' actions. Although the romantic and rationalistic advocates defined nature and nature design differently, they, and likely the latest activists, pursued the same goal. As long as cities like San Francisco fall short of social perfection—which they always will— and nature is treated as inherently good, we should expect our parks to remain shifting, malleable environments, as advocates use them to struggle toward that ever-elusive goal, the good society.

# notes

PREFACE

1. Throughout this book, unless stated otherwise, the term *park* will refer only to public urban parks and exclude regional, state, national and private parks. Although I make no claims in this study about the applicability of conclusions drawn from the American experience to park making in Canada, it is notable that one of that country's preeminent municipal greenspaces, Montreal's Mount Royal Park, also began at this time. See Laura Wood Roper, *FLO: A Biography of Frederick Law Olmsted* (Baltimore, 1973), pp. 356–359, passim. The statistic on parks in 1908 is in George F. Kunz, "Appendix I: American City Parks" in American Scenic and Historic Preservation Society, *Annual Report* (Albany, 1911), pp. 537–538. The literature touching on the history of American urban parks is too large to reference here, but for more on the mentioned cities see G. Chadwick, *The Park and the Town: Public Landscape in the Nineteenth and Twentieth Centuries* (New York, 1966); G. E. Montes, "San Diego's City Park, 1868–1902: An Early Debate on Environment and Profit," *Journal of San Diego History* 23 (Spring, 1977): 40–59; Galen Cranz, *The Politics of Park Design* (Cambridge, 1982); Cynthia Zaitzevsky, *Frederick Law Olmsted and the Boston Park System* (Cambridge, 1982); David Schuyler, *The New Urban Landscape: The Redefinition of City Form in Nineteenth-Century America* (Baltimore, 1986); and Roy Rosenzweig and Elizabeth Blackmar, *The Park and the People: A History of Central Park* (Ithaca, 1992).

Many of the above-mentioned park studies touch on the role greenspaces played in cultural battles, but only one book, Paul Boyer, *Urban Masses and Moral Order in America, 1820–1920* (Cambridge, Mass., 1978), speaks to the struggle to create the good society. Nonetheless, parks occupy only one portion of one chapter in Boyer's book. An example of a comprehensive study of the scientific and aesthetic aspects of gardens and plants in the landscape arts is Brenda Bullion, *The Science and Art of Plants and Gardens in the Development of an American Landscape Aesthetic (1620–1850)* (Ithaca, 1990). A study that discusses the relationship between the scientific and moral qualities of flowers is Nicolette Scourse, *The Victorians and Their Flowers* (Portland, Oreg., 1983).

2. Philosopher and intellectual historian Isaiah Berlin forcefully urges recognition of the roles of ideas and choice in historical events. He notes they are rarely simple and clear, confined to a particular class, or based on empirical evidence. For a discussion of Berlin's views, see John Gray, *Isaiah Berlin* (Princeton, 1996). The environmental historian, William Cronon, also argues for more accounts about the interaction between ideas, perceptions, and

beliefs, and the environment in "Modes of Prophecy and Production: Placing Nature in History" *Journal of American History* 76 (1990): 1122–1131.

3. Admittedly, San Francisco is beginning to view its parks as museum pieces, with a new master plan for Golden Gate Park aimed at "preservation" and "enhancement." See San Francisco Recreation and Park Department and Royston Hanamoto Alley & Abey, *Golden Gate Park Master Plan* (San Francisco, 1998). Elsewhere, a partial reconstruction to preserve the original design of Brooklyn's Prospect Park is underway. See I. Walmsley & Company, New York City, New York, and City of New York Parks and Recreation, *The First Historic Landscape Report for the Ravine, Prospect Park, Brooklyn, New York* (New York, 1986). New York City's Central Park long has had its preservationists. See Rosenzweig and Blackmar, *The Park*, pp. 426–435.

## 1   THE AMERICAN PARK MOVEMENT

1. This coterie included philanthropists, influential residents, newspaper editors and journalists, and magazine writers, along with municipal and park officials; but only a handful are known by name, and the total number was probably limited to hundreds when the city's population was in the hundreds of thousands. Their lives converged when they acted on their mutual belief that parks engender desirable qualities in society. Unless otherwise stated, further references to the supporters of parks will mean only this elite. According to Jon C. Teaford, *The Unheralded Triumph: City Government in America, 1870–1900* (Baltimore, 1984), pp. 6–7, such elites in American cities presided over the executive branches and other project commissions, as well as the park commissions, and they provided the professional expertise necessary to build the water and drainage systems, schools, public health services, and fire departments, as well as parks.

Although conflicts among the elite sometimes had little to do with working-class concerns, as William H. Wilson, *The City Beautiful Movement* (Baltimore, 1989), p. 77 observes, "many vocal opponents of [change] were strikingly similar to the proponents. . . . What may be said with certainty is that the active leadership for and against urban beautification came from roughly the same group. Both sides had access to a citywide audience, both expressed citywide concerns, and both used the press, the courts, and other devices such as pamphlets and public meetings to express their views." On the successes of nonleaders see Stephen Hardy, *How Boston Played: Sport, Recreation, and Community, 1865–1915* (Boston, 1982); Roy Rosenzweig, *Eight Hours for What We Will* (New York, 1983); Robert Weyeneth, "Moral Spaces: Reforming the Landscape of Leisure in Urban America, 1850–1920," (Ph.D. diss., University of California, Berkeley, 1984); and, Roy Rosenzweig and Elizabeth Blackmar, *The Park and the People: A History of Central Park* (Ithaca, 1992). Visitor records indicate advocates were not the only supporters or users of parks. For instance, more than 10,000,000 people entered New York's Central Park during 1873, Frederick Law Olmsted, *Forty Years of Landscape Architecture: Central Park*, ed. F. L. Olmsted, Jr., and T. Kimball, (Cambridge, Mass., 1973 [1928]), p. 536; and more than 500,000 visitors came to Golden Gate Park in 1875, San Francisco Board of Park Commissioners, *Third Biennial Report of the San Francisco Park Commissioners, 1874–75* (San Francisco, 1875), p. 14.

Further references to the San Francisco Board of Park Commissioners will be contracted to "SFBPC."

2. The first quote is from an 1867 Newark, New Jersey, park report in Frederick Law Olmsted, *The Years of Olmsted, Vaux & Company, 1865–1874*, ed. David Schuyler and Jane Turner Censer, vol. 6 of *The Papers of Frederick Law Olmsted* (Baltimore, 1992), p. 211; Charles Mulford Robinson, *Modern Civic Art, or The City Made Beautiful* (New York, 1909), p. 245. Paul Boyer, *Urban Masses and Moral Order in America, 1820–1920* (Cambridge, Mass., 1978), pp. 220–231, calls the larger movement "positive environmentalism" and considers park literature the most stridently environmentalist. See for example his description of landscape architect George Burnap on p. 242.

The reader may sense a connection to Progressivism. According to Richard Hofstadter, *Social Darwinism in American Thought* (Boston, 1955) or Boyer, *Urban Masses*, a characteristic thread of Progressivism was a faith in environmental determinism similar to that of the park proponents. Progressivism has usually been identified by researchers as beginning with the political party of the same name in the 1890s and continuing into the 1920s. See, for example, G. E. Mowry, *The California Progressives* (Chicago, 1951); Richard Hofstadter, *The Age of Reform* (New York, 1955); Samuel P. Hays, *Conservation and the Gospel of Efficiency* (Cambridge, Mass., 1959); S. C. Olin, *California's Prodigal Sons: Hiram Johnson and the Progressives, 1911–1917* (Berkeley, 1968); M. P. Rogin and J. L. Shover, *Political Change in California: Critical Elections and Social Movements, 1890–1966* (Westport, Conn., 1970); William Issel and Robert Cherny, *San Francisco, 1865–1932: Politics, Power, and Urban Development* (Berkeley, 1986); and, Philip J. Ethington, *The Public City: The Political Construction of Urban Life in San Francisco, 1850–1900* (New York, 1994). However, it seems reasonable to suggest that the park making that began in the 1850s indicates that at least this one thread of Progressive reform predates the well-known movement by approximately thirty years.

3. According to historian Thomas Bender, *Toward an Urban Vision: Ideas and Institutions in Nineteenth-Century America* (Lexington, 1975), p. 178, "Mid-century cultural leaders considered the nation's most urgent social need to be the development of institutions in cities that brought together all social classes." Parks were one of these arenas. H. W. S. Cleveland, *Landscape Architecture as Applied to the Wants of the West*, ed. Roy Lubove. (Pittsburgh, 1965), p. 38.

I have previously examined parks and social reform in "San Francisco's Golden Gate Park and the Search for a Good Society, 1865–1880," *Forest and Conservation History* 37 (1993): 4–13; "Trees, the Park, and Moral Order: The Significance of Golden Gate Park's First Plantings," *Journal of Garden History* 14 (1994): 158–170; and, "Social Reform through Parks: The American Civic Association's Program for a Better America," *Journal of Historical Geography* 22 (1996): 460–472, but Paul Boyer and I differ on the issue of moral order. In *Urban Masses*, p. ix, he uses *moral* "in the sense of its Latin root *mores*: the accepted usages and common behavior patterns of a people." The parameters of the moral order he studies are not clearly stated nor held steady. As concerns shift from one behavior to another in successive periods, Boyer follows. His analysis reveals disparate assemblages revolving around the general notion of the acceptableness of urban behavior. I use moral to refer to what is designated as a "good," which can be any action, object, or thought that conforms to the order perceived in the universe. One of these goods was usually justified on natural or supernatural grounds but in fact was largely the result of cultural-historical processes. I am arguing here that four such goods, collectively referred to as the virtues, exercised park advocates between 1850 and 1930 but were not generally identified by the names assigned here. I interpret the park champions' language so the reader can see how the constant pursuit of these cultural concerns informed the development of San Francisco's parks.

Other authors have focused upon one or more of the virtues in relation to urban life. The most comprehensive examination is Schuyler, *New Urban Landscape*. However, see also Martin Melosi, *Pragmatic Environmentalist: Sanitary Engineer George E. Waring, Jr.* (Washington, D.C., 1977), M. Melosi, ed., *Pollution and Reform in American Cities, 1870–1930* (Austin, 1980), and Judith Leavitt, *The Healthiest City: Milwaukee and the Politics of Health Reform* (Princeton, 1982) concerning public health; Marjorie Dobkin, "The Great Sand Park: The Origin of Golden Gate Park," (Master's thesis, University of California, Berkeley, 1979) concerning prosperity; Gunther Barth, *City People: The Rise of Modern City Culture in Nineteenth-Century America* (New York, 1980), Hardy, *How Boston Played,* and Judith K. Major, *To Live in the New World: A. J. Downing and American Landscape Gardening* (Cambridge, Mass., 1997) concerning social coherence; and Bender, *Urban Vision,* Geoffrey Blodgett, "Frederick Law Olmsted: Landscape Architecture as Conservative Reform," *Journal of American History* 62 (1976): 869–889; and David Schuyler, *Apostle of Taste: Andrew Jackson Downing, 1815–1852* (Baltimore, 1996) concerning democratic equality.

4. A recognition of the two phases helps to explain why Paul Boyer does not seriously include pre-1890s park makers in *Urban Masses and Moral Order* and why David Schuyler curtails his analysis of urban landscapes at the 1880s in *The New Urban Landscape*. On p. 236, Boyer goes so far as to marginalize parks before 1890. He recognizes and praises only one romantic advocate, Frederick Law Olmsted, but feels parks were of little interest to the majority of reformers, who "neglected [them] in favor of more direct strategies." The romantic and rationalistic periods coincide roughly with the "pleasure ground" and "reform park" periods identified in Galen Cranz's seminal study, *The Politics of Park Design.* Cranz's book, however, is more sociological than cultural and environmental. She emphasizes issues of class, politics, and the increasing bureaucratization of parks instead of the importance of ideas about nature, park form, and moral order. When Cranz discusses ideas, she treats them as "ideology," epiphenomena in a sociopolitical program of social control through environmental manipulation. They were not, she argues, truly believed by park leaders.

5. On Romanticism and its blending of art and science see Barbara Novak, *Nature and Culture: American Landscape and Painting, 1825–1875* (New York, 1980); Edmunds V. Bunkse, "Humboldt and an Aesthetic Tradition in Geography," *Geographical Review* 71, no. 2 (1981): 127–146; Marjorie Nicolson, "Alexander Von Humboldt, Humboldtian Science and the Origins of the Study of Vegetation," *History of Science* 25 (1987): 167–194; Stephen Jay Gould, "Church, Humboldt, and Darwin: The Tension and Harmony of Art and Science," in *Frederic Edwin Church* (Washington, D.C., 1989). Henry Ward Beecher, *Eyes and Ears* (Boston, 1869), pp. 281–284 (a collection of previously published newspaper articles by which Beecher wanted "to inspire a love of Nature" [p. iii]).

6. The use of the term *rationalistic* is inspired by Samuel P. Hays's *Conservation and the Gospel of Efficiency,* which examines a late-nineteenth-century and early-twentieth-century movement that pursued goals quite similar to those of the rationalistic park movement. Above all, Hays writes, conservation "was a scientific movement . . . Its essence was rational planning to promote efficient development and use of all natural resources" (p. 2). Peter Bailey, *Leisure and Class in Victorian England: Rational Recreation and the Contest for Control, 1830–1885* (Toronto, 1978) also sees rationalism at the center of this nature-recreation

movement. In *Shifting Gears: Technology, Literature, Culture in Modernist America* (Chapel Hill, 1987), Cecilia Tichi analyzes the rapid rise of technology during the late nineteenth and early twentieth centuries in terms of a cultural shift toward the mechanistic view of nature described here. The statement that parks must have civic beauty was made by Joseph Lee and is quoted in Peter J. Schmitt, *Back to Nature: The Arcadian Myth in Urban America* (Baltimore, 1990 [1969]), p. 74.

7. Many people see a park's open space as an opportunity to propose private or public development, but these propositions threaten the park's value as a natural setting by making it increasingly artificial. The *New York Times Magazine* for March 31, 1918, for example, includes a map of Central Park nearly filled by the structures proposed to that date. It is reproduced in Rosenzweig and Blackmar, *The Park,* p. 437. The authors claim that a similar Central Park map was produced as early as 1892. Like its predecessor, the 1918 version was published to counter another building proposal.

Parks have not suffered anything like "urban renewal" for at least two reasons. First, people continue to link parks to public health and prosperity. For instance, many people enjoy exercising and playing sports in parks, activities intended to increase health and prolong life. At the same time, merchants defend parks, especially the large, well known ones like Golden Gate Park and New York's Central Park, as tourist attractions. Parks also persist because they are in large part composed of living things. Landscape changes that add vegetation to the landscape, such as the rationalistic period's large flower gardens, were generally accepted but both users and advocates of parks frequently resisted removals. As will be shown in later chapters, the opposition to tree removal was sometimes so fierce in San Francisco that on one occasion it contributed to the downfall of one park administration and at a later date led another to publish a public defense of its tree thinning. Such opposition continues into our era. See, for example, Jane Kay, "GG Park's Trees on Chopping Block?" *San Francisco Examiner,* May 5, 1996, pp. 1, 12.

8. In a general sense, this division of parks into special purpose areas resembled the increasing segmentation and specialization of the urban space around them. For example, few identifiable districts existed in early-nineteenth-century cities, but by midcentury a recognizable central business district had appeared in the largest American cities and by 1900 this district had itself been further subdivided into identifiable zones of finance, administration, wholesale, and retail. Nor was the phenomenon confined to the business district. Boyer, *Urban Masses,* pp. 55–56, notes that urban residents, especially the elites, insisted that there were social class distinctions as early as the 1820s and 1830s. He does not indicate if there were spatial distinctions too. Also see George G. Foster, *New York by Gas-Light and Other Urban Sketches,* ed. and intro. Stuart M. Blumin (Berkeley, 1990), pp. 120–131. Foster was a newspaper reporter whose 1850 exposition includes a graphic description of poverty, disease, crime, and general chaos in the Five Points district of New York City. On the historic pattern of increasing social and spatial segmentation see Yi-Fu Tuan, *Segmented Worlds and Self: Group Life and Individual Consciousness* (Minneapolis, 1982) and Robert David Sack, *Place, Modernity, and the Consumer's World* (Baltimore, 1992). On the changing central business district see David Ward, *Cities and Immigrants* (New York, 1971), pp. 85–102 in particular. Olmsted is quoted in David Schuyler, *The New Urban Landscape: The Redefinition of City Form in Nineteenth-Century America* (Baltimore, 1986), p. 105. Olmsted's view is mirrored by his contemporary H. W. S. Cleveland, who, on p. 7 of his *Landscape Architecture* asserts

that someone designing a public or private landscape must use his artistic skill to "preserve a unity of design throughout, and then to give an expression of grace and beauty to the whole by the harmonious blending of its parts." George Burnap, *Parks: Their Design, Equipment, and Use* (Philadelphia, 1916), clearly takes a rationalistic park perspective with his book, which includes chapters on playgrounds, statues and monuments, buildings, fountains, outdoor seats, and plans for eye-catching flower displays. The insertion of these specialized areas supports the position that the mechanistic view of parks and nature gradually replaced the holistic view.

According to the sociologist, George Ritzer, *The McDonaldization of Society* (Thousand Oaks, Calif., 1992), pp. 35–120, the modern world inclines toward greater complexity through the creation of new social groups and hierarchical divisions in terms of both production and consumption. Drawing upon the work of the early-twentieth-century social scientist Max Weber, Ritzer identifies the recent source of this trend in the modern search for increased efficiency, quantifiability, predictability, and control. In concert with the increasing number of social divisions, has come a corresponding increase in the number and type of spatial segments. The social geographic history of the modern world has included an increasing diversity of places, regions, territories, and landscapes.

9. See, for example, W. Solotaroff, *Shade Trees in Towns and Cities* (New York, 1911); M. E. Weigold, *Pioneering in Parks and Parkways: Westchester County, New York, 1895–1945* (Chicago, 1980); Dominic Cavallo, *Muscles and Morals: Organized Playgrounds and Urban Reform, 1880–1920* (Philadelphia, 1981); Kenneth Jackson, *Crabgrass Frontier: The Suburbanization of the United States* (New York, 1985); Robert Fishman, *Bourgeois Utopias: The Rise and Fall of Suburbia* (New York, 1987); James Machor, *Pastoral Cities: Urban Ideals and the Symbolic Landscape of America* (Madison, 1987).

10. Laura Wood Roper, *FLO: A Biography of Frederick Law Olmsted* (Baltimore, 1973), p. 144. Landscape architects were not the only powerful public experts to emerge at this time. Others accompanied them, such as health officers, who proliferated in the effort to create improved urban environments.

11. The quote is Olmsted, *The Years of Olmsted, Vaux & Company*, p. 287.

12. Frederick Law Olmsted, *Public Parks and the Enlargement of Towns* (New York, 1970 [1870]), p. 22; SFBPC, *Second Biennial Report of the San Francisco Park Commissioners, 1872–73* (San Francisco, 1874), p. 86. Romantic park advocates and landscape architects generally did not oppose boisterous activities elsewhere, just in parks.

13. Burnap, *Parks*, p. 58. Burnap was chief landscape architect in the District of Columbia's Buildings and Grounds Division. See also Terence Young, "Modern Urban Parks," *Geographical Review* 85 (1995): 544–560. A city needed many parks that reflected and responded to the particular needs of the local social order according to the rationalistic landscape architects Frederick Law Olmsted (Jr.) and John Nolen, "The Normal Requirements of American Towns and Cities in Respect to Public Open Spaces" *Charities and the Commons* 16 (June 30, 1906): 411–426; and Burnap, *Parks*. Both publications are divided into subsections that describe the characteristics of such specialized greenspaces as "Small or Neighborhood Parks" and "Passing Through Parks." Unless otherwise indicated, all succeeding references to Frederick Law Olmsted are to the elder Olmsted rather than his son.

14. Frederick Law Olmsted, *Creating Central Park, 1857–1861*, ed. Charles E. Beveridge

and David Schuyler, vol. 3 of *The Papers of Frederick Law Olmsted* (Baltimore, 1983), p. 213; Olmsted, *The Years of Olmsted, Vaux & Company*, p. 428.

15. Andrew Jackson Downing, "The New-York Park" in G. W. Curtis, ed., *Rural Essays* (New York, 1857), p. 148 on the value of commerce. The appeal to prosperity should come as no surprise in this context. According to Charles Beard, "Some Aspects of Regional Planning," *American Political Science Review* 20 (1926): 277–278, "the fundamental aim of people engaged in economic enterprise is to get money out of it, and anybody who expects to go very far in discovering the nature of modern social forces will have to take note of that basic fact." T. J. Jackson Lears, *No Place of Grace: Antimodernism and the Transformation of American Culture, 1880–1920* (New York, 1981) explores exhaustion and devitalization in America in his analysis of "neurasthenia" after 1880. The 1866 Olmsted quote is in Frederick Law Olmsted, *The California Frontier, 1863–1865,* ed. Victoria Post Ranney, vol. 5 of *The Papers of Frederick Law Olmsted* (Baltimore, 1990), p. 522.

16. See Mona Domosh, *Invented Cities: The Creation of Landscape in Nineteenth-Century New York and Boston* (New Haven, 1996) on the growing presence of women in public life, especially in terms of consumption. Gary Cross, *A Social History of Leisure since 1600* (State College, Pa., 1990), p. 105. The "cushioning" ability of women is from Galen Cranz, "Women and Urban Parks: Their Roles as Users and Suppliers of Park Services," in S. Keller, ed., *Building for Women* (Lexington, Mass., 1981), p. 153. Mary A. Dodge, *Woman's Worth and Worthlessness* (New York, 1872), p. 94. The quote on ladies is from SFBPC, *Second Biennial Report,* p. 79. Frederick Law Olmsted discussed women in this same tone. In *Public Parks and the Enlargement of Towns* (New York, 1970 [1870]), p. 32, he does not mention women who might enter a park alone but discusses its benefits for "Mothers with their children." The implication in all this, of course, is that women's lives are not particularly difficult or stressful.

17. J. Horace McFarland, "Are National Parks Worth While?" *American Civic Association,* ser. 11, no. 6 (1912), p. 24.

The logic for this approach to play came from G. Stanley Hall, a widely influential psychologist at Clark University. According to his progressive evolutionary theory, individual development recapitulated humanity's history. Each individual had to pass from one cultural environmental stage to the next at the right moment to develop into a proper member of society. The centrality of G. Stanley Hall to theories on the value of play both indoors and out is developed in Cavallo, *Muscles and Morals;* and, Donald J. Mrozek, "The Natural Limits of Unstructured Play, 1880–1914," in *Hard at Play: Leisure in America, 1840–1940,* ed. Kathryn Grover (Rochester, 1992), pp. 210–226.

Joseph Lee, the American Civic Association's officer of public recreation, in *Play and Playgrounds* (Harrisburg, Pa., 1906), pp. 7–28, expanded Hall's theory to include three stages in childhood. In the first stage, the "dramatic age" child of under six learned to manipulate materials such as sand as well as to play expressively and socially. This stage represented the transition from pre-human to human, when people had their "first taste" of social unity. Next came the "Big Injun" stage, a recapitulation of the frontier era. Children between the ages of six and eleven passed through a period of investigation, mischief, skepticism, learning, and self-measurement, as self-reliance and competition came to the fore. The last stage, the "Age of Loyalty," was a period of "the group game and the gang." Social unity was reasserted for the final time as children learned to be both competitive and cooperative, laying the foundation for an industrial society. On p. 242 of *Urban Masses,* Boyer calls Lee the "father of American playgrounds." In 1906, Lee joined with Henry S. Curtis, a Ph.D. student of Hall, and others to found the Playground Association of America.

18. Along with arguing that parks reduced delinquency and increased productivity, Henry S. Curtis in *The Play Movement and Its Significance* (New York, 1917), pp. 311–339, claimed that parks with playgrounds would save money by preventing accidents and "worker unrest," by enticing people to remain in the city on their vacations, by lessening the frequency of tuberculosis, and by lowering the consumption of alcohol and tobacco.

19. Heath Schenker, "Women's and Children's Quarters in Golden Gate Park, San Francisco," *Gender, Place and Culture* 3 (1996): 293–308 explores the continuation of romantic middle-class views toward women, children, and domesticity into the rationalistic period. The quote on exercise as a remedy is from D. J. Mrozek, *Sport and American Mentality, 1880–1910* (Knoxville, 1983), p. 141. According to Mrozek, "Natural Limits," p. 210, Luther Halsey Gulick was among the rationalistic era's most influential writers on play. In the chapter "Sex Differences" in *A Philosophy of Play* (Washington, D.C., 1972 [1920]), pp. 97–98, 113–127, Gulick admits that since women were entering "wide competition . . . in the modern world, it would be wise for them to have the discipline afforded by athletic sports." But, he asked, is this good? "The question whether young women shall play competitive games hinges on what woman is going to be." If, as he favored, both women and men should come to possess similar "fundamental qualities," then athletics were appropriate for women. Later in the book, however, he contradicts this position. When discussing "the play of adults," he carefully and in detail argues why both young and older men need recreation, but never mentions women of any age.

20. For more on immigration during this period see Roger Daniels, *Coming to America: A History of Immigration and Ethnicity in American Life* (New York, 1991). According to Boyer, *Urban Masses,* p. 224, the shift of interest from individuals to groups was spread throughout early-twentieth-century intellectual thought and "reflected not merely an interest in *studying* social groups, but also in *controlling* them through the benevolent manipulation of their physical and social environment." For histories of active pastimes in general see J. Higham, "The Reorientation of American Culture in the 1890s," in *Writing American History: Essays on Modern Scholarship* (Bloomington, Ind., 1970), pp. 73–102; Lears, *No Place of Grace;* Hardy, *How Boston Played;* Mrozek, *Sport;* and, Schmitt, *Back to Nature.*

21. Marjorie C. Driscoll, *The M. H. de Young Memorial Museum, Golden Gate Park, San Francisco, California* (San Francisco, 1921), pp. 3, 11.

22. Galen Cranz contends that park site locations were "compromised by political, economic, and demographic considerations" and that "in practice the sites selected were simply those for which there was no competition at all, those unusable for other purposes." *The Politics of Park Design,* pp. 26, 29. While the effects of political, economic, and other factors must be considered when examining site selections, this explanation is inadequate for at least two reasons. First, it reduces culture to an epiphenomenon, portraying parks as if they were small craft able to land only where a sea of more important social forces allowed. However, the endurance of older and newer parks in the face of numerous proposals for their "development" illustrates how the attitudes supporting parks are stable, common, and as powerful as other social forces. For an indication of what these developments could have done to a park, see Rosenzweig and Blackmar, *The Park,* p. 437, a 1918 depiction of New

York's Central Park if the proposed developments had been constructed. The result is virtually no parkland. Second, it seems unlikely that advocates could reach "compromises" unless they had some preferred locations in mind.

23. On the declining significance of urban parks relative to other types of parks, see T. Young, "Social Reform through Parks." Cranz, *The Politics of Park Design* also concludes that her "reform park" period ended at about the same date. She observes that around 1930 park administrators and other outspoken advocates "abandoned their idealistic efforts to use parks as a mechanism of social reform." Parks no longer needed justification, they were "an expected feature of urban life." I am not arguing, however, that park development ceased during the 1920s. Many facilities were added to existing parks and new parks were created, but they tended to be in the rationalistic mold. Robert Caro details such development in New York in *The Power Broker: Robert Moses and the Fall of New York* (New York, 1974), as does Rosenzweig and Blackmar, *The Park*. See also Randolph Delehanty, "San Francisco Parks and Playgrounds, 1829–1990: The History of a Public Good" (Ph.D. diss., Harvard University, 1992); and Mike Eberts, *Griffith Park: A Centennial History* (Los Angeles, 1996) on Los Angeles.

24. The size of the park is given in San Francisco Board of Park Commissioners (SFBPC), *Third Biennial Report of the San Francisco Park Commissioners, 1874–75,* (San Francisco, 1875), p. 55. "Public Parks," *California Horticulturist and Floral Magazine* 1, no. 4 (1871), p. 111. The statistics for Minneapolis, Detroit, and St. Louis came from United States Census Office, *Report on the Social Statistics of Cities in the United States at the Eleventh Census: 1890* (Washington, D.C., 1895), p. 35.

25. The expense figure is from SFBPC, *Twenty-Sixth Annual Report of the Board of Park Commissioners of San Francisco For the Year Ending June 30, 1897* (San Francisco, 1897), p. 28. For a discussion of the general financial history of parks and park acquisition see Cranz, *Politics of Park Design,* pp. 175–181. According to George F. Kunz, "Appendix I: American City Parks" in American Scenic and Historic Preservation Society, *Annual Report* (Albany, 1911), pp. 537–541, spending on parks by municipal governments was such that by 1908, the value of the lands, buildings, and equipment of parks, gardens, and playgrounds in American cities with populations greater than 30,000 was nearly $800,000,000. These same municipalities annually spent on these facilities approximately $9,000,000 for salaries, wages, and other expenses. Terrence MacDonald, in *The Parameters of Urban Fiscal Policy: Socioeconomic Change and Political Culture in San Francisco, 1860–1906* (Berkeley, 1986), p. 47, writes that in San Francisco in 1905, the expense of having parks represented approximately 5% of the annual municipal budget. This was slightly less than the amount spent on streets (8%), equal to that spent on street lights, and more than that spent on school buildings or libraries. By contrast, San Francisco's 1998 budget for parks, including the zoo, golf courses, and other recreational features that did not exist in 1905, was approximately 2.3% of total municipal expenditures. See City and County of San Francisco, *Consolidated Budget and Annual Appropriation Ordinance: Fiscal Year Ending June 30, 1998* (San Francisco, 1998), pp. 2, 4.

26. San Francisco's early-arriving Irish, German, British, Chinese, French, and Scandinavian immigrants rubbed shoulders with its late-arriving Poles, Portuguese, Greeks, Italians, and others. See Ward, *Cities and Immigrants,* p. 76. Ethnic conflicts arose in San Francisco in relation to numerous issues. For example, see William Issel, "Class and Ethnic Conflict in San Francisco Political History: The Reform Charter of 1898," *Labor History* 18

(1977): 341–359; and Issel and Cherny, *San Francisco,* pp. 80–100, passim. Rosenzweig and Blackmar, *The Park,* passim, has shown that conflicts over parks occurred between working and capitalist classes in New York. Many of these working-class people were foreign born. The text reference is to David Ward, *Poverty, Ethnicity, and the American City, 1840–1925: Changing Conceptions of the Slum and the Ghetto* (New York, 1989). The ethnic composition of San Francisco and any resultant struggles over the city's parks remain largely unexplored in this book, because the emphasis is on the elite's beliefs and ideas.

27. The population figures are in M. G. Holli and P. d'A. Jones, eds. *Biographical Dictionary of American Mayors, 1820–1980: Big City Mayors* (Westport, Conn., 1981), p. 433. Gunther Barth, *Instant Cities: Urbanization and the Rise of San Francisco and Denver* (New York, 1975). Issel and Cherny, *San Francisco,* p. 24.

28. Ward, *Cities and Immigrants,* p. 77; The description of the city is in C. Wollenberg, *Golden Gate Metropolis: Perspectives on Bay Area History* (Berkeley, 1985), p. 142; Issel and Cherny, *San Francisco,* p. 26.

29. The residential population numbers are from Delehanty, "San Francisco Parks," p. 256. The park refugee numbers and the date are from Charles J. O'Connor et al., *San Francisco Relief Survey* (New York, 1913), p. 404.

Despite the variations described, San Francisco makes a fine case study. The city is and was sufficiently typical that urban scholars have frequently used it in their analyses of the American experience. Sociologist Galen Cranz, in *Politics of Park Design,* found it sufficiently typical to use with New York and Chicago as the bases for her history of American urban parks. Other historians and sociologists studying San Francisco include Jane Jacobs, *The Death and Life of Great American Cities* (New York, 1961); J. L. Spates and J. J. Macionis, *The Sociology of Cities* (New York, 1982); H. P. Chudacoff and J. E. Smith, *The Evolution of Urban Society* (Englewood Cliffs, 1988); Eric H. Monkkonen, *America Becomes Urban: The Development of U.S. Cities and Towns 1780–1980* (Berkeley, 1988); and Alan Mayne, *The Imagined Slum: Newspaper Representation in Three Cities, 1870–1914* (New York, 1993).

30. Raymond Williams, "Aesthetic," in *Keywords* (New York, 1983), pp. 31–33; Christopher Hussey and Luigi Salerno, "The Picturesque," in *Encyclopedia of World Art, Volume XI,* Massimo Pallottino, ed. (New York, 1966), pp. 336–342.

31. Barbara Novak, *Nature and Culture: American Landscape and Painting, 1825–1875,* rev. ed. (New York, 1995), pp. 3–17 develops the romantic connection among God, nature, and landscape in America.

32. George B. Tatum, "Introduction: The Downing Decade (1841–1852)," in *Prophet With Honor: The Career of Andrew Jackson Downing, 1815–1852,* ed. George B. Tatum and Elisabeth Blair MacDougall (Washington, D.C., 1989), pp. 1–2, and Schuyler, *Apostle of Taste,* pp. 39–44 argue that Downing modeled his work on that of Repton and, especially, Loudon. Downing's debt to Repton and others is acknowledged in *A Treatise.* See in particular, the first chapter for Downing's extensive narrative on the historical background and literature of landscape gardening. For a full chronology of Downing's life and publications see George Tatum, "Andrew Jackson Downing: Arbiter of American Taste, 1815–1852" (Ph.D. diss., Princeton University, 1950), p. 14. The Tatum quote is in *Landscape Gardening and Rural Architecture* (New York, 1991), p. v. This Dover edition is a reproduction of the seventh edition (1865) of *A Treatise on the Theory and Practice of Landscape Gardening.*

33. Andrew Jackson Downing, "The New-York Park," *Horticulturist and Journal of Rural*

*Art and Rural Taste* 6, no. 8 (1851): 345–347. See David Schuyler, "The Washington Park and Downing's Legacy to Public Landscape Design," in *Prophet With Honor: The Career of Andrew Jackson Downing, 1815–1852,* ed. George B. Tatum and Elisabeth Blair MacDougall (Washington, D.C., 1989), pp. 304–307, on the legacy of Downing's editorials.

There is a debate over who was responsible for initiating Central Park. Frederick Law Olmsted, "Passages in the Life of an Unpractical Man," in *Ctreating Central Park,* p. 84, attributes the park primarily to Downing. M. M. Graff, *Central Park, Prospect Park: A New Perspective* (New York, 1985), p. 3, attributes it to Downing and William Cullen Bryant. Rosenzweig and Blackmar, *The Park,* pp. 15–17, acknowledge the importance of Downing but point to Robert Bowne Minturn as most responsible.

34. Downing, "The New-York Park," p. 343.

35. Ibid., p. 348; idem, "A Talk About Public Parks and Gardens," in *Rural Essays,* ed. G. W. Curtis (New York, 1853), p. 156. Clearly Downing viewed parks as a tool to eliminate social and cultural diversity, but his advocacy was not as heavy handed as later efforts. It was instead a naïve attempt to "lift" everyone up to the social and economic level enjoyed by someone like Downing.

36. Downing, "A Talk," p. 155; On the ravages of cholera, see C. E. Rosenberg, *The Cholera Years: The United States in 1832, 1849, and 1866* (Chicago, 1962). The quote on Downing's influence is from W. G. Jackson, "First Interpreter of American Beauty: Andrew Jackson Downing and the Planned Landscape," *Landscape* 1, no. 3 (1952): 11. According to Jackson, p. 12, there were ultimately ten editions of Downing's *Treatise,* the last published in 1921. When the Commissioners of Central Park announced a design competition, the submissions were, in the words of David Schuyler, "Washington Park and Downing's Legacy" p. 307, "a testament . . . to the degree to which Downing had influenced the way Americans thought about parks." See also Norman T. Newton, *Design on the Land; The Development of Landscape Architecture,* (Cambridge, Mass., 1971), pp. 261–266.

37. On the joint efforts of Downing and Vaux see Francis R. Kowsky, *Country, Park, and City: The Architecture and Life of Calvert Vaux* (New York, 1998), pp. 28–51. On the influence of Downing upon Olmsted and Vaux see Schuyler, *Apostle of Taste,* pp. 156–186 and Schuyler, "Washington Park and Downing's Legacy," pp. 307–310; Charles Beveridge, "Introduction," in Olmsted, *Creating Central Park,* p. 4; Charles Beveridge and David Schuyler, "Biographical Directory," in *Creating Central Park,* pp. 64–65; and David Schuyler, *The New Urban Landscape: The Redefinition of City Form in Nineteenth-Century America* (Baltimore, 1986), pp. 75–76. The quote is from the last.

Olmsted clearly respected the role of Downing in the development of landscape design. In "Park" (*Creating Central Park,* p. 359), an encyclopedia article originally published in 1861, Olmsted describes landscape gardening near the end of the eighteenth century as "monotonous." It was in need of "genius again . . . to criticize and create, as in the time of Pope, Addison, and Kent. In the various 'Picturesque Tours' of Gilpin, and the voluminous 'Essays on the Picturesque' by Sir Uvedale Price, the true principles of art applicable to the creation of scenery were laboriously studied and carefully defined. . . . In more recent times the good service of Repton, Loudon, Paxton, Kemp, our own Downing and other artists . . . merits warm acknowledgement. Downing's works especially should be in every village school library." The depth of Olmsted's and Vaux's sense of personal debt to Downing is demonstrated by the latter's christening of his son "Downing" and by Vaux and Olmsted's joint efforts to create a memorial to Downing in Central Park. See Schuyler, "Washington Park and Downing's Legacy," p. 310; and Frederick Law Olmsted, "Circular Proposing the Erection in Central Park of a Memorial to Andrew Jackson Downing, April 5, 1860" in *Creating Central Park,* pp. 251–252.

38. Kowsky, *Country, Park, and City,* p. vii. See also ibid., pp. 53 ff.; and Beveridge and Schuyler, "Biographical Directory," p. 65 ff. on Vaux's activities after Downing's death. According to Beveridge, "Introduction," p. 2, Olmsted gained the post of superintendent because of his skill and because he was "a Republican who was not politically threatening to the Democratic members of the park board." See "Introduction," p. 4 on Olmsted's reading of Ruskin.

39. Olmsted's visit to Birkenhead is briefly discussed in Beveridge, "Introduction," p. 4. The article mentioned is [Frederick Law Olmsted], "The People's Park at Birkenhead, near Liverpool" *Horticulturist* 6, no. 5 (1851): 224–228. The quotations concerning Birkenhead Park are from Laura Wood Roper, *FLO: A Biography of Frederick Law Olmsted* (Baltimore, 1973), p. 71.

40. Olmsted and Vaux's employment arrangement with the park commission changed after they won the design competition. Olmsted was made "Architect-in-Chief" in May 1858 and Vaux was soon hired as one of his assistants. In January 1859, Vaux was elevated to "Consulting Architect"; and the following May, Olmsted's title was made even grander, "Architect-in-Chief and Superintendent." He retained this title until 1862. See Beveridge, "Introduction", pp. 27–28.

41. The first quote is from Charles E. Beveridge, "Frederick Law Olmsted's Theory on Landscape Design," *Nineteenth Century* 3, no. 2 (1977): 40; idem, "Introduction," p. 22. According to Kowsky, *Country, Park, and City,* p. 8, "no succinct testimony from Vaux himself exists that might be regarded as a statement of his esthetic philosophy." Nevertheless, Kowsky assembles a variety of sources to conclude that Vaux felt nature scenes in a park "transfigured and elevated" viewers.

The grade separations for the transverse roads, although a clever solution, nevertheless prompted some of the initial efforts to change the park's design after the Greensward plan had won the competition. Critics suggested that the depressions would be blocked with water or snow, but such criticisms were ultimately refuted. See Beveridge, "Introduction," pp. 16–17, 24.

42. Beveridge, "Introduction," pp. 17–18. Schuyler, "Washington Park and Downing's Legacy," p. 308, also considers Olmsted's "pastoral" to be his "nomenclature for Downing's Beautiful in landscape design." See Graff, *Central Park,* pp. 46–55, and Herbert J. Orange, "Frederick Law Olmsted: His Horticultural Philosophy and Practice" (Master's thesis, University of Delaware, 1973), pp. 42–48 passim. While Olmsted and Vaux handled the basic plan and the architectural features of the park, they relied on the landscape gardener Ignaz Pilat (1820–1870) to supervise the ornamental horticulture.

The Parade Ground was required by the competition rules, but Vaux and Olmsted hoped it would instead become "a great country green or open common."

43. Olmsted's use of terraces followed in the tradition of Humphry Repton. Later in life Olmsted used terraces only around houses, because he thought the mix of formal and informal styles was inappropriate in a public park. A terrace at the north end of the Mall indicates that Olmsted and Vaux considered the latter to be analogous with a house. In the

description accompanying the Greensward Plan they declared, "In giving [The Mall] this prominent position, we look at it in the light of an artificial structure on a scale of magnitude commensurate with the size of the park, and intend in our design that it should occupy the same position of relative importance in the general arrangement of the plan, that a mansion should occupy in a park prepared for private occupation." See Olmsted, *Creating Central Park,* p. 181 on Olmsted and Repton, and p. 126 on the Promenade and Terrace.

44. According to Frederick Law Olmsted, *Forty Years of Landscape Architecture: Central Park,* ed. Frederick Law Olmsted, Jr., and Theodora Kimball (Cambridge, Mass., 1973 [1928]), p. 535, Central Park had 7,593,139 visitors in 1865. Rosenzweig and Blackmar, *The Park,* p. 268, relate that in 1866 new investors were paying $5,000 to $7,000 for uptown cross-street lots near the new park which had sold for $400 in 1857. The brokers in these deals were also doing well: "Between 1857 and 1868, John McClave claimed, he handled $15 million worth of uptown property and earned nearly $1 million in commissions" despite the fact that there had been an economic panic between 1857 and 1863. See Mary Corbin Sies and Christopher Silver, eds., *Planning the Twentieth-Century American City* (Baltimore, 1996), especially Part 1, on the impact of Olmsted and Vaux's work on the history of planning.

45. Prospect Park's authorization and Olmsted and Vaux's involvement are discussed in Schuyler, *New Urban Landscape,* pp. 115–119.

46. Clay Lancaster, *Prospect Park Handbook* (New York, 1972), p. 30; Olmsted quoted in Schuyler, *New Urban Landscape,* p. 124. Two design changes illustrate Olmsted and Vaux's improved understanding of design. First, they requested the purchase of land *outside* Prospect Park for a parade so that the Green would not be used for military exercises. This additional area sat immediately south of the Lake, across Parkside Avenue. Second, they reserved a portion of the site north of Flatbush Avenue for a museum and botanical garden. They recognized the reasonable desire for these institutions but wished to protect the naturalistic landscape by placing them beyond its boundaries. See Schuyler, *New Urban Landscape,* pp. 124–125.

47. Schuyler, *New Urban Landscape,* p. 126; Rosenzweig and Blackmar, *The Park,* pp. 229, 232–233.

48. Quoted in Schuyler, *New Urban Landscape,* pp. 127–128.

49. Ibid., pp. 128–129; Charles Beveridge, "Frederick Law Olmsted's Vision for Buffalo," in *The Best Planned City: The Olmsted Legacy in Buffalo,* ed. Francis R. Kowsky (Buffalo, 1992), p. 19.

50. Quoted in Schuyler, *New Urban Landscape,* p. 130; Beveridge, "Buffalo," p. 19.

51. Quoted in Schuyler, *New Urban Landscape,* pp. 129–131; Beveridge, "Buffalo," p. 20.

## 2   SAN FRANCISCO'S PARK MOVEMENT BEGINS

1. On the early growth of San Francisco see Gunther Barth, *Instant Cities: Urbanization and the Rise of San Francisco and Denver* (New York, 1975) and Roger W. Lotchin, *San Francisco 1846–1856: From Hamlet to City* (New York, 1974). Soulé quotes are from Frank Soulé, *Annals of San Francisco* (New York, 1854), pp. 160–161. Dorothy H. Huggins, "Continuation of the Annals of San Francisco," in *The Annals of San Francisco by Frank Soulé, John H. Gihon, M.D., and James Nisbet Together with the Continuation, Through 1855 Compiled by Dorothy H. Huggins,* intro. Richard Dillon (Palo Alto, Calif., 1966), pp. 21, 23–24. On the various public

spaces see San Francisco Board of Supervisors (hereafter SFBS), *San Francisco Municipal Reports, for the fiscal year 1861–2, Ending June 30, 1862* (San Francisco, 1862), p. 262.

2. U.S. Bureau of the Census, Table 8, "Population of 100 Largest Urban Places: 1850" and Table 9, "Population of the 100 Largest Urban Places: 1860" Released on June 15, 1998, at http://www.census.gov/population/documentation/twps0027. Andrew Jackson Downing, "The New-York Park," *Horticulturist and Journal of Rural Art and Rural Taste* 6, no. 8 (1851): 345. John P. Young, *San Francisco: A History of the Pacific Coast Metropolis* (San Francisco, 1911), p. 410.

3. On the attitudes toward these spaces see *Daily Evening Bulletin,* April 16, 1856, p. 1; SFBS, *Municipal Reports* (1864), p. 170. According to William Issel and Robert W. Cherny, *San Francisco, 1865–1932: Politics, Power and Urban Development* (Berkeley, 1986), p. 14, "San Francisco experienced a dizzying rate of population turnover between 1850 and 1870."

4. Albert Shumate, *Rincon Hill and South Park: San Francisco's Early Fashionable Neighborhood* (Sausalito, Calif., 1988), pp. 30–31.

5. Ibid., 32, 34, 101.

6. John Bonner, "San Francisco As It Was and May Be" *San Francisco Chronicle,* March 14, 1897, p. 10, remarks on the throngs that went to the Willows. The rail time and cost is noted in "The Willows," *Mining and Scientific Press* (June 15, 1861): 1. Edgar M. Kahn, *Cable Car Days in San Francisco* (Stanford, 1944), pp. 9–10, writes that the railroad began service on July 4, 1860, but that horsecars replaced it in 1867 because they were more cost effective. On p. 11, Kahn places the entrance to the Willows on Valencia.

7. Kahn, *Cable Car Days,* 10–11, Pioche was one of the owners of Pioche, Bayerque & Company, a San Francisco banking firm, which also financed the development of the Market Street Railroad and wished to increase ridership on the line. "The Willows", p. 1; Bret Harte is quoted in Lewis Francis Byington and Oscar Lewis, eds. *The History of San Francisco, Volume 1* (Chicago, 1931), p. 233; J. Young, *San Francisco,* p. 262; and, Mark Twain, *Roughing It* (New York, 1980 [1871]), p. 339.

8. Soulé, *Annals,* p. 536. J. Young, *San Francisco,* p. 262. Kahn, *Cable Car Days,* p. 14, reports that the Central Railroad Company, incorporated in 1861, ran from Davis and Vallejo Streets, south through downtown, and then southeast along Sixth Street past Harrison Street. Bonner, "San Francisco," p. 10, argues that Woodward was motivated to open his own resort by the popularity of Russ's Gardens and the other local gardens.

9. Kahn, *Cable Car Days,* pp. 15–16. On the life of Woodward and his gardens see Bonner, "San Francisco"; Ethel Malone Brown, "Woodward's Gardens," in *Vignettes of Early San Francisco Homes and Gardens,* comp. Mrs. S. H. Palmer (San Francisco, 1935), pp. 15–19; and, Louise E. Taber, *Gold Rush Days* (San Francisco, 1935), pp. 26–29.

10. Taber, *Gold Rush Days,* p. 27.

11. The comparison to New York's Central Park is in "Woodward's Gardens, San Francisco, Cal." *California Horticulturist and Floral Magazine* 1, no. 10 (1870): 9. Taber, *Gold Rush Days,* p. 28.

12. Brown, "Woodward's Gardens", p. 18.

13. Brown, "Woodward's Gardens," mentions the visit by the General and his companions in one of P. T. Barnum's most famous acts (p. 18) and the influence of Golden Gate Park (p. 19). According to Taber, *Gold Rush Days,* p. 29, Woodward's Gardens was closed and its contents and property auctioned off in 1893. "Woodward's Gardens," *San Francisco Chroni-*

*cle,* May 18, 1889. The article blames the garden's demise on squabbles between the heirs, but the grounds were in poor shape toward the end, and this likely drove away customers too. A spring 1887 visitor, Amy Bridges, described the resort as "not well kept" and "a dirty place altogether." Amy Bridges, "April 10, 1887" *Journal Kept on Fourth Raymond Excursion to Colorado, New Mexico and California,* unpublished manuscript, Huntington Library, San Marino, Calif., p. [166].

14. Terrence J. McDonald, *The Parameters of Urban Fiscal Policy: Socioeconomic Change and Political Culture in San Francisco, 1860–1906* (Berkeley, 1986), pp. 124–128, 136–140; Issel and Cherny, *San Francisco,* pp. 15, 18–22, and 119–125; and, Philip J. Ethington, *The Public City: The Political Construction of Urban Life in San Francisco, 1850–1900* (Cambridge, 1994), pp. 161–169. The city budget figures are in Marjorie Dobkin, "The Great Sand Park: The Origin of Golden Gate Park" (Master's thesis, University of California, 1979), p. 50, and the departmental figures are in Randolph Delehanty, "San Francisco Parks and Playgrounds, 1829–1990: The History of a Public Good" (Ph.D. diss., Harvard University, 1992), p. 93. Although the department's budget rebounded to $25,000 in 1860, funding for small parks and squares would remain insignificant and inadequate until the 1890s. The act is reprinted in A. E. T. Worley, compiler, *The Consolidation Act and Other Acts Relating to the Government of the City and County of San Francisco* (San Francisco, 1887), pp. 3–31. The one Democratic mayor during the twenty-year rule of the People's Party was Frank McCoppin (1868–1870), of whom there is more below. The party's executive was Clancey J. Dempster. He is quoted in Ethington, *The Public City,* p. 164.

15. J. Young, *San Francisco,* p. 449.

16. "A Public Park and Pleasure Grounds Needed for San Francisco" *Daily Evening Bulletin,* July 25, 1865, p. 2. The article on parks referred to in the editorial was on p. 1. The article was a condensed version of a piece that had appeared in the *New York World,* May 9, 1865, p. 1. Olmsted's response to Fitch's editorial is reproduced as "The Project of a Great Park For San Francisco" in Frederick Law Olmsted, *The California Frontier, 1863–1865,* ed. Victoria Post Ranney, vol. 5 of *The Papers of Frederick Law Olmsted* (Baltimore, 1990), pp. 425–430.

17. Victoria Post Ranney, "Introduction," in Olmsted, *California Frontier,* p. 1.

18. Ranney, "Introduction," p. 33–35. Both plans are reproduced in *California Frontier.* The cemetery covers pp. 473–487 and the college is on pp. 546–573.

19. See Olmsted, *California Frontier:* p. 429 on the need of a park, p. 427 on the links to prosperity, p. 428 on public health, p. 426 on democratic equality, and, p. 425 on social coherence. Olmsted was an executive on the U.S. Sanitary Commission from June 1861 to August 1863. He had been tapped for the post because of the organizational skills he had perfected during his work on New York's Central Park. However, by 1863 he was exhausted and at the same time received the intriguing offer to manage the Mariposa gold mine. For a history of this period, see Laura Wood Roper, *FLO: A Biography of Frederick Law Olmsted* (Baltimore, 1973), pp. 163–237.

20. See Olmsted, *California Frontier,* pp. 426, 429–430. The exact figure given for the cost of Central Park is $7,389,727.96 in Eugene Kinkead, *Central Park, 1857–1995* (New York, 1990), p. 17.

21. William Ashburner (1831–1887) was a mining consultant and a former member of the California Geological Survey. Olmsted engaged him to work on the Mariposa mine at the recommendation of the state geologist, Josiah Dwight Whitney. Later in life, Ashburner

became a professor and regent at the University of California and a trustee of Stanford University. Olmsted considered him a very close friend. Frederick Billings (1823–1890) was a lawyer who owned a large share of the Mariposa mine. He was serving on the Board of Trustees of the College of California when it hired Olmsted. He remained a leader in the campaign for San Francisco parks. Both Ashburner and Billings lived in San Francisco. For further biographical details see Olmsted, *California Frontier,* pp. 93–94, 200–202. The petition is reprinted in SFBS, *Municipal Reports* (1866), p. 395.

This proposal by the petitioners for a comprehensive system of parks instead of a single large park suggests that Olmsted had been devising an approach to the San Francisco park problem since his August letter and had consulted with Ashburner and Billings before they circulated the petition. The approach it outlines is very similar to the plan Olmsted would prepare for San Francisco in 1866.

22. "A Great Public Park Wanted in San Francisco," *Daily Alta California,* November 18, 1865, p. 2. *Daily Morning Call,* December 22, 1865, p. 2.

23. I rely primarily on Eugene N. Kozloff and Linda H. Beidleman, *Plants of the San Francisco Bay Region: Mendocino to Monterey* (Pacific Grove, Calif., 1994) for my vegetational community types and botanical nomenclature. See also Michael G. Barbour and Jack Major, eds., *Terrestrial Vegetation of California* (New York, 1977); and V. L. Holland and David J. Keil, *California Vegetation* (Dubuque, Iowa, 1995).

24. Richard Henry Dana, *Two Years Before the Mast: A Personal Narrative* (New York, 1964 [1840]), p. 342. Soulé, *Annals,* p. 157. Olmsted is quoted in Ranney, "Introduction," p. 11.

25. The petition is printed in SFBS, *Municipal Reports* (1866), p. 395. The Coon quote is from SFBS, *Municipal Reports* (1868), p. 623. Frederick Law Olmsted, "Preliminary Report in Regard to a Plan of Public Pleasure Grounds for the City of San Francisco," in *California Frontier,* pp. 518–546. For a discussion of Olmsted's designs for semiarid California see Charles E. Beveridge, "Introduction to the Landscape Design Reports," in Olmsted, *California Frontier,* pp. 449–473.

26. Beveridge, "Introduction to the Landscape Design Reports," pp. 451–461.

27. Olmsted, "Preliminary Report," p. 534.

28. Beveridge, "Introduction to the Landscape Design Reports," p. 461; Olmsted, "Preliminary Report," p. 536–537. The evergreen and irrigation quotes are in Olmsted, "Preliminary Report," p. 531.

29. Quoted in Beveridge, "Introduction to the Landscape Design Reports," p. 461; Olmsted, "Preliminary Report," pp. 529–530, 538–541.

30. Olmsted, "Preliminary Report," pp. 532–533.

31. Ibid., pp. 532–534.

32. Ibid., p. 534.

33. Roper, *FLO,* pp. 303–304. The dates for the arrival and the departure of the packages are noted in Olmsted, "Preliminary Report," p. 518; the Coon letters are quoted in p. 544, n. 1.

34. The description of the struggle is from William Hammond Hall, "The Beginnings of Golden Gate Park," in *The Romance of a Woodland Park,* unpublished manuscript (ca. 1926), William Hammond Hall Papers, Bancroft Library, University of California, Berkeley, pp. 3–4. For more on the competing groups see Richard M. Gibson, "Golden Gate Park," *Overland Monthly* 37, no. 3 (1901): 741; William Hammond Hall, "The Site Location Wrangle," *The Story of a City Park,* unpublished manuscript (ca. 1919), William Hammond Hall

Papers, pp. 1–10; Linda M. Benton, *The Presidio: From Army Post to National Park* (Boston, 1998), pp. 28–30; and, Erwin N. Thompson and Sally B. Woodbridge, *Presidio of San Francisco: An Outline of Its Evolution as a U.S. Army Post, 1847–1990* (Denver, 1992), p. 34.

35. The 1851 Charter set the city's boundary at two miles west of Portsmouth Square and parallel with Kearny Street. Divisadero Street currently runs north-south near the line. The approximate size of the Outside Lands is given in SFBS, *Municipal Reports* (1868), p. 565. For a botanical discussion of the beach vegetation, see Kozloff and Beidleman, *Plants*, pp. 19–20; and, Michael G. Barbour and Ann F. Johnson, "Beach and Dune," in Michael G. Barbour and Jack Major, eds., *Terrestrial Vegetation of California* (New York, 1977), pp. 223–261).

36. The case and the court's ruling is recounted in SFBS, *Municipal Reports* (1865), pp. 190–200. It is analyzed in Dobkin, "Great Sand Park," pp. 47–54.

37. According to Frank McCoppin in SFBPC, *Twenty-Second Annual Report* (San Francisco, 1893), p. 24, the Outside Land squatters included Eugene Sullivan and Eugene Lies. We will hear more about them in the next chapter. *The Congressional Globe* (Washington, D.C., 1866), pp. 337, 734, 853, 898, 1147, 1150, 1178, 1190, 1273. The quote is on p. 853. For biographical information on Conness and Bidwell, see Joel D. Treese, ed., *Biographical Dictionary of the American Congress, 1774–1996* (Alexandria, Va., 1997), pp. 172, 659, and 854. The successes of the Outside Land squatters did not end efforts by the other groups to have a city park in their area. See, for example, "The Presidio Reservations," *California Horticulturist and Floral Magazine* 1, no. 4 (1871), pp. 123–124; and, "Our City Park," *California Horticulturist and Floral Magazine* 1, no. 7 (1871), pp. 203. On January 16, 1871, the San Francisco Board of Supervisors, joining with the state Assembly and Senate, adopted a resolution asking California's U.S. senators and representatives to have the federal Presidio property turned over to the city for a public park. This was five months after the municipal and state authorities had created Golden Gate Park.

38. Byington and Lewis, *History, Volume 1*, p. 322. J. Young, *San Francisco*, p. 409. Hall, "Site Location Wrangle," p. 18. Others shared Hall's opinion of the situation at the time. See "The Outside Lands," *Golden Era* 17, no. 16 (March 13, 1869), p. 4.

39. McCoppin (1834–1897), an emigrant from Ireland in 1852, rose quickly in San Francisco politics. Trained as an engineer, he moved to San Francisco in 1858 to be employed as the superintendent of construction on the Market Street Railroad, the city's first transit system. He was first elected supervisor in 1860 and was steadily reelected until his successful campaign for mayor. His mayoral tenure, however, was short, as he lost, albeit narrowly, in the September 1869 election. According to Melvin G. Holli and Peter d'A. Jones, *Biographical Dictionary of American Mayors, 1820–1980* (Westport, Conn., 1981), p. 232, McCoppin must have been very aware of the physical nature of the Outside Lands because he "planted ground cover along the [streetcar] lines to prevent drifting sand—a major problem in those early days."

Contract scheme in Raymond H. Clary, *The Making of Golden Gate Park: The Early Years, 1865–1906* (San Francisco, 1984), p. 5.

40. J. Young, *San Francisco*, p. 311. California continued to have this power of indirect rule over San Francisco until the state's constitution was rewritten in 1879.

41. The majority report is in SFBS, *Municipal Reports* (1868), on pp. 560–564, and the minority report is on pp. 564–565. The majority members were two San Francisco supervisors, Charles H. Stanyan, chairman, and A. J. Shrader, and a physician, R. Beverly Cole; the

minority, Monroe Ashbury and Charles Clayton, also both San Francisco supervisors. On the Brooklyn developments see David Schuyler, *The New Urban Landscape: The Redefinition of City Form in Nineteenth-Century America* (Baltimore, 1986), p. 128. The nearly contemporaneous development of a park system in Buffalo also had no effect on San Francisco, because in May 1868 it was still in the future. According to Schuyler, pp. 128–133, Olmsted and Vaux began their work in this upstate New York city during summer 1868 and did not submit their first, preliminary park report until October of that year. Quote about Central Park's width is on p. 562 of *Municipal Reports*.

42. SFBS, *Municipal Reports* (1868). The points of agreement are on p. 560. The large parcel in both reports included at least parts of Olmsted's Rural Ground.

43. The McCoppin quote comes from a speech he gave twenty-five years later. See SFBPC, *Twenty-Second Annual Report*, p. 24. The details come from J. Young, *San Francisco*, p. 409. See Gibson, "Golden Gate Park," p. 737; and, Michael Black, "Searching for a Genius of Place: The Ambiguous Legacy of Golden Gate Park," in *The Environmental Spirit: Past, Present and Prospects; Conference Proceedings, University of California, Berkeley, 1995*, John F. Keilch, ed. (Berkeley, 1995), pp. 123–124, for further details on the development of the Outside Lands agreement. The opposition meeting is presented in "The Outside Land Assessment," *The Golden Era* 17, no. 13 (February 20, 1869), p. 3. This journal was in favor of the settlement "as there seems no likelihood of a better reservation now being made."

The commissioners' appointment date is noted in San Francisco Board of Park Commissioners, *First Biennial Report of the San Francisco Park Commissioners, 1870–71* (San Francisco, 1872), p. 1. The board had a difficult time selling these bonds because the state ordered that they not be sold at a discount like other municipal bonds. Abraham Seligman, an Outside Land holder, bought $75,000 worth at full price in 1870 and 1871 and then became the Park Commission's treasurer. According to SFBPC, *Second Biennial Report of the San Francisco Park Commissioners, 1872–73* (San Francisco, 1874), pp. 13–14, after the state removed the prohibition on discounts, the commission sold bonds worth $150,000 for $137,915 during 1872 and 1873. During the romantic era of park development, American park bureaucracies usually consisted of a board of commissioners who were the titular heads of a city's parks, a superintendent who answered to the board, and perhaps one or two other specialists who answered to the board, for example, a secretary. The commissioners, generally political appointments from the local upper-middle class, were frequently businessmen and responsible for accounts. The superintendent was the chief executive in charge of all labor and was viewed as the local expert on parks. California Legislature, Chapter 808, in *Statutes of California* (Sacramento, 1870); SFBS, *Municipal Reports* (1870), pp. 605–606.

44. SFBPC, *Third Biennial Report of the San Francisco Park Commissioners, 1874–75* (San Francisco, 1875), p. 55, gives 1,019 acres as the size of Golden Gate Park; but SFBPC, *Forty-Second Annual Report of the Board of Park Commissioners*, ed. Hugh M. Burke (San Francisco, 1912), p. 13, lists it as 1,013 acres; while a recent appraisal, San Francisco Recreation and Park Department, and Royston Hanamoto Alley & Abey, *Golden Gate Park Master Plan* (San Francisco, 1998), p. 1–12, provides the figure of 1,017 acres. The topographic map of the undeveloped park site in SFBPC, *First Biennial Report* shows the park enclosed by a grid of streets. Central Park's size and shape are included in an 1859 letter by Frederick Law Olmsted, "Description of the Central Park," in *Creating Central Park, 1857–1861*, ed. Charles E.

Beveridge and David Schuyler, vol. 3 of *The Papers of Frederick Law Olmsted* (Baltimore, 1983), pp. 204–205.

45. Hall, "Site Location Wrangle," pp. 18–20; "The Park Swindle," *Golden Era* 17, no. 10 (1869): 4; "The Outside Land Assessment," *Golden Era* 17, no. 13 (1869): 3; "The Outside Lands," *Golden Era* 17, no. 16 (1869): 4; Dobkin, "Great Sand Park," pp. 72–74.

46. J. Young, *San Francisco*, p. 410. The extensive quote is from William Hammond Hall, "Our Park Sites as Nature Made Them," *The Making of a City Park*, unpublished manuscript (ca. 1915), Hall Papers, pp. 4–5. The botanical nomenclature for "prostrate escalonia" is unclear since there are no native *Escallonia* in the area. Hall may be recognizing an ornamental introduced from South America. If so, it suggests that either someone had been planting the area or the species had naturalized. Clary, *The Early Years*, p. 12, ascribed the lack of woody vegetation to the widespread cutting of timber during the gold rush era. The critique of the site is from Hall, "Site Location Wrangle," p. 8.

47. Hall, "Our Park Sites," pp. 6–7.

48. J. Young, *San Francisco*, p. 432.

## 3   ROMANTIC GOLDEN GATE PARK

1. Hall's bid is listed in San Francisco Board of Supervisors (SFBS), *Municipal Reports* (San Francisco, 1871), p. 396. Robert Kelley, *Battling the Inland Sea: American Political Culture, Public Policy, and the Sacramento Valley, 1850–1986* (Berkeley, 1989), p. 189. Gray Brechin, *Imperial San Francisco: Urban Power, Earthly Ruin* (Berkeley, 1999), p. 81. The biographical information is drawn from "Hall, William Hammond," in *Notables of the Southwest: Being the Portraits and Biographies of Progressive Men of the Southwest, Who Have Helped in the Development and History Making of this Wonderful Country* (Los Angeles, 1912), pp. 120. [William Hammond Hall], "Reminiscences of Golden Gate Park: An Interview with the First Engineer and Superintendent," unpublished manuscript (1900), William Hammond Hall Papers, Bancroft Library, University of California, Berkeley, p. 10.

Much that Hall wrote about Golden Gate Park was written well after the events occurred, some over four decades later. Hall changed some of his views over the years, but he is cautiously relied on here for several reasons. First, the views expressed in his later writings agree with his earlier public and private statements. There are no major philosophical or empirical disagreements. The richness of his understanding undoubtedly increased as he aged, but his judgments remained unchanged. Second, he was a determined researcher and writer who had adequate evidence. Beginning early in his professional career he took to writing prolifically and retaining his letters and the replies. He collected voluminous newspaper accounts, public reports, and other evidence over the course of his life; the boxes containing his papers in the Bancroft Library fill more than forty feet of shelf space. Third, the statements in his later writings generally agree with other sources from the 1870s and 1880s, the decades when he most influenced San Francisco's parks.

2. William Hammond Hall, "Our Park Sites as Nature Made Them," In *The Making of a City Park*, unpublished manuscript (ca. 1915), Hall Papers, Bancroft Library, p. 4. He mentions his thoughts about a plan in "Reminiscences," p. 10.

Late in life Hall wrote several histories of Golden Gate Park's first decades which are preserved in the Bancroft Library. These unpublished manuscripts record Hall's experiences, clearly expressing his view that events were often driven by personality and politics. His accounts are well documented and generally accord with other sources. It is not clear why Hall wrote these histories, but they may have been an effort to reassert his importance in comparison with John McLaren, the popular and personally powerful superintendent of San Francisco's parks from 1890 to 1943. The manuscripts certainly focus on Hall's role in Golden Gate Park's history. Such a purpose would fit Hall's general makeup. He was a very bright individual who relished receiving credit and who tried to retain control. The production order of the manuscripts appears to be first, *The Making of a City Park* (ca. 1915), then *The Story of a City Park* (ca. 1919), and finally *The Romance of a Woodland Park* (ca. 1926).

3. As the historian Roy Lubove notes in his "Introduction" in H. W. S. Cleveland, *Landscape Architecture as Applied to the Wants of the West*, ed. Roy Lubove (Pittsburgh, 1965), p. viii, most such experts "drifted" into the field. Their expertise came prior to the development of abstracted principles and training, when the example of others played a major role in professional definition and practice. However, it would not have been unusual for a superintendent and some of his staff to have been tutored in a field, like engineering or architecture, whose practices had direct application to park making. Hall mentions in "Reminiscences" having read the New York and Brooklyn park reports (p. 10). He continued to collect park reports over the years. See, for example, the letter from John C. Cresson, chief engineer of Fairmount Park in Philadelphia, to William Hammond Hall, February 14, 1874, Hall Papers. In addition, Olmsted delivered in 1870 a seminal address on the social value of parks which was was soon published. See Frederick Law Olmsted, *Public Parks and the Enlargement of Towns* (New York, 1970 [1870]). Although it is uncertain whether Hall possessed a copy in 1870–71, there is one among his personal papers. This copy is among the William Hammond Hall papers in the Helen Crocker Russell Library in Golden Gate Park.

4. William Hammond Hall, "Making a Park Plan" in *The Story of a City Park*, p. 1.

5. The timing of the plan and memorandum is mentioned in [Hall], "Reminiscences", p. 11. The quote, in formal language including a third-person reference to himself, is from Hall, "Making a Park Plan," p. 2.

6. [Hall], "Reminiscences," p. 10.

7. Ibid., p. 7.

8. The interactions between Hall, the commissioners, Alexander, and Rousset are covered in ibid., pp. 7–10. The quote is on p. 11. In addition to the cited reasons, Hall *may* have been named superintendent because he was a Democrat. Governor Haight was a Democrat and he had appointed the commissioners. Presumption of Hall's political affiliation is based on the large contributions he made to the Democratic Party. See letter from M. C. Haley to William Hammond Hall, October 11, 1882, in Hall Papers. It is uncertain how long he had been a Democrat.

9. Letter from William Hammond Hall to Edward Pennington, Esquire, Bookseller and Importer, August 16, 1871, Hall Papers, Bancroft Library, p. 1; The letter from William Hammond Hall to D. Van Nostrand, Publisher, Importer & Bookseller, November 29, 1871, Hall Papers, Bancroft Library, mentions their correspondence "several months" earlier. It is assumed these letters were written in approximately mid-to-late August 1871. Letter from William Hammond Hall to Frederick Law Olmsted, August 22, 1871, Frederick Law Olmsted

Papers, Manuscripts Division, Library of Congress, pp. 1–4 (emphasis in original). No evidence corroborates Hall's claim that he had traveled to the parks or the estates, so it appears he was simply trying to make himself more credible.

10. Letter from Frederick Law Olmsted to William Hammond Hall, October 5, 1871, Hall Papers, Bancroft Library, p. 1–3.

11. Ibid., pp. 2–3. Olmsted's note continues:

Much the most valuable work for you will be Alphand's Les Promenades de Paris; Rothschild edition, Paris; a large quarto with numerous plates, giving details of construction.

Much has been compiled and condensed from it in Mr. Robinson's Parks & Promenades of Paris, published two years ago in London. A very valuable work.

Sir Uvedale Price On the Picturesque

Repton's Landscape Gardening

Loudons Encyclopedia of Gardening;

"     Suburban Villas;

"     Cottage Gardener;

"     Horticultural Magazines (serial)

"     Arboretum Britannicum. (8 vols)

Sir Henry Steuart's Planters' Guide;

John Arthur Hughes' Garden Architecture;

Smith's Landscape Gardening.

Kemp's How to Lay Out a Garden.

As to general principles and spirit of design all of Ruskin's art works are helpful.

Downing's writings are conspicuously absent from this list, but, given Hall's reference to Downing in his letter, it seems reasonable to conclude that Olmsted thought Hall was already well aware of Downing's work.

12. Hall, "The Site Location Wrangle," in Story of a City Park, pp. 10–11. "San Francisco's Park," California Horticulturist and Floral Magazine 2, no. 2 (1872): 90. This publication was the official outlet for the Bay District Horticultural Society, an organization composed of local gardeners and nurserymen. William Hammond Hall, "First Five Years of Work," Romance of a Woodland Park, p. 18, says that at the time the magazine was "the accepted prophet of all that pertained to the improvement of gardens and grounds." On the pressures facing the commissioners and Hall, see "The Park Swindle," The Golden Era 17, no. 10 (1869); "Public Parks," California Horticulturist and Floral Magazine 1, no. 4 (1871): 110–112; or, "Public Improvements," California Horticulturist and Floral Magazine 2, no. 4 (1872): 118–120.

13. San Francisco Board of Park Commissioners (SFBPC), First Biennial Report (San Francisco, 1871), p. 25. The plan is presented on pp. 24–38. Hall, unlike Olmsted, did not adapt his plan to this region's semi-aridity. Instead, he irrigated with groundwater and supplies transferred from distant watersheds to create the scenery typical of an eastern park. Consequently, the Golden Gate Park site encouraged San Franciscans to accept the idea of

greened cities in the arid West. The park's need for copious irrigation set San Francisco on a collision course with its private water suppliers and led indirectly to the city's later support for the Hetch Hetchy reservoir in Yosemite National Park. See Michael Black, "Searching for a Genius of Place: The Ambiguous Legacy of Golden Gate Park," in *The Environmental Spirit: Past, Present and Prospects; Conference Proceedings, University of California, Berkeley, 1995,* ed. John F. Keilch (Berkeley, 1995), pp. 109–159.

14. SFBPC, *First Biennial Report,* pp. 15, 24–26. The memorandum is unpublished but quoted in William Hammond Hall, "The Plan and Purpose of the Avenue," in *Making a City Park,* pp. 7–12.

15. SFBPC, *First Biennial Report,* pp. 27–28. Pope's 1771 admonition to "In all, let *Nature* never be forgot. Consult the Genius of the Place in all," whenever creating architecture or landscape was in "An Epistle to Lord Burlington" and is reprinted in John Dixon Hunt and Peter Willis, eds., *The Genius of the Place: The English Landscape Garden, 1620–1820* (Cambridge, 1988), p. 212.

16. SFBPC, *First Biennial Report,* pp. 32, 23.

17. The conservatory had been owned by James Lick but, when he died in 1867, it was purchased by a group of San Franciscans, including Leland Stanford, Charles Crocker, Claus Spreckels, and park commissioner William Alvord, who then gave it to the park. Raymond Clary, *The Making of Golden Gate Park: The Early Years, 1865–1906* (San Francisco, 1984), p. 35. SFBPC, *First Biennial Report,* p. 22. The formal garden was not constructed for several decades, and no children's tract would ever appear here.

18. The opposite of Central Park, these lawns were called "Dressed Grounds" by Hall. SFBPC, *First Biennial Report,* pp. 22–23.

19. Ibid., pp. 23, 34.

20. The description of Gerster is in William Hammond Hall, "After the Dark Decade," in *Romance of a Woodland Park,* p. 17. Although he had already looked for a rustic carpenter in San Francisco, the record of Hall's search for one begins with a letter to Olmsted. Olmsted recommended Anton Gerster, who had been employed in both Central and Prospect Parks. Gerster was willing to work for a year in San Francisco for "$6 a day and expenses of travel one way." William Hammond Hall to Frederick Law Olmsted, January 26, 1874, Olmsted Papers, p. 2; Olmsted to Hall, February 24, 1874, Hall Papers, Bancroft Library, p. 4. SFBPC, *First Biennial Report,* p. 35.

21. SFBPC, *First Biennial Report,* p. 23. In the same report, p. 32, he names the San Miguel Hills as worthy of viewing from a high point within the park.

22. Hall to Van Nostrand, pp. 1–2.

23. Hall's library is not intact and there is no list of his personal or professional library at this time. However, his copy of Humphry Repton, *The Landscape Gardening and Landscape Architecture of the late Humphry Repton, Esq.,* ed. J. C. Loudon (London, 1840) is in the William Hammond Hall Collection, Helen Crocker Russell Library, Strybing Arboretum, Golden Gate Park. The unpublished report is quoted in Hall, "The Plan and Purpose of the Avenue," pp. 7–12.

24. SFBPC, *First Biennial Report,* p. 27.

25. William Hammond Hall, "The Influence of Parks and Pleasure-Grounds" *Overland Monthly* 11 (1873): 529. Idem, "The City Woodland Park," in *Romance of a Woodland Park,* p. 1.

In "Early American Park Makers" in *Romance of the Woodland Park,* pp. 2–10, Hall listed the American notables to whom he intellectually deferred in the area of park making. They were, in order of Hall's presentation: the landscape gardener Andrew Jackson Downing; Henry Winthrop Sargent, landscape gardening author and editor and owner of "Wodenethe," a rural estate along the Hudson River; Charles Sprague Sargent, horticulturist, director of Harvard's Arnold Arboretum, and editor of *Garden and Forest;* and the landscape architects, Frederick Law Olmsted and Calvert Vaux.

Hall dedicated *The Romance of the Woodland Park* to Olmsted, saying,

> Although he never had business connection with the planning or making of the San Francisco park whose story [this manuscript] tells, his kindly personal advice by letters, commencing years before I met him, with his printed reports and other professional papers, shaped or supported the ideas whereby I planned in 1870–71, and later conducted the basic works and primal developments for that which is now seen as Golden Gate Park. (p. 10)

26. Hall, "The City Woodland Park," pp. 1, 4–5.

27. SFBPC, *Second Biennial Report of the San Francisco Park Commissioners, 1872–73* (San Francisco, 1874), pp. 78–79; Galen Cranz, "Women and Urban Parks: Their Roles as Users and Suppliers of Park Services," in *Building for Women,* ed. S. Keller (Lexington, Mass., 1981), pp. 153–154.

28. William Hammond Hall, "Reclaiming a Waste for a Park," in *Story of a City Park,* p. 1.

29. The estimate on the sea walls is in ibid., p. 4. In "Appendix A: The Report of the Engineer" in SFBPC, *Second Biennial,* pp. 23–26, Hall relates the park staff's knowledge of sand reclamation work on the "sand downs" of France, Denmark, Prussia, Holland, and Great Britain. When Brémontier began his work, the shifting sands along the Bay of Biscay stretched for approximately 150 miles and were several miles in width. The climate is similar to San Francisco's—summer dry. The winds are westerly and fierce. For more on Brémontier and his efforts see George Vivian Poore, "The Story of Brémontier, and the Reclamation of the Sand-Wastes of Gascony," in *Essays on Rural Hygiene,* 2nd ed. (London, 1894), pp. 353–369; and, Pierre Buffault, *Histoire des Dunes Maritimes de la Gascogne* (Bordeaux, 1942). The dune-fixing efforts in Golden Gate Park are also discussed in Ronald Amundson and Brian Tremback, "Olmsted's Law Refuted" *Pacific Horticulture* 50, no. 4 (1989): 52–56.

30. "Appendix A," pp. 38–39 discusses the plants. For introduced species, particularly ornamental ones, see Liberty Hyde Bailey and Ethel Zoe Bailey, *Hortus Third: A Concise Dictionary of Plants Cultivated in the United States and Canada,* rev. ed. (New York, 1976).

31. Ibid., p. 29; Hall, "Reclaiming a Waste," pp. 10–11.

32. Hall, "Reclaiming a Waste," p. 12; SFBPC, *Second Biennial Report,* pp. 9, 19–41; SFBPC, *Third Biennial Report,* pp. 38–40.

33. SFBPC, *Second Biennial Report,* p. 46.

34. Letter from William Hammond Hall to Frederick Law Olmsted, January 15, 1872, Olmsted Papers, pp. 1–2. William Hammond Hall, "The Plan and Purpose of the Avenue," p. 2. An F. A. Miller was elected secretary of the new Bay District Horticultural Society of California in 1870 and was probably the individual of whom Hall wrote. See "Bay District Horticultural Society of California," *California Horticulturist and Floral Magazine* 1, no. 1 (1870), p. 13. Letter from Frederick Law Olmsted to William Hammond Hall, February 20,

1872, Hall Papers, Bancroft Library, pp. 1–2. Charles E. Beveridge, "Introduction," in Frederick Law Olmsted, *Creating Central Park, 1857–1861,* ed. Charles E. Beveridge and David Schuyler, vol. 3 of *The Papers of Frederick Law Olmsted* (Baltimore, 1983), p. 463 notes that this fee is high for the day.

35. Hall to Olmsted, January 26, 1874, pp. 1–2; Olmsted to Hall, February 24, 1874, pp. 2–3; letter from J. M. Cleaveland to Frederick Law Olmsted, February 24, 1874, pp. 1–2; letter from William Hammond Hall to Frederick Law Olmsted, February 5, 1875, p. 1. All in Olmsted Papers.

36. The Poppey quotes are in "Testimony taken before the Assembly Special Committee appointed to investigate the affairs of the Golden Gate Park, San Francisco," in California, *Appendix to the Journals of the Senate and Assembly of the Twenty-First Session of the Legislature of the State of California, Volume 4* (Sacramento, 1876), pp. 130–134. See also Terence Young, "'I am my own authority': The Landscape Gardening of Frederick William Poppey," *Journal of Garden History* 15, no. 4 (1995): 226–230. An important difference between Andrew Jackson Downing and Frederick William Poppey was the latter's disregard for columnar, upright trees and his insistence upon a difference between trees whose foliage tended to hang downward and those that did not, but both relied on gross morphology as the basis for their categorization.

37. Guy Giffen and Helen Giffen, *The Story of Golden Gate Park* (San Francisco, 1949), p. 18. SFBPC, *Second Biennial Report,* pp. 35–38. SFBPC, *Third Biennial Report,* p. 38. While it is possible that the *Eucalyptus globulus* might have been transplanted, it seems unlikely for two reasons. First, there is no discussion of tree moving or tree-moving equipment anywhere in the reports. The effort would have been mentioned, because the cost would have been significant. Second, there were likely few if any trees to transplant. They could have been purchased from nurseries, but if they had come from San Francisco, the local nurserymen would have been less antagonistic. It seems unlikely that the trees could have come from San Jose, since it would have been difficult to ship such large specimens the approximately twenty-mile distance. "Public Improvements," p. 120. The water and fertilizers are mentioned in SFBPC, *Second Biennial Report,* pp. 10–11, 50–51, 54–56.

38. Hall supervised the park nurserymen and directed the gardeners for the first "several years." See William Hammond Hall, "Pioneer Park Works," in *Story of a City Park,* pp. 19–20. The nursery industry's attacks are in January 1871, "Public Parks," p. 111; March 1871, "Public Improvements," pp. 140–141; December 1871, "San Francisco's Park," p. 13; and February 1872, "Editorial Portfolio," *California Horticulturist and Floral Magazine* 2, no. 3 (1872): 81–82.

39. Henry Winthrop Sargent's note about the shortage of specific information is in his "Preface to Sixth Edition," in *A Treatise on the Theory and Practice of Landscape Gardening Adapted to North America; With a View to the Improvement of Country Residences, 6th Edition, With a Supplement by Henry Winthrop Sargent* (New York, 1859), p. xii. Idem, "Supplement to Landscape Gardening," in *A Treatise, 6th Edition,* pp. 540–545.

40. Hall to Olmsted, August 22, 1871, p. 4. The pupil mentioned by Hall in his memorandum was Frank J. Scott. See Hall, "The Plan and Purpose," p. 12. It is possible that Hall developed his tree planting list after reading Scott's, *The Art of Beautifying Suburban Home Grounds of Small Extent* (New York, 1870). Hall was familiar with the book; he quoted Scott in July 1871. In addition, Scott dedicates the book to Andrew Jackson Downing, his "friend

and instructor," uses a typological system similar to Downing's, and discusses some of the species named in the Giffens' list. Specifically, they are the Norway maple, sycamore, English yew, Austrian pine, elder, alders, cottonwood, and oaks. However, Hall certainly did not develop his selection solely from Scott. Scott's book was relatively new and the author did not have the reputation of Downing, and Scott provided no more cultural information than Downing and less than Sargent offered in his appendix to the edited Downing. There is no section in Scott's book on the cultivation of plants by region or in general. When such information is provided for a particular genus or species, it is usually limited to a few words. Finally, on p. 575 Scott specifically recommends against planting English yews in windy, exposed situations. If Hall had read Scott closely for his horticultural information, he might not have planted yews on the site.

41. The Monterey cypress is included in H. W. Sargent, "Supplement," p. 541. It was not recommended, as it was too tender in the northeastern U.S. areas where it had been test grown. Andrew Jackson Downing, *A Treatise, 6th Edition,* p. 117–121. I cite this 1859 edition because it is the last definitive revision until 1921 and the one most likely read by Hall. It included major deletions, Sargent's supplement, and material on New York's Central Park. Hall may have referred to 1865's seventh edition rather than this one but the only difference between them is one additional plate in the latter. The texts are identical.

42. Ibid., p. 248.

43. SFBPC, *Second Biennial Report,* p. 52.

44. SFBPC, *Third Biennial Report,* p. 18.

## 4    THE PUBLIC REACTS TO ITS NEW PARK

1. The comment about visitor approval is quoted in William Hammond Hall, "Early Use of Golden Gate Park," in *The Story of a City Park,* unpublished manuscript (ca. 1919), William Hammond Hall Papers, Bancroft Library, University of California, Berkeley, p. 2. The first visitor numbers are in San Francisco Board of Park Commissioners (SFBPC), *Second Biennial Report of the San Francisco Park Commissioners, 1872–73* (San Francisco, 1874), p. 6. According to United States, Bureau of the Census, *Ninth Census, Volume I: The Statistics of the Population of the United States* (Washington, D.C., 1872), p. 14, the approximate population of San Francisco at the time was 150,000. The later visitor numbers are in SFBPC, *Third Biennial Report of the San Francisco Park Commissioners, 1874–75* (San Francisco, 1875), p. 14. Of course, not everyone thought the park perfect. Charles Donohue, a September 1880 tourist from Jersey City, found it unimpressive. "The Park seems to be but little, but as the season of the year was bad it may excuse the look but it seems to me no season can make it much." In "Diary of a Trip to California," unpublished manuscript, Huntington Library, San Marino, Calif., p. 29, September 18, 1880.

2. The 1873 visitor figures are from SFBPC, *Second Biennial Report,* p. 15, while the 1875 visitor figures are from SFBPC, *Third Biennial Report,* p. 14. The latter report broke down the visitors by mode of transport. The categories were "Carriages, Double Buggies, Single Buggies, Equestrians," and "Pedestrians." Raymond H. Clary, *The Making of Golden Gate Park: The Early Years, 1865–1906* (San Francisco, 1984), p. 34, reports that the total number of visitors for 1877 was 703,658 of which 17,259 were pedestrians, but it does not list the source of the statistic.

Robert McClure, *The Gentleman's Stable Guide* (Philadelphia, 1870), pp. 11–15, sets the total value of the approximately 8,000,000 American horses at between $2 billion and $3 billion. While a very fast, well-bred horse might fetch $75,000 at the time, McClure estimates the value of the three million horses that were "stylish in action and well adapted for general wagon and road purposes" at $300 to $2,000 each and the five million that were "most useful . . . the horse of slow work" at $50 to $200 each. Henry G. Langley, *Langley's City Guide Map and Street Directory, 1870, San Francisco* (San Francisco, 1870), p. 77, lists the city-regulated hack and cab fares. The majority of the city's population was approximately one-half to four miles from the edge of Golden Gate Park, so the fare for two or more people would have been between $1.50 and $4.00 each way. Since the per capita income for 1870 was approximately $165, owning a horse, even an inexpensive one, or hiring a carriage was well beyond the means of most people. See *Historical Statistics of the United States: Colonial Times to 1957* (Washington, D.C., 1962), p. 139, for income figures.

3. Clary, *The Early Years*, p. 38. The annual per capita income in the United States between 1872 and 1876 was $171. United States Bureau of the Census, *Historical Statistics of the United States: Colonial Times to 1957* (Washington, D.C., 1960), p. 139. The history of San Francisco's transportation system between 1850 and 1880 is described in Edgar M. Kahn, *Cable Car Days in San Francisco* (Stanford, Calif., 1944), pp. 8–56; John Bernard McGloin, *San Francisco: The Story of a City* (San Rafael, Calif., 1978), pp. 118–130; and, Oscar Lewis, *San Francisco: Mission to Metropolis* (San Diego, 1980), p. 115 ff. The caustic comment about the lack of transport comes from "Editorial Portfolio," *California Horticulturist and Floral Magazine* 2 no. 3 (1872), p. 81. Hall quote is in SFBPC, *Third Biennial Report,* p. 19.

4. Amy Bridges, "Journal Kept on 4th Raymond Excursion to Colorado, New Mexico and California," unpublished manuscript, Huntington Library, San Marino, California, [p.159], March 21, 1887. Hill grades are generally given in percentages: a 10 percent grade translates into a 10-foot vertical rise for every 100 feet of horizontal distance. U.S. railroads generally restrict their grades to between 1 and 3 percent. The Hall description is from William Hammond Hall, "Ten Dark Park Years—1876–'86," in *The Romance of a Woodland Park,* unpublished manuscript (ca. 1926), Hall papers, pp. 14, 16.

5. Cemetery Avenue was also known as Lott Avenue during the 1870s. Kahn, *Cable Car Days*, pp. 14, 20, 41–42, 54–55; A. L. Bancroft and Company, *Bancroft's Guide Map of the City and County of San Francisco* (San Francisco, 1873); and Langley, *Langley's City Guide*, p. 80, all identify the public transportation routes. The description of the walk from the Eddy Street terminus to the park is in Clary, *The Early Years*, p. 13. "Golden Gate Park," *Daily Morning Call,* December 12, 1875.

6. It is unclear why the Geary Street, Park and Ocean Railroad decided to run a steam line out to the park in 1880. According to Lewis, *San Francisco*, p. 115, steam trolleys had been in use in San Francisco since at least 1860, so it may have been that the company felt there was or would soon be adequate riders. Alternatively, they may have planned to sell land along their line, or perhaps the cost of constructing and running a line had come down sufficiently in twenty years to make such a line profitable. The quote on the success of this railroad is from Hall, "Ten Dark Park Years," p. 15. According to San Francisco Board of Supervisors (SFBS), *Municipal Reports for The Fiscal Year 1880–1881, Ending June 30, 1881* (San Francisco, 1881), p. 188, the park recorded 1,608,912 visitors during the fiscal year. The arrival of the Market Street Cable Railway Company is also from Clary, *The Early Years*, p. 61. A San

Francisco cable-wire manufacturer, Andrew Hallidie, invented the cable car for use on the city's steep hills. Lewis, *San Francisco,* p. 156, tells us that their use began in October 1873.

7. William Hammond Hall, "First Five Years of Work," in *Romance of a Woodland Park,* p. 2.

8. *Daily Morning Call,* August 7, 1872. The 1869 editorial is quoted in ibid., p. 3.

9. *Daily Evening Bulletin,* October 23, 1872, and January 25, 1873. The park also struck a positive cord with the English writer Anthony Trollope, who visited San Francisco in summer 1875. He was touring, writing a series of articles for Liverpool's *Weekly Mercury.* The November 11, 1875, issue derides the city but finds the park promising. "I do not know that in all my travels I ever visited a city less interesting to the normal tourist. . . . There is almost nothing to see in San Francisco . . . [However,] there is a new park in which you may drive for six or seven miles on a well-made road, and which, as a park for the use of a city, will, when completed, have many excellencies." Quoted in Oscar Lewis, *This Was San Francisco* (New York, 1962), pp. 179–180.

10. *San Francisco Chronicle,* October 24, 1875.

11. "Public Parks," *California Horticulturist and Floral Magazine* 1, no. 4 (1871), p. 111. The Hall quote is from William Hammond Hall, "Pioneer Park Works," in *Story of a City Park,* p. 19. The links between the three magazines is "Pioneer Park Works," p. 18.

12. The value of dune fixing is mentioned in "Public Parks," *California Horticulturist and Floral Magazine,* p. 111. The call for experiments is in "Public Improvements," *California Horticulturist and Floral Magazine* 1, no. 5 (1871), p. 140. The condemnation of the commissioners and the superintendent by the *California Horticulturist* was merciless and frequent. See, for example, "Our City Parks," 1, no. 7 (1871), pp. 202–203; "San Francisco's Park," 2, no. 1 (1871), p. 13; "Editorial Portfolio," 2, no. 3 (1872), pp. 81–82; "San Francisco's Park," 2, no. 3 (1872), pp. 89–90; "Our Public Grounds," 2, no. 4 (1872), pp. 115–116; "The Golden Gate Park," 2, no. 4 (1872), pp. 119–120; "Golden Gate Park," 2, no. 5 (1872), pp. 150–151; and "Grasses for Fixing a Shifting Soil," 2, no. 9 (1872), pp. 266–267.

13. Hall, "Pioneer Park Works," p. 20. The nurseries are listed in the self-published Thomas A. Brown, *A List of California Nurseries and Their Catalogs, 1850–1900* (1982), pp. xiii–xiv.

14. Hall, "Pioneer Park Works," p. 21. "Public Improvements," *California Horticulturist and Floral Magazine* 2, no. 4 (1872), p. 119.

15. The Pollyanna quote is in "Golden Gate Park," *California Horticulturist and Floral Magazine* 2, no. 5 (1872), p. 150. The call for more sand-dune grass experiments is in "Grasses for Fixing a Shifting Dune," *California Horticulturist and Floral Magazine* 2, no. 9 (1872), p. 266–267. The demonstration near Strawberry Hill is noted in William Hammond Hall, "Sand Dune Reclamation," in *Romance of a Woodland Park,* p. 10.

16. "Golden Gate Park," *California Horticulturist and Floral Magazine* 4, no. 5 (1874), pp. 143–144.

17. Hall, "The Civic Shake-Up of 1875–76," in *Romance of a Woodland Park,* p. 8. See Gunther Barth, *Instant Cities: Urbanization and the Rise of San Francisco and Denver* (New York, 1875), p. 142, on the economic character of San Francisco during the early 1870s. Lewis F. Byington and Oscar Lewis, eds. *The History of San Francisco* (Chicago, 1931) quote on p. 333, see also pp. 342–345.

18. Hittell is quoted in Byington and Lewis, *History of San Francisco,* pp. 333–334. Their

comment is on p. 346. They also note on p. 337 that between 1873 and 1878 the Consolidated Virginia produced $100,000,000 worth of silver. Again, the $1,000 per capita loss needs to be seen in comparison with the annual per capita income in the United States—approximately $171. United States Bureau of the Census, *Historical Statistics*, p. 139.

19. On the failure of the bank see Byington and Lewis, *History of San Francisco*, pp. 337–338, 345; and John P. Young, *San Francisco: A History of the Pacific Coast Metropolis* (San Francisco, 1912), pp. 504–506. The figures are from Terrence McDonald, *The Parameters of Urban Fiscal Policy: Socioeconomic Change and Political Culture in San Francisco, 1860–1906* (Berkeley, 1986), p. 146.

20. According to SFBPC, *Third Biennial Report*, p. 12, $447,705.62 in park bonds were sold between May 3, 1870, and November 30, 1875. The park's other sources of income, for example interest accounts, collectively provided only $5,128.12 during the same period. McDonald, *Parameters*, describes this time as a period when San Francisco politics was reduced to a series of attempts to prove that one's party and one's self were less likely to tax and spend than one's opponents. On p. 40 McDonald characterizes the political mentality: "a low tax rate was the 'Moses and the Prophets' of politicians . . . and the party that did not condemn governmental 'extravagance' and pledge to lower the rate even further was rare indeed." The original park legislation had authorized the City and County of San Francisco to issue bonds at the request of the commissioners. See SFBPC, *Statutes, Ordinances, and Laws* (San Francisco, 1889), p. 44.

21. According to *List of Constitutional Officers, Congressional Representatives, Members of the California State Legislature and Members of the Supreme Court, 1849–1985* (Sacramento, [1986]), pp. 32, 128, D. C. Sullivan served only during the twenty-first session of the Assembly (Dec. 6, 1875–Apr. 3, 1876). The hearings are recorded in California, "Testimony taken before the Assembly Special Committee appointed to investigate the affairs of the Golden Gate Park, San Francisco," in *Appendix to the Journals of the Senate and Assembly of the Twenty-First Session of the Legislature of the State of California, Volume 4* (Sacramento, 1876), pp. 1–160; the park board's response is in SFBPC, *To His Excellency William Irwin, Governor of the State of California, From the Park Commissioners of San Francisco* (San Francisco, 1876).

22. The fiscal data come from SFBPC, *Third Biennial Report*, p. 11; and from the SFBS, *Municipal Reports* of 1875–1889 as follows: 1875, pp. 230–231; 1876, p. 206; 1877, pp. 159 (also includes the vote on the legislature's change of the tax rate and the quote on the horses) and 161; 1878, p. 408 (includes the gift); 1879, p. 90; 1880, pp. 614 (the gift and its purpose) and 619; 1881, p. 190; 1882, p. 250; 1883, p. 614; 1884, p. 176; 1885, p. 185; 1886, p. 41; 1887, p. 272; 1888, p. 364; and 1889, p. 813. The $125,000 figure is mentioned in Hall, "The Civic Shake-Up," p. 12. Hall has different fiscal information in "Ten Dark Park Years," p. 3 for 1876 through 1880 because he included only the expenditures for sand reclamation, tree planting, maintenance of plantations and roads, and park guards. Among other things he omitted the salaries of the management and the cost of water. According to SFBPC, *Third Biennial Report*, p. 16, the park was using approximately 14,000,000 gallons of water per year at the time. Michael Black, "Searching for a Genius of Place: The Ambiguous Legacy of Golden Gate Park," in *The Environmental Spirit: Past, Present, and Prospects: Conference Proceedings, University of California, Berkeley, 1995* (Berkeley, 1995), pp. 139–141, tells us that much of the water had to be purchased, undoubtedly a major expense. On p. 138, Black indicates why it is not sur-

prising that Hall failed to include the cost of the water in his figures. "Little mention was made of [water] in Hall's writings and in routine reports offered by Park Commissioners themselves. Water was simply viewed as a necessity which one never questioned." The gift of the Conservatory is discussed in Hall, "Ten Dark Park Years," p. 6; and, *Daily Alta California*, January 1, 1878, and April 24, 1878.

23. It is not clear if the governor tried to entice Hall back. William Hammond Hall, "After the Dark Decade," in *Romance of a Woodland Park*, p. 19.

24. Hennessey's temper is noted in Tom Girvan Aikman, *Boss Gardener: The Life and Times of John McLaren* (San Francisco, 1988), p. 53. Letter from Frederick Law Olmsted to William Hammond Hall, December 7, 1874, Hall Papers, Bancroft Library, p. 1; Hall had first expressed his distrust in his letter to Olmsted on November 26, 1874, and then again on December 18, 1874, Frederick Law Olmsted Papers, Manuscripts Division, Library of Congress.

25. *Daily Alta California*, August 17, 1879. *Daily Evening Bulletin*, May 2, 1879.

26. On the belief that parks prevent disease see John H. Rauch, *Public Parks: Their Effects Upon the Moral, Physical and Sanitary Condition of the Inhabitants of Large Cities* (Chicago, 1869), p. 30; and, Frederick Law Olmsted, *Public Parks and the Enlargement of Towns* (New York, 1970 [1870]), pp. 14–15. A reference to miasmas is noted in SFBPC, *Second Biennial Report*, p. 63. The quote on invalids is from "Public Parks," *California Horticulturist and Floral Magazine* 1, no. 2 (December 1870), p. 54. The report linking climate with health is in SFBS, *San Francisco Municipal Reports, for the Fiscal Year 1866–7, Ending June 30, 1867* (San Francisco, 1867), p. 266.

27. See, for example, *Daily Evening Bulletin*, January 25, 1873. The quote is from "Public Parks" (1870), p. 54. Olmsted, Vaux & Co., "Preliminary Report in Regard to A Plan of Public Pleasure Grounds for the City of San Francisco," in Frederick Law Olmsted, *The California Frontier, 1863–1865*, ed. Victoria Post Ranney, vol. 5 of *The Papers of Frederick Law Olmsted* (Baltimore, 1990), p. 522.

28. *Daily Alta California*, November 18, 1865, p. 2. *Daily Morning Call*, December 12, 1875.

29. B. E. Lloyd, *Lights and Shades in San Francisco* (San Francisco, 1876), p. 355.

30. Roy Rosenzweig and Elizabeth Blackmar, *The Park and the People: A History of Central Park* (Ithaca, 1992), p. 87. They also note that the rising prices and speculation drove poorer property owners off these sites, because their property taxes were linked to market values. We must assume the same for San Francisco. The quote from Frederick Law Olmsted's August 4, 1865, letter to the *Daily Evening Bulletin* is reproduced as "The Project of a Great Park for San Francisco," in *California Frontier*, pp. 426–427. The prohibition against discounting and the quote on appreciation are in SFBPC, *First Biennial Report*, pp. 4–5. The report goes on to note that bonds worth a total of $225,000 were offered and that the prohibition "prevented the sale of the full amount." See also "Editorial Gleanings," *California Horticulturist and Floral Magazine* 1, no. 4 (February 1871), p. 122. Seligman's property in the Outside Lands is mentioned in "Reminiscences of Golden Gate Park," unpublished manuscript, William Hammond Hall Papers, Bancroft Library, University of California, Berkeley, p. 6. Clary, *The Early Years*, p. 12, discusses Seligman as the only bidder on the bonds. P. J. Sullivan, "Homes For All: Catalogue of Choice Residence Lots in the Vicinity of Golden Gate Park, to be Sold at Auction on Tuesday, March 2d, 1880 at 8 o'clock P.M. . . . by P. J. Sullivan, Real Estate Agent . . . H. A. Cobb & Co., Auctioneers" (San Francisco, 1880), p. 1.

31. See Olmsted, "The Project," p. 427, on the link between the enhanced tax base and the cost of constructing a park. SFBPC, *Second Biennial Report,* p. 3. See also "Parks," *California Horticulturist and Floral Magazine* 1, no. 7 (1871), p. 202.

32. SFBPC, *Second Biennial Report,* pp. 63–64.

33. *Daily Morning Call,* December 12, 1875.

34. *Daily Evening Bulletin* 25 January 1873.

35. "The Park and Moral Reform," in *Scrapbook* (ca. 1873), Hall Papers, Bancroft Library, p. 6.

## 5   RATIONALISTIC GOLDEN GATE PARK

1. This period's politics commonly included some sort of antirailroad sentiments. William Deverell, *Railroad Crossing: Californians and the Railroad, 1850–1910* (Berkeley, 1994), pp. 60, 194, explains that both the Republican gubernatorial candidate, Morris Estee, as well as the winner, Stoneman, ran on antirailroad platforms. "Stoneman, in part because of his reputation as an (if not the only) honest commissioner from the new railroad commission, won easily." See W. A. Bullough, *The Blind Boss and His City: Christopher Augustine Buckley and Nineteenth Century San Francisco* (Berkeley, 1979).

2. Deverell, *Railroad,* pp. 131, 233 notes that the Southern Pacific Railroad was paying Pixley upwards of $10,000 per year until the late 1880s. Collis P. Huntington cut his corporate support before 1890 but Leland Stanford continued to pay Pixley personally. The story of Alvord's resignation is in Raymond Clary, *The Making of Golden Gate Park: The Early Years, 1865–1906* (San Francisco, 1984), p. 48.

3. The quote from the foreman is in Clary, *The Early Years,* p. 52. For more on the Park and Ocean Railroad, see Walter Rice and Emiliano Echeverria, "When Steam Ran on the Streets of San Francisco," *Live Steam* (November–December 1999): 48–54. McDowell was no longer on the board that Stoneman sought to replace. He had resigned in January 1885. McDowell was replaced by Charles Goodall, a business partner of George Perkins. See William Issel and Robert Cherny, *San Francisco, 1865–1932: Politics, Power, and Urban Development* (Berkeley, 1986), p. 33, on the relationship between Perkins and Goodall.

4. William Hammond Hall, "Forming a Park Commission," *The Story of a City Park,* unpublished manuscript (ca. 1919), William Hammond Hall Papers, Bancroft Library, University of California, Berkeley, pp. 1–2.

5. The intrigue surrounding the creation of a new board was byzantine in its complexity. A detailed account is in ibid., pp. 1–24. The Hall quote is on p. 10. William T. Coleman's life is detailed in a laudatory account by James A. B. Scherer, *"The Lion of the Vigilantes": William T. Coleman And The Life of Old San Francisco* (New York, 1939). Background on Joseph Austin and William Dimond is in Clary, *The Early Years,* p. 57.

6. Clary, *The Early Years,* p. 69.

7. Tom Girvan Aikman, *Boss Gardener: Life and Times of John McLaren* (San Francisco, 1988), pp. 22–23. This book is as much a family history as biography; the author is a descendant of McLaren.

8. Ibid., pp. 24–50. The connection between Howard and Olmsted is in Victoria Post Ranney, "Introduction," in Frederick Law Olmsted, *The California Frontier, 1863–1865,* ed. Victoria Post Ranney, vol. 5 of *The Papers of Frederick Law Olmsted* (Baltimore, 1990), p. 33.

George Henry Howard died in 1878; his widow, Agnes, married Henry Pike Bowie the following year, remained on the estate, and McLaren continued to work there. See Mitchell P. Postel, *San Mateo: A Centennial History* (San Francisco, 1994), p. 23.

9. McLaren was a complex, influential, and enduring character in San Francisco. See Roy L. Hudson, "John McLaren As I Knew Him," *California Horticultural Journal* 31, no. 2 (1970): 48; Clary, *The Early Years,* pp. 76–77. McLaren's landscape skills were highly admired outside of the park and San Francisco. McLaren's 1909 book, *Gardening in California, Landscape and Flower,* was so well received that it went through at least three editions in the following years. Aikman, *Boss Gardener,* p. 57, recognized that McLaren had political skills. According to him, McLaren's "greatest contribution of course was keeping politics out of the Park! 'What do politicians know about gardening?' he would snort!" McLaren's control over employment led many people, even the former superintendent, William Hammond Hall, to ask McLaren to favor them, a relative, or a friend with a job. See such a letter from William Hammond Hall to John McLaren, November 25, 1889, Hall Papers, Bancroft Library. In 1917, when McLaren reached the mandatory retirement age of seventy, the Board of Supervisors passed legislation that permitted him to remain superintendent of parks as long as he lived. He was still working when he died in 1943 at the age of 96. Since McLaren would never be able to collect his pension, the board also doubled his salary for life. See Clary, *The Early years,* p. 77. In the rationalistic period, the parks in many American cities continued to have appointed commissioners or departmental heads, but the locus of the real authority came to rest in the park's superintendent and his staff, many of whom were experts with formal training in such fields as landscape architecture, ornamental horticulture, museum directing, and civil engineering.

10. The increasing fragmentation of Golden Gate Park's landscape also prompted a growth in the park's bureaucracy. A comparison of a park report from the beginning of the rationalistic period with one from its end indicates that the number of park bureaucrats grew and the span of control for each shrank as the level of spatial and organizational specialization increased. For example, the San Francisco Board of Park Commissioners (SFBPC), *Twentieth Annual Report for The Year Ending June 30, 1891* (San Francisco, 1891), pp. 8–9, noted the following organizational subdivisions, each presumably with its own supervisor and associated employees: structures, waterworks, drainage, drives, grounds, forests, conservatory, police, nursery, and play area, and that was within Golden Gate Park alone. In contrast, the *Fifty-fourth Annual Report* (San Francisco, 1924), pp. 60–68, is divided between "small parks and squares" and "Golden Gate Park," and then the latter section is further subdivided into the museum, music concerts, grounds, drives, stock and implements, conservatory, nursery, stables, play area, miscellaneous, administration (including a chauffeur for McLaren), structures, water works, stadium, aquarium, forests, tennis courts and club house, beach chalet, and the "Herbert Fleischhacker Play Field." For further explanation of the connection between the segmentation of modern societies and their built environments, see chapter 1 in George Ritzer, *The McDonaldization of Society* (Thousand Oaks, Calif., 1993); and Robert David Sack, *Human Territoriality: Its Theory and History* (New York, 1986). SFBPC, *Twenty-Fourth Annual Report for The Year Ending June 30, 1895* (San Francisco, 1895), p. 19.

11. See "Inventory of Plants in the Golden Gate Park Nursery, June 1882," William Hammond Hall Collection, Helen Crocker Russell Library, San Francisco. The number of species

was undoubtedly higher in this and later records, because many genera are listed as "in variety," for example, "Euonymus in variety." From the types of genera involved in the inventory and the obviously field-written marginalia beside various species, I estimate that the nursery contained no fewer than 250 species and their cultivars at the time of the inventory. These botanical and common names are modern ones.

12. SFBPC, *Eighteenth Annual Report* (San Francisco, 1889), pp. 35–40; SFBPC, *Twenty-Eighth Annual Report for The Year Ending June 30, 1899* (San Francisco, 1899), pp. 37–44; SFBPC, *Fifty-Fourth Annual Report,* pp. 69–82. See San Francisco Board of Supervisors (SFBS), *Municipal Reports for The Fiscal Year 1881–82, Ending June 30, 1882* (San Francisco, 1882), p. 246, on the nursery. Vilmorin-Andrieux & Cie, "Facture d'envoi fait a' M Park Commissioners, San Francisco," January 14, 1888, Carl Poch Collections, Helen Crocker Russell Library, San Francisco. The letters are from John McLaren to Francesco Franchesci, Camillo F. Franchesci, or Franchesci's Montarioso Nursery, bought after he sold the Southern California Acclimatizing Association in 1908 to a former partner: December 14, 1904, January 16, 1906, March 8, 1906, June 12, 1911, February 13, 1912, November 7, 1913, and November 14, 1913, Franchesci Papers, Bancroft Library. According to Victoria Padilla, *Southern California Gardens: An Illustrated History* (Santa Barbara, 1994), much of this nursery's reputation rested upon the diverse selection it developed through a steady introduction of exotic species into California. Hudson, "John McLaren," p. 47. George A. Burnap, *Parks: Their Design, Equipment and Use* (Philadelphia, 1916), p. 222. SFBPC, *Fifty-Fourth Annual Report,* pp. 52–53.

13. For an example from the period and place, see "The Bedding-Out System," *California Horticulturist and Floral Magazine* 1, no. 9 (1871): 285–286. The history of the use of flowering annual plants in beds is complicated by the variety of terminology. "Carpet bedding," "the bedding system," "picturesque bedding," "ribbon bedding," "mosaiculture," and other terms have, at times, been casually interchanged by garden writers. For the clearest explications of these terms see Brent Elliot, "Mosaiculture: Its Origins and Significance," *Garden History* 9 (Spring 1981): 76–98; Brent Elliot, *Victorian Gardens* (London, 1986); Ann Leighton, *American Gardens of the Nineteenth Century* (Amherst, 1987), pp. 241–248; and, David Stuart, *The Garden Triumphant: A Victorian Legacy* (New York, 1988), 111–145.

14. William Hammond Hall, "Another Forest Management Controversy," in *Story of a City Park,* p. 4.

15. SFBPC, *Twenty-Fourth Annual Report,* p. 13.

16. William Hammond Hall, "The Memorial Museum," in *Story of a City Park,* p. 16, concurred with the value of museums in locations outside parks, where they, "would have made another and separate attraction for the City and been of greater advantage to its people." The emphasis on order and revivalist architecture within the naturalistic setting of a park shows how similar were the concerns of rationalistic park proponents to those of the larger City Beautiful movement that arose across America at about the same time. In both instances, activists believed that the "Good Society" was a function of good environments. See William H. Wilson, *The City Beautiful Movement* (Baltimore, 1989), pp. 86–95, on the architectural aesthetics of the City Beautiful movement. Tunnard is quoted on p. 88 of Wilson.

17. On the attendance and collections of the museum see "Third in Size in America, Memorial Museum Eight Years Old To-Day and Stands High in Rank," *San Francisco Chronicle,* March 23, 1903, p. 5; On the original proposals to build a museum in the park see Hall,

"The Memorial Museum," p. 7; and, "Golden Gate Park, Improvements Made and Suggested," *San Francisco Chronicle*, January 30, 1887, p. 4.

18. De Young was vice president of the National Commission at the Columbian Exposition as well as commissioner of the California exhibit, and according to *The Official Guide to the California Midwinter Exposition* (San Francisco, 1894), p. 19, he had been a U.S. commissioner to the Paris Exposition in 1889. The history of the fair comes from Marjorie C. Driscoll, *The M. H. de Young Memorial Museum* (San Francisco, 1921), pp. 10–11; and, Arthur Chandler and Marvin Nathan, *The Fantastic Fair: The Story of the California Midwinter International Exposition Golden Gate Park, San Francisco, 1894* (San Francisco, 1993), pp. 1–6.

19. Chandler and Nathan, *Fantastic Fair*, pp. 5–6. Clary, *The Early Years*, pp. 111–112. On Mayor Ellert's role see Melvin G. Holli and Peter d'A. Jones, *Biographical Dictionary of American Mayors, 1820–1980* (Westport, Conn., 1981), pp. 109–110.

20. De Young also planned to benefit indirectly from the fair. According to Gray Brechin, *Imperial San Francisco: Urban Power, Earthly Ruin* (Berkeley, 1999), p. 181, de Young "owned all or major parts of thirty-one blocks in the dunes south of the park and a lesser but still considerable amount of sand north of it. These properties constituted hundreds of lots whose value would skyrocket when buyers were assured of access and nearby attractions, which the Midwinter Fair was designed to provide." McLaren's views on the fair are recorded in Chandler and Nathan, *Fantastic Fair*, p. 5. He was correct in his prediction of the physical harm that would come to the park during the fair. "New Threat to the Park" in Raymond H. Clary, *The Making of Golden Gate Park: The Growing Years, 1906–1950* (San Francisco, 1987), pp. 37–41, reports on the attempt to hold the 1915 Panama-Pacific Exposition in the west end of Golden Gate Park. That effort was repulsed and the fair was held in the area that became the Marina District. The Stow–de Young debate is recorded in the *San Francisco Call*, July 14, 1893, p. 4. The story of other resistors is in Clary, *The Early Years*, pp. 112–113.

21. The dismissive comments by the fair advocates are from *Official Guide*, p. 21. The account of the use of Union Square is in an editorial in *Daily Evening Bulletin*, January 14, 1868, p. 2. The comparison of Jackson Park to Golden Gate Park is in *Official History of the California Midwinter International Exposition* (San Francisco, 1895), p. 5.

22. The official designation date is from *Official Guide*, p. 22. The final attendance and profits are from Chandler and Nathan, *Fantastic Fair*, p. 77. Total receipts were $1,260,112.19, while total disbursements were $1,193, 260.70. Paid attendance was 1,315,002 and 904,148 entered free. Information about the destruction of the buildings and the quote about McLaren's delight are from Chandler and Nathan, *Fantastic Fair*, p. 69.

23. Marsh developed real estate in the area north of Golden Gate Park. He called it the "Richmond District" after a suburb of his native city, Melbourne, Australia. The origins and design of the Tea Garden have been a point of cultural contest for decades. See the intriguing and insightful account by Kendall H. Brown, "Rashomon: The Multiple Histories of the Japanese Tea Garden at Golden Gate Park," *Studies in the History of Gardens and Designed Landscapes* 18, no. 2 (1998): 93–119. For more standard histories see Robert J. Morey, "Japanese Tea Garden" *California Horticultural Journal* 31, no. 2 (1970): 52–59, 73; Tanso Ishihara, *The Japanese Tea Garden in Golden Gate Park (1893–1942)* (San Francisco, 1979); Chandler and Nathan, *Fantastic Fair*, p. 42.

24. Chandler and Nathan, *Fantastic Fair*, p. 56. The use of Egyptian motifs is from Leland M. Roth, *A Concise History of American Architecture* (New York, 1979), pp. 117–118. Richard G. Carrott, *The Egyptian Revival: Its Sources, Monuments and Meaning, 1808–1858* (Berkeley, 1978), p. 3, considers the period 1808 to 1858 to be the central period of Egyptian revival. He notes that there were later revivals in the United States and abroad but calls them "merely a few isolated instances of the picturesque, or, at least, of the attention-attracting. They cannot be considered as a serious part of the Revival." Many of the Fine Arts Building's art object remained, donated after the fair concluded. SFBPC, *Twenty-Fourth Annual Report* (San Francisco, 1895), p. 10. The Stow and de Young quotes are from Driscoll, *de Young Memorial Museum*, p. 12.

25. The exchange between de Young and Stow is in Driscoll, *de Young Memorial Museum*, p. 12. It is not known how much Stow truly resisted de Young's entreaties, since W. H. Hall's characterization of Stow stands in sharp contrast to de Young's. According to Hall, "The Outlook for Golden Gate Park," *The Romance of a Woodland Park*, unpublished manuscript, William Hammond Hall Papers, Bancroft Library, p. 13, Stow regularly "spoke of the desirability of having museums and libraries in . . . parks." Stow died on February 11, 1895. His death and the acceptance of the museum are recorded in SFBPC, *Twenty-Fourth Annual Report*, pp. 11 and 9–10, respectively. President Austin's speech is on p. 10 of the same report. The second and third buildings, the renaming, and the date of the original building's demolition can be found in Chandler and Nathan, *Fantastic Fair*, pp. 10, 75; and, Driscoll, *M. H. de Young*, p. 9, 19–20.

26. SFBPC, *Fifty-Fourth Annual Report*, pp. 18–20. See SFBPC, *Forty-Second Annual Report*, ed. Hugh M. Burke (San Francisco, 1912), p. 33, on the agreement to build the Academy of Sciences across Conservatory Valley from the M. H. de Young Memorial Museum. According to Clary, *The Growing Years*, p. 31, 63, the money for the Steinhart Aquarium, a part of the Academy of Sciences, was given as a gift in 1910 and the structure was built in 1917.

27. The national primacy of the playground is from Randolph Delehanty, "San Francisco Parks and Playgrounds, 1829–1990: The History of a Public Good in One North American City" (Ph.D. diss., Harvard University, 1992), p. 286. The quote is from Oscar Lewis, *San Francisco: Mission to Metropolis* (San Diego, 1980), p. 112. On the history of the politics leading up to the construction of the building and grounds see Hall, "Special Park Parts," *Romance of a Woodland Park*, pp. 1-7.

At about the same time, J. L. Meares, San Francisco's Public Health Officer, was arguing for a playground before the San Francisco Board of Supervisors, "Health Officer's Report" *San Francisco Municipal Reports, for the fiscal year 1885–6, Ending June 30, 1886* (San Francisco, 1886), p. 375. He connected playgrounds to the virtues of public health and especially to social coherence. Following a line of reasoning that would become more common in the early twentieth century, Meares wrote that playgrounds would mean that San Francisco "would have fewer 'hoodlums,' and many children would be saved from the disgrace and ruin of a commitment to our so-called reformatory institutions, where more are educated by bad association to be confirmed criminals than are ever reformed."

28. The Avenue, which was one block wide, extended eight blocks east from the park proper. SFBPC, *Souvenir Programme* (San Francisco, 1888), pp. [1–2] is a program from the opening day activities. Clary, *The Early Years*, pp. 86, 88, 90, discusses the making of the site

and the Children's Quarter's amenities. SFBPC, *Twenty-Fourth Annual Report*, p. 14, gives a brief summary of the activities available in 1891. Heath Schenker, "Women's and Children's Quarters in Golden Gate Park, San Francisco" *Gender, Place, and Culture* 3, no. 3 (1996): 293–308, offers an intriguing analysis of the design and use of the playground by gender and age.

29. SFBPC, *Souvenir Programme*, p. [2]. Fred Emerson Brooks, "Sharon Quarters," in SFBPC, *Souvenir*, p. [1]. The sentiment of the poem—social differences are eliminated on the playground—also was formally argued by the Director of Gymnastics, Athletics, and Playgrounds for Chicago's South Park system, E. B. De Groot, in "Nationalities May Be United in Rational Recreation," in *American Playgrounds*, 2nd ed., ed. Everett B. Mero (Washington, D.C., 1909), pp. 287–288.

30. SFBPC, *Fifty-Fourth Annual Report*, p. 15. Charles S. Greene, "The Parks of San Francisco," *Overland Monthly* 17, no. 99 (1891): 236–237. According to *Who Was Who in America, Volume 1: 1897–1942* (Chicago, 1943), p. 482, Greene (1856–1930) lived in Berkeley, California, and graduated from the University of California in 1886. He went on from there to hold various editorial posts with the *Overland Monthly* from 1887 to 1899. He became the librarian of the Oakland (California) Free Library in 1899 and remained so until 1926. He wrote many poems, descriptive articles, reviews, editorials, etc. in the *Overland Monthly*, the *Californian*, the *Argonaut*, and other publications. His criticism of the Sharon Building may have arisen from his interest in young people; his children's literature was well regarded.

31. SFBPC, *Twenty-Sixth Annual Report for The Year Ending June 30, 1899* (San Francisco, 1897), p. 22.

32. Ibid., p. 22. See also Stephen Hardy, *How Boston Played: Sport, Recreation and Community, 1865–1915* (Boston, 1982) on how sports encouraged competition and cooperation.

33. SFBPC, *Fifty-Fourth Annual Report*, p. 27.

34. According to Galen Cranz, "Women in Urban Parks" *Signs* 5, no. 3 (1980): pp. S81–S83, basketball, croquet, and boating were also popular women's activities in Golden Gate Park. In a colder climate, like New York, women ice skated as well. See also Donald J. Mrozek, *Sport and American Mentality* (Knoxville, 1983), pp. 136–160. The bicycle ridership is mentioned in *San Francisco Examiner*, August 12, 1895; and, SFBPC, *Twenty-Fourth Annual Report*, p. 19; SFBPC, *Thirty-First Annual Report for The Year Ending June 30, 1902* (San Francisco, 1902), p. 22. According to Clary, *The Early Years*, p. 146, handball, golf, and other sports enthusiasts "immediately . . . demanded equal space in the park" after the administration built tennis courts.

35. Clary, *The Early Years*, p. 75. Cranz, "Women in Urban Parks," p. S82, notes that women's ideal role at the time "was not as a user of facilities for games and sports but as a stabilizing presence."

36. The park commissioners' reports kept separate construction and maintenance accounts for plantations, forestry, and reclamation of the dunes from 1891 to 1924. The emphasis shifted from construction to maintenance as the transformation proceeded. For example, under "construction" in 1890–91, the commissioners spent $4,161.45 "planting trees to prevent the drifting of sand." For maintenance, "trimming, cleaning, and dressing out plantations," they spent $495.25. SFBPC, *Twentieth Annual Report* (1891). SFBPC, *Fifty-fourth Annual Report* (1924), pp. 64, 66, records that the commission spent $1,151.83 on forestry

construction and $4,348.15 on maintenance. The stadium was first discussed in SFBPC, *Fortieth Annual Report for the Year Ending June 30, 1910* (San Francisco, 1910), pp. 39–40.

37.  On the social signification of carpet beds, see Anne Leighton, *American Gardens of the Nineteenth Century: "For Comfort and Affluence"* (Amherst, 1987), David Stuart, *The Garden Triumphant: A Victorian Legacy* (New York, 1988), and Terence Young, "From Manure to Steam: The Transformation of Greenhouse Heating in the United States, 1870–1900" *Agricultural History* 72, no. 3 (1998): pp. 574–596. Amy Bridges, "Journal kept on 4th Raymond Excursion to Colorado, New Mexico, and California," unpublished manuscript, Huntington Library, San Marino, California, March 21 and April 13, 1887 [p. 167].

38.  SFBPC, *Thirty-first Annual Report*, p. 12.

39.  Ibid.

40.  The Spreckels Music Temple is described in ibid., pp. 15–17.

41.  *The Official Guide to the California Midwinter Exposition* (San Francisco, 1894), p. 172.

42.  SFBPC, *Twenty-second Annual Report* (San Francisco, 1893), pp. 5–10, discusses Stow Lake and Huntington's Water Fall and Cascade. The lake is named after park commissioner and railroad lobbyist W. W. Stow. The waterfall and cascade are named after their benefactor, Collis P. Huntington, one of the "Big Four" railroad owners.

## 6   THE MANY SMALL PARKS OF SAN FRANCISCO

1.  On progressivism and the new San Francisco charter see William Issel and Robert Cherny, *San Francisco, 1865–1932: Politics, Power, and Urban Development* (Berkeley, 1986), pp. 140–152. Reformers had tried unsuccessfully to alter the charter in 1880, 1883, 1887, and 1896 but finally gained voter approval in the 1898 elections. For the details of the new charter see SFBS, *Charter of The City and County of San Francisco as Amended in 1903, 1907, 1911, 1913 and 1915* (San Francisco, 1915).

San Francisco had an unusually low public debt in the late nineteenth century as a result of the pay-as-you-go restrictions. For example, Randolph Delehanty, "San Francisco Parks and Playgrounds, 1829–1990: The History of a Public Good" (Ph.D. diss., Harvard University, 1992), pp. 217–218, lists the city's 1900 population as 342,783 and its assessed valuation at $413,099,993, but records that it had a minuscule public indebtedness of only $250,000. In contrast, Buffalo, New York, a city that allowed itself to sell bonds, had approximately the same population and assessed valuation but $16,874,302 in bonded indebtedness. The restrictions on the addition of new park land were not absolute. For instance, SFBPC, *Third Biennial Report of The San Francisco Park Commissioners, 1874–5* (San Francisco, 1875), p. 5, relates that the board had been placed in charge of the Mountain Lake Park in 1875.

Only Buena Vista, Mountain Lake, and Golden Gate Parks were under the jurisdiction of the Board of Park Commissioners prior to the new charter. All others were the responsibility of the Department of Streets, Sewers, and Squares, whose budgets varied widely between 1854 and 1897. Delehanty, "San Francisco," p. 97, identifies 1887–88 as a typical year: of the department's $317,734 budget, only $19,107 was spent on all squares, with $8,220 going for salaries, $6,024 for water from a private utility, the Spring Valley Water Company, and $4,863 for materials. The *San Francisco Chronicle* is quoted on pp. 74, 80.

2.  On progressivism in California see G. E. Mowry, *The California Progressives* (Chicago,

1951). Democrat Washington Bartlett (1824–1887) was mayor from 1883 until his death. Another Democrat, Edward B. Pond (1833–1910), succeeded him until 1890. On Buckley's career see W. A. Bullough, *The Blind Boss and His City: Christopher Augustine Buckley and Nineteenth Century San Francisco* (Berkeley, 1979). See Issel and Cherny, *San Francisco: 1865–1932*, p. 135, on the 1892 and 1894 elections. The description of Sutro is quoted in M. G. Holli and P. d'A. Jones, eds., *Biographical Dictionary of American Mayors, 1820–1980: Big City Mayors* (Westport, Conn., 1981), p. 351.

3. Phelan's inheritance is described in Gray Brechin, *Imperial San Francisco: Urban Power, Earthly Ruin* (Berkeley, 1999), pp. 99, 335. His description is from Terrence McDonald, *The Parameters of Urban Fiscal Policy: Socioeconomic Change and Political Culture in San Francisco, 1860–1906* (Berkeley, 1986), p. 95. On p. 159, McDonald describes how the improvement groups had entered the political arena with the 1892 election. He also discusses Phelan's platform, on p. 196, and the election results, on p. 166.

4. A history of the various charter reform movements is presented in Issel and Cherny, *San Francisco: 1865–1932*, pp. 140–152. James D. Phelan, *Municipal Conditions and The New Charter* (San Francisco, 1896), p. 4.

5. A brief biography of Phelan is presented in Judd Kahn, *Imperial San Francisco: Politics and Planning in an American City, 1897–1906* (Lincoln, Neb., 1979), pp. 60–61. See Issel and Cherny, *San Francisco: 1865–1932*, pp. 109–110; and Kahn, pp. 57–79, on Phelan's involvement in the City Beautiful movement. Phelan's involvement with Hetch Hetchy is mentioned in Issel and Cherny, *San Francisco: 1865–1932*, pp. 175 and 182–183; Norris Hundley, *The Great Thirst: Californians and Water, 1770s–1990s* (Berkeley, 1992), pp. 171–174; and Brechin, *Imperial San Francisco*, pp. 100–102. The last presents an alternative, discerning interpretation of Phelan's environmental efforts, which have frequently been characterized as noblesse oblige. On pp. 99–100, Brechin sees this member of "San Francisco's lace-curtain Irish" as motivated in part by his desire to increase "the value of the [environmental] assets that were the basis of his family's power."

6. Delehanty, "San Francisco," pp. 98, 216. The word *outside* in the *Post* quote refers to the portion of the city beyond the 1851 charter line, which ran north-south in a parallel with Kearny Street, but two miles to the west of Portsmouth Square. Divisadero Street runs along this line today. According to the same source, pp. 205–208 and SFBPC, *Fifty-Fourth Annual Report* (San Francisco, 1924), p. 52, the board gained approximately 111 acres in the transfer of responsibility. The annual report, p. 52, also relates that the Park Commission's total expenditures reached a pre-1900 charter peak of $302,726 in 1896. They declined to $205,863 in 1898 and did not exceed the level of 1896 until 1902.

7. See McDonald, *The Parameters*, p. 159, on the improvement groups. The parks proposal is in Daniel H. Burnham and Edward H. Bennett, *Report on a Plan for San Francisco* (San Francisco, 1905), p. 191. Burnham's proposal sought to transform approximately one-third of San Francisco's entire area into greenspaces. See Kahn, *Imperial San Francisco*, pp. 80–102, on the AIASF and the Burnham plan. The Mission Park Association's work is reported in "Park in Mission Has Warm Friends," *San Francisco Chronicle*, August 29, 1903, p. 12. Delehanty, "San Francisco," pp. 218, 220, notes that this same bond measure had been passed in a December 1899 ballot but the results were later invalidated. See also "A Chain of Parks For San Francisco" *The Wave* 20 (December 27, 1899): 22. This "society, literary, and

political journal" felt that the Mission District was "justly entitled" to a park. Mission Park is described in SFBPC, *Forty-Second Annual Report,* ed. Hugh M. Burke (San Francisco, 1912), p. 37; and, SFBPC, *Fifty-Fourth Annual Report,* p. 41.

8. SFBPC, *Thirty-First Annual Report for The Year Ending June 30, 1902* (San Francisco, 1902), pp. 7–8.

9. See Delehanty, "San Francisco," p. 218, 220. The voters in the invalidated 1899 ballot (see note 7 this chapter) had approved the parkway, the transformation of Dolores Street and, absent from the 1903 ballot, a thirteen-block extension of Golden Gate Park's Panhandle (formerly known as the Avenue) to the intersection of Market Street and Van Ness Avenue. SFBPC, *Fortieth Annual Report for The Year Ending June 30, 1910* (San Francisco, 1910), pp. 31–35 and 53–62. In addition to twenty-eight parks and squares, the Park Commission held responsibility for Seal Rocks, the Great Highway along the Ocean Beach, and four undeveloped lots scattered about the city. On pp. 28–29, the Park Commission stated that it was their goal to have a park wherever there existed a need that only park pastimes could satisfy.

10. See John Nolen, "Park Systems," in *City Planning: A Series of Papers Presenting the Essential Elements of a City Plan* (New York, 1917), pp. 159–180. See SFBPC, *Fortieth Annual Report,* pp. 32–33, for a description of the Presidio and the Presidio Parkway. On p. 30, this report states that it was necessary to remove 186,000 cubic yards of sand to create the parkway. See "A Chain of Parks," p. 22 for a discussion of the parkway proposal published just prior to the 1899 ballot.

11. SFBPC, *Fortieth Annual Report,* p. 33. By comparison, the width of Olmsted and Vaux's parkways in Brooklyn and Buffalo were 260 feet and 200 feet, respectively. The rationalistic elements in the parkway are reminiscent of the flowers and trees recommended for the 390-foot "promenade" in Olmsted's San Francisco plan (1866) (see Chapter 2).

12. SFBPC, *Fortieth Annual Report,* p. 31, on Balboa Park; p. 53 on Mission Park; pp. 53–54 on Lincoln Park. The golf course originally had nine holes but was expanded to eighteen in 1913. See Delehanty, "San Francisco," p. 231; p. 362, discusses the art museum.

13. The properties are described or in some other way identified in SFBPC, *Fifty-Fourth Annual Report,* pp. 37–51, 67–68. The four missing properties included a lot between Rhode Island and De Haro Streets, lots on Fillmore Street from Bay Street to Lewis Street, a lot between Clement Street and Point Lobos Avenue (now Geary Boulevard) in the Richmond District, and two blocks between Channel and Irwin Streets. The absence of Parkside Square from this report may indicate nothing more than a lack of development. The Park Commission was never keen to transfer its parks to the Playground (later Recreation) Commission after the latter came into existence in 1908, but between then and 1937, it did so with all or part of five properties—Sunnyside Park, Hamilton Square, Lobos Square, Jackson Square, and half of Jefferson Square. See Delehanty, "San Francisco," p. 289. Sadly, no parks were created in the South of Market area, despite the earlier report's concern.

14. SFBPC, *Fifty-Fourth Annual Report,* pp. 46–47.

15. Ibid., pp. 50–51. McLaren's actions are discussed in Raymond H. Clary, *The Making of Golden Gate Park: The Early Years, 1865–1906* (San Francisco, 1984), p. 77.

16. Expenditures on Coso and St. Mary's Squares are listed in SFBPC, *Fifty-Fourth Annual Report,* pp. 67–68; the description of Huntington Square is on p. 41.

17. Issel and Cherny, *San Francisco: 1865–1932,* p. 37–40, describes Crocker as "perhaps

the most important single figure in the city's business elite during the early twentieth century." The child of Charles Crocker (one of the "Big Four" tycoons of the Central Pacific Railroad), William greatly enhanced his father's railroad and real estate investments following the older man's death. The Heights had been Sutro's home. SFBPC, *Fifty-Fourth Annual Report,* pp. 37 (Bay View) and 46 (Sutro Heights).

18. SFBPC, *Fifty-Fourth Annual Report,* pp. 44–46 (Sharp) and 48–49 (Harding). A golf course was opened in Sharp Park in 1932. See Delehanty, "San Francisco," p. 231. Delehanty also writes that golf enthusiasts had been trying since 1901 to create a golf course in Golden Gate Park. Superintendent McLaren, however, opposed it, so none opened until 1951, eight years after his death. Sharp Park is now a Pacifica, California, city park.

19. SFBPC, *Thirty-First Annual Report,* p. 7; SFBPC, *Fortieth Annual Report,* p. 29. According to Issel and Cherny, *San Francisco: 1865–1932,* pp. 54 and 56, San Francisco had as increasingly complex a workforce as any in America in 1900 and its residents came from a wide diversity of ethnic backgrounds. Of the population, only 24.4 percent were white and the children of parents born in the United States. See also David Ward, *Cities and Immigrants* (New York, 1971), pp. 75–81. Jack London, "South of the Slot," *International Socialist Review* 15, no. 1 (1914): 7.

20. Sam Bass Warner, *The Urban Wilderness: A History of the American City* (New York, 1972). See James E. Vance, Jr., *Geography and Urban Evolution in the San Francisco Bay Area* (Berkeley, 1964); and William Cherny and William Issel, *San Francisco: Presidio, Port and Pacific Metropolis* (San Francisco, 1981) on the increasing social-spatial segmentation of San Francisco. On the South of Market parks, see Delehanty, "San Francisco," p. 205.

21. The title of the *Call* article was a reference to the 1830 poem of the same name by George Pope Morris. The first stanza of the poem is:

Woodman, spare that tree!
Touch not a single bough!
In youth it sheltered me,
And I'll protect it now.

These two newspapers had the same owner and management, so the prevalence of the attitude they held in this controversy may not have been as great as it might initially appear.

22. William Hammond Hall, "Another Forest Management Controversy," *The Story of a City Park,* unpublished manuscript, William Hammond Hall Papers, Bancroft Library, University of California, Berkeley, p. 11. SFBPC, "The Development of Golden Gate Park and Particularly the Management and Thinning of Its Forest Tree Plantations. A Statement from the Board of Park Commissioners, Together With Reports from Messers. Wm. Ham. Hall, Consulting Civil Engineer, Fred. Law Olmsted, Landscape Architect, and John McLaren, Landscape Gardener" (San Francisco, 1886). McLaren had been working at the Bowie estate (formerly the Howard estate) since 1873. George H. Howard hired McLaren; after he died, in 1878, his widow married Henry Pike Bowie, in 1879. See Tom Girvan Aikman, *Boss Gardener* (San Francisco, 1988), pp. 39–41.

23. SFBPC, "Development of Golden Gate Park," pp. 11–12.

24. Hall, "Another Forest Management Controversy," p. 13.

25. The quote is from F. L. Olmsted and J. B. Harrison, *Observations on the Treatment of Public Plantations, More Especially Relating to the Use of the Axe* (Boston, 1889), pp. 3–4. See

Roy Rosenzweig and Elizabeth Blackmar, *The Park and the People: A History of Central Park* (Ithaca, N.Y., 1992), pp. 519–520, for a contemporary, similar controversy in New York City and Jane Kay, "Golden Gate Park's Trees on Chopping Block?" *San Francisco Examiner,* May 5, 1996, pp. A1; Jane Kay, "City's Plan to Cut Tallest Trees Comes Under Fire; Sierra Club Tries to Save 21 Set to Fall in Golden Gate Park," *San Francisco Examiner,* December 4, 1997, p. A1.

26. For example, SFBPC, *Fifty-Fourth Annual Report,* p. 33, notes that as new athletic facilities were constructed on a park site without trees, "approximately 1,000 nearly full-grown trees, [were] transplanted from the more congested regions of Golden Gate Park." The quote is from Hall, "Another Forest Management Controversy," pp. 13–14.

27. According to William H. Wilson, *The City Beautiful Movement,* (Baltimore, 1989), pp. 86–87, the ideology of the movement linked "natural beauty, naturalistic constructivism, the urban counterpart of natural beauty, and classicism." City Beautiful advocates had a great interest in naturalistic themes but were also drawn to neoclassic architecture. For other park backers, like Robinson, see Frederick Law Olmsted (Jr.) and John Nolen, "The Normal Requirements of American Towns and Cities in Respect to Public Open Spaces," *Charities and The Commons* 16 (June 30, 1906): 411–426; and George W. Burnap, *Parks: Their Design, Equipment, and Use* (Philadelphia, 1916), passim. Both lay out hierarchical typologies of urban parks, playgrounds, and squares.

28. Charles M. Robinson, *Modern Civic Art, Or The City Made Beautiful,* (New York, 1909), pp. 321–322. Robinson was not commenting upon San Francisco specifically, but this city was in the process of developing its own City Beautiful plan at the time, so his work would have been well known there. For more on San Francisco's City Beautiful experience see Kahn, *Imperial San Francisco,* pp. 57–102; or, Oscar Lewis, *San Francisco: Mission to Metropolis,* 2nd ed. (San Diego, 1980), pp. 72–79.

29. Burnham and Bennett, *Report on a Plan for San Francisco,* pp. 111, 145, 191.

30. SFBPC, *Fortieth Annual Report,* pp. 28–29.

31. "Beauties of the Park," *Daily Morning Call,* August 31, 1886, p. 5. The situation in New York City was considered so horrendous that the concern for disease prevention formed one pillar of New York park advocates' successful arguments for an increase in the number of parks in the 1890s. See T. Will, H. L. White, and W. Vrooman, "Public Parks and Playgrounds: A Symposium," *The Arena* 10 (1894): 274–288. Richard M. Gibson, "Golden Gate Park," *Overland Monthly* 37, no. 3 (1901), p. 760. According to Issel and Cherny, *San Francisco: 1865–1932,* p. 53, the size of the San Francisco work force increased by 388 percent between the mid-1860s and the early 1930s.

32. SFBPC, *Thirty-First Annual Report,* p. 8. According to "A Chain of Parks," p. 22, another connection between Golden Gate Park and South of Market would have been a thirteen-block extension of the Avenue to the intersection of Van Ness and Market Streets. A newly tree-lined Dolores and Buchanan Streets would have connected the extension to the new Mission District park. Mayor Phelan unsuccessfully backed the Avenue extension in 1899. See Issel and Cherny, *San Francisco: 1865–1932,* p. 110.

33. E. Strother French, "Where Shall the Children Play?" *California Weekly* 1, no. 16 (1909), p. 251.

34. On the more recent features see Katherine Wilson, *Golden Gate: The Park of a Thousand Vistas* (Caldwell, Idaho, 1950); and Raymond H. Clary, *The Making of Golden Gate Park: The Growing Years, 1906–1950* (San Francisco, 1987). The sewage plant in particular was

highly inappropriate, since it handles effluents from the Richmond and Sunset Districts not Golden Gate Park. On the continuing use of the small parks in a rationalistic fashion see, for example, "U.S. to Face Canada in Rugby Tournament at Balboa Park," *San Francisco Examiner,* May 10, 1996, p. F-8; Julie Chao, "Kids Delight in Rebuilt Mission Playground," *San Francisco Examiner,* October 31, 1997, p. A-1; and, Dan Levy, "'Disc Golf' Course Proposed at S.F.'s McLaren Park," *San Francisco Chronicle,* February 7, 1998, p. A-15.

35. San Francisco Recreation and Park Department and Royston Hanamoto Alley & Abey, *Golden Gate Park Master Plan* (San Francisco, 1998), pp. 13-5, 13-10. A draft master plan was completed in 1994. As parts of it were approved, work on them proceeded; so some projects, like removal of the sewage treatment plant and renovation of the Beach Chalet, were completed prior to publication of the entire final *Master Plan.*

36. The controversy about vehicular access is detailed in Ken Garcia, "Foes View A and J as Pure Evil; They Just Want Cars Out of Golden Gate Park," *San Francisco Chronicle,* May 28, 1998, p. A-1. The Sierra Club's concerns are presented in Kay, "City's Plan to Cut Tallest Trees," p. A-1. On his views and proposal see Michael Laurie, "Ecology and Aesthetics," *Places* 6 (1989), pp. 48–51; and, Michael Laurie, "Landscape Architecture and the Changing City," in *Ecological Design and Planning,* ed. George E. Thompson and Frederick R. Steiner (New York, 1997), pp. 155–166. Catharine Ward Thompson, "Updating Olmsted," *Landscape Design* (October 1996), pp. 26–31, supports Laurie's proposal and others like it.

As Kay's newspaper article about the Sierra Club suggests, the new park advocates are not necessarily opposed to everything about a park that is rationalistic. The two views can complement each other. See, for example, Joan Aragone, "Releafing Goldengrove," *Landscape Architecture* 86, no. 9 (1996), pp. 54–59, which discusses the long-term, multi-age replacement of the even-aged plantings done in Golden Gate Park during the 1870s and 1880s.

# index

*Italicized page numbers refer to tables, maps, or illustrations.*